"From the first page until the last, *American Exceptionalism Reconsidered* will grab the reader's attention. I hope that David Forsythe and Patrice McMahon are correct that the pursuit of U.S. national interests can still be blended with attention to universal human rights and even an occasional commitment to come to the rescue of those outside its borders."

Thomas G. Weiss, *Graduate Center of the City University of New York*

"Forsythe and McMahon have written an exceptional book on American exceptionalism. Against the broad canvas of American history but with a focus on events since 9/11, this intelligent and wide-ranging book shows quite convincingly what no politician would ever acknowledge: that the U.S. is no better than any other country. Those seeking an antidote to 'make America great again' will certainly find it here."

Mark Gibney, *University of North Carolina–Asheville*

"This fresh analysis of a recurring central theme in U.S. policy brings important insight to bear on the fate of human rights in a post-hegemonic world. Forsythe and McMahon's rigorous analysis of the U.S. record builds the case for a more nuanced 'American globalism' that advances academic understanding and strategies for human rights advocacy."

Alison Brysk, *University of California–Santa Barbara*

"The U.S. does not have a unique interest in promoting the good abroad; it is a normal country blending self-interest with internationalism, nationalism with cosmopolitanism. Forsythe and McMahon expertly make this case by analyzing history, policy, and law pertaining to issues like humanitarian intervention, torture, and corporate regulation. This excellent, readable, and current classroom text is enlivened by frequent reference to American public opinion and comparison with other large countries' foreign policies."

Rhoda E. Howard–Hassmann, *Wilfrid Laurier University*

"This book, a searing but thoughtful indictment of the myth of American exceptionalism, is an indispensable analysis of a self-identified 'indispensable' country. It exposes double standards in U.S. foreign policy when it comes to the protection of human rights, while also recognizing that hypocrisy is not reserved just for the U.S. This excellent book raises profound questions about the ability of human rights law to affect state behavior, with sometimes-uncomfortable conclusions. It notes the paradox that U.S. power has been central to both attempts to protect human rights and failure to do so."

Kurt Mills, *University of Glasgow*

AMERICAN EXCEPTIONALISM RECONSIDERED

Is the United States really exceptional in terms of its willingness to take universal human rights seriously? According to the rhetoric of American political leaders, the United States has a unique and lasting commitment to human rights principles and to a liberal world order centered on the rule of law and human dignity. But when push comes to shove—most recently in Libya and Syria—the United States failed to stop atrocities and dithered as disorder spread in both places. This book takes on the myths surrounding U.S. foreign policy and the future of world order. Weighing impulses toward parochial nationalism against the ideal of cosmopolitan internationalism, the authors posit that what may be emerging is a new brand of American globalism, or a foreign policy that gives primacy to national self-interest but does so with considerable interest in and genuine attention to universal human rights and a willingness to suffer and pay for those outside its borders—at least on occasion. The occasions of exception—such as Libya and Syria—provide case studies for critical analysis and allow the authors to look to emerging dominant powers, especially China, for indicators of new challenges to the commitment to universal human rights and humanitarian affairs in the context of the ongoing clash between liberalism and realism.

The book is guided by four central questions: 1) What is the relationship between cosmopolitan international standards and narrow national self-interest in U.S. policy on human rights and humanitarian affairs? 2) What is the role of American public opinion and does it play any significant part in shaping U.S. policy in this dialectical clash? 3) Beyond public opinion, what other factors account for the shifting interplay of liberal and realist inclinations in Washington policy making? 4) In the twenty-first century and as global power shifts, what are the current views and policies of other countries when it comes to the application of human rights and humanitarian affairs?

David P. Forsythe is Professor Emeritus of Political Science at the University of Nebraska–Lincoln.

Patrice C. McMahon is Associate Professor of Political Science at the University of Nebraska–Lincoln.

International Studies Intensives

Series Editors: Shareen Hertel and Michael J. Butler

Series Advisory Board

Robin Broad, *American University*
A. Cooper Drury, *University of Missouri*
Natalie Hudson, *University of Dayton*
Mahmood Monshipouri, *San Francisco State University*
Javier Morales-Ortiz, *Baldwin Wallace University*
Anna Ohanyan, *Stonehill College*

Series Description

International Studies Intensives (ISI) is a book series that springs from the desire to keep students engaged in the world around them. ISI books pack a lot of information into a small space—they are meant to offer an intensive introduction to subjects often left out of the curriculum. ISI books are relatively short, visually attractive, and affordably priced.

Recent Books in the Series

AMERICAN EXCEPTIONALISM RECONSIDERED

U.S. Foreign Policy, Human Rights, and World Order

David P. Forsythe and Patrice C. McMahon

Routledge
Taylor & Francis Group

NEW YORK AND LONDON

Published 2017
by Routledge
711 Third Avenue, New York, NY 10017

and by Routledge
2 Park Square, Milton Park, Abingdon, Oxon, OX14 4RN

Routledge is an imprint of the Taylor & Francis Group, an informa business

Library of Congress Cataloguing in Publication Data
Names: Forsythe, David P., 1941– author. | McMahon, Patrice C., author.
Title: American exceptionalism reconsidered : US foreign policy, human
rights, and world order / David P. Forsythe, University of
Nebraska-Lincoln ; Patrice C. McMahon, University of Nebraska-Lincoln.
Description: New York, NY : Routledge, 2016.
Identifiers: LCCN 2016020613| ISBN 9781138956797 (hardback) |
ISBN 9781138956827 (pbk.) | ISBN 9781315665528 (ebook)
Subjects: LCSH: Human rights–Government policy–United States. |
United States–Foreign relations–Moral and ethical aspects. |
United States–Foreign relations–Public opinion. |
Exceptionalism–United States. | World politics–21st century.
Classification: LCC JC599.U5 F67 2016 | DDC 327.73–dc23
LC record available at https://lccn.loc.gov/2016020613

ISBN: 9781138956797 (hbk)
ISBN: 9781138956827 (pbk)
ISBN: 9781315665528 (ebk)

Typeset in Bembo
by Out of House Publishing

CONTENTS

TABLES

PREFACE

This short book takes on the rather large topic of the United States and the future of world order with regard to the development and implementation of internationally recognized human rights, including the sister notion of international humanitarian law. It does so in admittedly critical fashion, suggesting that Americans' view of themselves is often undeservedly high—a view that is sometimes referred to as "American exceptionalism" by proponents and detractors alike. In this book we consider the extent to which the United States is really exceptional in terms of its willingness to take universal human rights seriously—especially when inconvenient. This inquiry comes at a time when many people have expressed frustration with the yawning gap between human rights law on the books compared with that law in action. Given recent events in places like Libya and Syria, but also political developments in Europe and the United States, it is easy to see why so many people are puzzled by the disparity between claims to greatness and the continuation of gross violations of human rights. If the United States and its allies are so great and so committed to human rights, how is it that so much evil continues in a world supposedly dominated by those very same states?

Readers may be coming to this book in the context of a variety of different interests—human rights, U.S. foreign policy, international law, world politics, or even ethics and politics. No matter what the angle, we hope all readers will be able to see how all these perspectives and considerations fit together under the rubric of "American exceptionalism." Even though we—like certain other scholars—criticize that notion, we seek to understand how and why the rhetoric of American exceptionalism keeps reappearing in different contexts. In explaining this, we utilize the distinction between what we call cosmopolitanism and parochial nationalism. The former idea seeks to *blend* identification with—and love of—country with a serious commitment to international standards and for the rights and suffering of those outside one's own border. The second elevates patriotism and national self-interest *over* international standards, consigning the latter to an aspirational and impotent idealism. In short form, what we find is that U.S. foreign policy on rights and world order does not reflect the persistent workings of moral greatness. Rather, the very mixed U.S. foreign policy record on these questions reflects the shifting complex of a number of factors including its power in the world, international events, and domestic politics. We then look at the potential of certain so-called rising powers to improve upon the U.S. human rights record. What we conclude on that point is not encouraging.

We were stimulated to undertake this study by a perplexing array of political developments including but not limited to the following. President Obama sometimes utilized the notion of American exceptionalism, as when he sought to build support for a no-fly zone in Libya. He said that America was special, and unlike other nations could not turn its back on impending atrocities. At other times he downplayed that idea, as when he said he believed in American exceptionalism the same way that Greeks believed in Greek exceptionalism. This implied that he did not see America as truly morally exceptional. This sort of political rhetoric led to some of Obama's Republican opponents saying that the president did not love the country the way that they did. Then there was the persistent refrain that the president, whoever he might be in whatever era, had failed to uphold great American values abroad and was not committed to contesting evil. It followed that the then out-group, whether Republicans in the Obama era or Democrats in say the Nixon era, were the ones who would restore American moral exceptionalism in foreign affairs. The 2016 American presidential primaries, especially the Republican ones, were full of rhetoric about making American great again—entailing all sorts of claims about the decline of American power and virtue, why it had happened, and what should be done to correct the errors. All of this and more caused us to want to systematically examine the rhetoric about American identity, American nationalism, and the U.S. role in the world. What was truth, what was fiction, and thus what did the empirical record show?

Previous scholars who had delved into the topic may have mostly concluded that the discourse about American exceptionalism was a matter of myth making. But if so, this conclusion seemed to have had precious little effect on many contemporary political leaders and voters. Surely confusion continued on the part of students and others new to the topic. So we decided to take a new look, with particular attention not just to elite decision making but also especially to public opinion polls. Our most fundamental hope is that the next time political discourse turns to American exceptionalism, as it certainly will, all within hearing distance will have an empirical basis for evaluating that rhetoric.

This book comprises a brief look and not an encyclopedia. Thus we use a few topics to make our point(s). Our first chapter outlines the subject and provides an overview. Than we look at the idea of American exceptionalism and its roots in history, with passing reference to other nations. We next turn to one of the self-proclaimed roles of the United States—namely to engage in democracy promotion so as to create an empire of liberty and leave the world a freer place than previously. We then take up the key issue of forceful intervention abroad on human rights grounds, asking whether the country is really prepared to expend blood and treasure abroad for the rights of others. We follow up with a careful look at whether the United States really opposes torture, and whether the United States is in favor of holding for-profit corporations to human rights standards in their foreign operations. All of this sets the stage for asking whether the so-called aspiring powers, or the BRICs, are likely to compile a better record when and if they actually rise and the United States and its allies actually decline. Our focus on Brazil, Russia, India, and China suggests that the U.S. record on human rights and world order, warts and all, is likely to be better.

We were encouraged and supported by a number of colleagues. At the risk of forgetting someone we would like to thank, in no particular order: Jean Cahan, John Gruhl, Barb Flanagan, Courtney Hillebrecht, Alice Kang, Annette Kovar, Roger Clark, Jay Ovsiovitch, and Jerry Petr. Our editors at Routledge were unfailingly helpful.

INTRODUCTION

The Quest for a Liberalized Realism?

Arguing for U.S. action in Libya in 2011, President Obama resurrected the hoary notion of American exceptionalism when he said:

> To brush aside America's responsibility as a leader and—more profoundly—our responsibilities to our fellow human beings under such circumstances would have been a betrayal of who we are. Some nations may be able to turn a blind eye to atrocities in other countries. The United States of America is different.[1]

Despite this reference to the core idea in American nationalism, namely that the nation manifests exceptional morality in political affairs, Obama is often criticized by Republicans for insufficient belief in American exceptionalism. According to a 2010 Gallup poll, 91 percent of Republicans doubt that President Obama believes in American exceptionalism.[2] To be sure, this is not the first time a Democratic has talked about America's unique and exceptional mission. In 1998, Secretary of State Madeleine Albright, with regard to use of force in Iraq, said:

> If we have to use force, it is because we are America; we are the indispensable nation. We stand tall and we see further than other countries into the future, and we see the danger here to all of us.[3]

President Obama, like other politicians both past and present, Democratic and Republican, has emphasized America's unique and lasting commitment to human rights principles and to a liberal world order centered on rule of law and human dignity. Because of relatively recent developments in Syria and Libya, but other situations as well, we are deeply skeptical of such assertions. At the same time, we do not denigrate the considerable good that Americans have done in the world over many decades. We think the U.S. government, under both Democrats and Republicans, tries to do good *when convenient*. Based on the behavior of the United States in the past and given significant changes in the world in the last decade, however, we doubt that in the twenty-first century Americans will be willing to take *costly* measures for the rights of "others." In other words, although there were many occasions in the past when it was convenient for the United States to think about the human rights of those outside its borders, there may well be fewer such opportunities in the future.

Up until this point, little research has put claims about American exceptionalism and human rights abroad to the test. This book thus takes on the rather large and complex topic of American exceptionalism and the future of world order with regard to the development and implementation of universal human rights, including the sister notion of humanitarian affairs—against the background of claims to American exceptionalism.[4] It does so in admittedly critical fashion, suggesting that Americans' view of themselves is often undeservedly high. Such an elevated view is also dangerous, as Russian President Vladimir Putin noted in a September 2013 *New York Times* op-ed, because this leads to the notion that Washington's special status makes it essentially free to do as it pleases in the world.[5] Putin may not be the right pot to call the kettle black, given Russia's historical messianic impulses and the Russian leader's cavalier treatment of both international law and liberal values. However, Putin's essay raises a point worth considering: to what extent is the United States really exceptional in terms of its willingness to take universal human rights seriously—even when inconvenient? Does the United States truly embrace what are called cosmopolitan values? If so, when is it more likely to do so and follow through on such impulses?

This inquiry comes when more than one author has expressed frustration with the yawning gap between human rights law on the books compared with that law in action. Given the human rights language in the 1945 UN Charter, and then the normative revolution which followed in the form of adoption of numerous human rights (and humanitarian) standards, clearly there is a sizable and troubling gap between standard-setting and implementation. The end of the Cold War and then arguably the "uni-polar moment" of U.S. power superiority in the world in the following two decades, did not—on a fair reading of the facts—lead to a closing of this gap. That is, the United States' acclaimed "primacy" in the 1990s did not, in fact, consistently or clearly improve the actual protection of most human rights in most places. We examine some of these specific situations and the reasons for this.

In so doing, we make a distinction between what we call cosmopolitan and parochial nationalism. The former idea seeks to blend identification with—and love of—country with a serious commitment to international standards and for the rights and suffering of those outside one's own border. The second elevates patriotism and a narrow national self-interest over international standards, consigning the latter to an aspirational and impotent idealism. In this latter view, expecting states to take seriously the international law of human rights is utopian precisely because such rights are international and not grounded in national citizenship.[6] Certainly, more than one author has argued that American lip service of commitment to international law is rarely matched by consistent implementation. And many have also concluded that the United States uses international law to advance its interests and values abroad, while exempting itself from any major restriction by international law on its freedom of policy making—including on human rights. This is a serious claim that we scrutinize in this book.

In the pages that follow, we will show that U.S. foreign policy normally sees the international law of human rights as something for others to adhere to and implement while it usually resists that law's effect on U.S. decision making. We also argue that the U.S. record is not, in fact, exceptional among states that see themselves as great powers and thus believe that they have the power to go it alone. Putin's Russia also sees itself as exceptional, but it is certainly not known for its principled attention to international human rights. The United States may remain exceptional, not because it is unusually virtuous but because it openly practices exceptionalism as exemptionalism—exempting itself from international legal standards.[7] Thus, on balance, the U.S. record reflects the triumph of parochial nationalism over cosmopolitan nationalism. By looking closely at mythical American exceptionalism, which supposedly leads to a consistent and systematic defense of personal freedom, we show that the country's decidedly mixed human rights record in foreign policy is influenced by a number of shifting factors, including its power in the world, international events, and domestic politics. Context matters as does U.S. power for backing up rhetoric with action.

Understanding American Views

All great powers decline sooner or later. As a result of decline, they usually then express more commitment to the international standards that protect them from the whims of the upstart nations. Today the British and French, their empires long gone, are usually relatively serious about international law. In the future, if the world becomes more multipolar in power distribution, the United States may show more, rather than less, interest in international standards seeking to protect human dignity. We return to this idea in our concluding chapter.

In the meantime, increased globalization as well as changes in the balance of power among states highlight, if not exacerbate, the tension between cosmopolitan and parochial nationalism in the area of human rights and humanitarian affairs. That is, as the world becomes more interconnected, pressures build for serious attention to international standards. A world interconnected in important ways is a world needing considerable regulation and coordination. Increased trade and the development of the World Trade Organization testify to this point. But additional rules for states, particularly states whose power is growing economically and politically, whether pertaining to security, economics, or social affairs, can and usually do chafe. A dislike for rules from public authorities is often true within nations, as some decry the loss of "freedom" and the expansion of "big government." Similar resistance to international standards can obviously be true in foreign policy, as some see national independence and legal sovereignty being unwisely restricted by "foreigners." It is clear that increased interdependence can produce frustration and pushback against dominant trends. This tension between the international and the national, between cosmopolitan ideals and national preferences for unilateral action, has special acuity in matters of human rights and humanitarian affairs, particularly for the United States.

Traditionally, many within the United States, most prominently in recent years President Ronald Reagan, have seen the nation as a city on a hill and beacon to others concerning personal freedom and rights.[8] The United States has often defined for itself a special role in the world: that of advancing personal, individual "freedom." It is therefore not easy for U.S. policy makers to accept the binding nature of universal human rights defined in an international process, much less submit to international means of implementation that it does not fully control. Such international standards, and above all muscular international enforcement, call into question national claims to uniqueness.

Noting the difference between cosmopolitan and parochial versions of nationalism identifies a key comparison in this book. Although there are complex ways of expressing this, in this book we examine the opposing forces shaping U.S. foreign policy and its human rights record. On the one hand, there is the normative or ideational revolution in internationally recognized human rights—on paper. Since 1945, there has been a remarkable proliferation of human rights norms in international relations both globally and regionally.[9] There has also been a great expansion of humanitarian law—aka, the laws of war or the law of armed conflict. Both of these bodies of international law exist primarily to regulate the state in order to produce human dignity for all regardless of nationality (or gender, religion, etc.).

These advances have taken place not simply because of the United States but rather with the support and assistance of scores of international and national human rights institutions that are both public and private, created to advance these causes. On paper, a universal liberal system is on the march, embodying cosmopolitan values for all—and countries are supposed to adjust appropriately. Relatedly, there is also much talk about American hegemony since 1945 leading to a liberal world order, although it should be noted that much of this writing is about a rules-based global trading system with relatively little attention to the actual protection of human rights.

On the other hand, there is the continuation of traditional or parochial nationalism, in which the idea of narrow national self-interest looms large. For advocates of the latter view, what drives action in world affairs is—and should be—primarily the notion of the nation-state, its independence, and the protection of that population's security and economic well-being. Among scholars of international relations, this view is in line with realist principles. What is most important is thus protecting and preserving the country and those within its borders. What happens to foreigners and other non-citizens is not a major concern. Robert Gates, for example, was Secretary of Defense when President Obama decided on military intervention in Libya to forestall massacres of Libyans. Gates was opposed to military intervention precisely because U.S. self-interests were insufficiently affected.[10] It is likely that, despite Libya in 2011, these are also the views of President Obama. In foreign policy, Obama held mostly realist values and was not moved to major intervention in Syria despite extensive suffering there.[11] For such persons, ethics and concerns about liberal values are mostly limited to internal, national affairs. Moral concern largely stops at the border—unless one's national colleagues are harmed abroad. Deep moral communities are national while transnational identities and loyalties are thin and superficial.

The synthesis between these clashing views on nationalism and how they play out on specific human rights issues is our main interest, with primary attention to the United States and its role in the world, especially since 1990 and the end of the Cold War. For John Locke and other classical liberal theorists, human rights are supposed to be trumps in the political game; they are values that dominate all others. Human rights are so fundamental to human dignity that they exist for all and public authorities are not to violate them. In reality, we show that for U.S. foreign policy the real trumps remain national security and national economic advantage. Although competition between human rights and the national interest traditionally defined repeatedly shows that the latter dominates the former, there are situations and ways in which U.S. foreign policy is heavily influenced by liberal ideas and practices. Thus, U.S. foreign policy is characterized by what we see as a certain form of *liberalized realism* or *American globalism* that pays considerable attention to human rights. As we suggested however liberalized realism is not consistently followed; it is adopted and implemented when convenient, depending on the context and American power.

An interesting question we consider toward the end of this book is: What does the rise of so-called aspiring countries like China and India mean for the future of human rights and world order? Does the "rise of the rest" inevitably hurt cosmopolitan values and human rights? Despite our skepticism about an elevated American self-image, we also wonder whether we are moving at a glacial pace toward a more liberal and cosmopolitan world order, with or without the relative decline of U.S. power. What evidence exists to demonstrate that this is so?

Unfortunately, we find we have to argue that, despite the great proliferation of liberal standards and principles emphasizing the importance of universal human dignity, or what some call human security, as well as the existence of countless institutions and organizations to implement these standards, what continues to matter most will be national identity, state power, and national well-being narrowly defined. And the growing power of aspiring countries will probably make this even more apparent. We think it is likely that a cosmopolitan nationalism, conceived here as the focus on individual well-being across nations, has triumphed on paper or in legal theory, but that the real winners will remain those, often called realists, who concentrate on states, their independence and national advantage. We think the proper question in the future is whether the liberal international law of human rights and humanitarian affairs can have some impact on U.S. and other foreign policies, not whether liberal norms can fully dominate or replace realist, self-interested policies.

The bright side of possibilities is that perhaps human rights norms can, in relative terms, have further impact on national foreign policies. National leaders, whether they are in the United States or in other states, may be effectively pressured (or themselves feel it proper and necessary) to pay *relatively* more attention to human rights—even the rights of foreigners. We consider the possibility that world order, even if built on state calculation, could: 1) become even more liberal and 2) survive the decline of the United States as arguably the single hegemon which enjoyed, however briefly, a unipolar moment of primacy of power during the 1990s. We recall that the "pure" nation-state system that evolved in the world from more or less 1648 and lasted until about 1919 did not produce changes immediately. Instead, change evolved gradually, in fits and starts with pockets of atavistic exception. We cannot expect parochial nationalisms and ideas about state sovereignty to change immediately and consistently either. Conceptions of proper international authority and global governance obviously evolve in bits and pieces and at different paces in different areas. But, on balance, we are not terribly optimistic about this prospect for a more liberal world order.

In our wide-ranging analysis, we maintain a focus on the U.S. contribution to world orders, past, present, and future, albeit sometimes in a comparative perspective. We subscribe to the view that the United States of FDR and Harry Truman was *primus inter pares* in laying the cornerstone for modern human rights norms in the world, via the 1945 UN Charter (Article 55) and the 1948 Universal Declaration of Human Rights. This is not to denigrate the considerable roles played by the likes of the French official Rene Cassin (France) or the UN Secretariat official John P. Humphrey (Canada) and various Latin American Social Democrats in getting these norms initially approved. However, we argue that the basic norms would not have been formally approved without U.S. diplomatic leadership by Eleanor Roosevelt and others.

The same U.S. leadership role figured in the Nuremberg and Tokyo trials of the 1940s, which set the stage for an interesting rejuvenation of international criminal law some 50 years later. Although the United States was but one among many in advancing a revised international humanitarian law via the 1949 Geneva Conventions and Protocols for war victims (Switzerland and parts of the Red Cross network also exercised leadership, as did many other states like Pakistan, depending on time and norm considered), some U.S. support for the laws of war and attempts to protect both civilians and sidelined combatants from unnecessary suffering was undeniably crucial.

The United States also helped negotiate other human rights standards after the 1940s and remained a key human rights and humanitarian actor, whether one speaks of: 1) institutional developments, such as the creation of the UN High Commissioner on Refugees (UNHCR) and the accompanying refugee regime; 2) involvement in particular crises, such as conflicts in the Balkans (1991–1999); or 3) the promotion of certain ideologies and practices such as democracy promotion or large-scale humanitarian action. By all this we are definitely not saying that the United States always ratified the standards that were negotiated, or ratified in good faith without debilitating RUDs (reservations, understandings, and declarations).

We are also not suggesting that Washington never turned a blind eye to atrocities, as when in 1971 it knew about but ignored genocide and other crimes in the creation of Bangladesh. Indeed, it is a central point of this book to show that there has always been and there will continue to be tension and dualism as well as a mixed record when it comes to U.S. policy and international human rights standards. We wrestle with a proper summary of the complicated U.S. human rights record and the causes for this but it undoubtedly has been inconsistent and motivated by many factors.

We believe that when there were major international efforts in international relations in the name of protecting human rights, the United States was almost always centrally involved—e.g., Somalia in the early 1990s, Kosovo in 1999, Libya in 2011, etc. And where international muscular efforts on behalf of human rights were conspicuous by their absence, as in the Rwandan genocide of 1994, the U.S. role was also central. As others have argued, the United States has often played the role of the indispensable nation in trying to protect human rights in the world. It has been crucial not in the sense of consistent moral superiority but in the sense of bringing to the table its considerable military, economic, and diplomatic leverage or power—at least sometimes but not always.

We study the U.S. record on human rights and humanitarian affairs, not as it ought to be according to international law and human rights norms in the abstract or according to pure legal logic, but in the context of the ongoing clash between liberalism and realism. That is, we focus on the details and dilemmas associated with the conflict between universal human interests and narrow national interest, between an emphasis on human rights and human dignity without regard to nationality and advancing parochial national objectives—or the struggle between cosmopolitanism and parochial nationalism.

To the extent that U.S. foreign policy on human rights adds up to a blend of narrow self-interest *and* more liberal, cosmopolitan concerns, we allow for that complicated possibility as well. Indeed, there might be such a thing, despite the oxymoron, as American globalism, or a foreign policy that gives primacy to national self-interest but does so with considerable interest in and genuine attention to universal human rights and a willingness to suffer and pay for those outside its borders—at least on some occasions under specific circumstances. It might be possible then to suggest that American foreign policy manifests some kind of "liberalized realism" in its human rights policies. The question is: on which issues and under what circumstances?

As examples of a liberalized realism, we point to Bill Clinton's foreign policy in the Balkans from 1993 to 1999 and Barack Obama's foreign policy in Libya early on in 2011. These cases are not cited as how problems *should be* handled but rather as to how parochial and cosmopolitan considerations come together to produce a particular policy of liberalized realism in a particular context. That such a hybrid approach rarely produces a perfect or totally satisfying outcome is worth noting, as are the importance of context, American power, and public opinion. At the same time, a totally narrow and self-serving U.S. policy, as in Bangladesh in 1971 or Rwanda in 1994, we point out, is in fact far worse—certainly for the victims of the atrocities who were supposed to be beneficiaries of universal human rights but also for world order that seems to be rudderless without American leadership.

At the end of the day our inquiry is guided by four central concerns. 1) What is the relationship between international or cosmopolitan human rights standards and narrow national self-interest in U.S. policy on human rights and humanitarian affairs? 2) What is the role of American public opinion and does it play any significant role in shaping U.S. policy in this dialectical clash? 3) Beyond possibly public opinion, what other factors account for the shifting interplay of liberal and realist inclinations in Washington policy making? 4) Finally, in the twenty-first century and as the distribution of power ebbs and flows among countries and other actors, what are the current views and policies of other countries, such as the BRICs (referring to Brazil, Russia, India, China (and those aligned with them), when it comes to the application of human rights and humanitarian affairs? Importantly, should we worry that after the current *Pax Americana* and when Goliath has weakened, international commitment to human rights and human suffering will be even more problematic?

Outline and Chapter Summaries

After our Introduction, we start our specific analyses in Chapter 1 with a discussion of American political culture, meaning the dominant political ideas and especially the notion of American exceptionalism. In each chapter and focusing on different manifestations of human rights policies we show that: 1) American exceptionalism is more myth than fact, as Americans are not any more willing to sacrifice blood and treasure for others than citizens in other countries; 2) despite its mythical status, this trope is widely believed at home by some key players and its invocation does affect policy making from time to time; and 3) American exceptionalism can and often does lead to a dangerous exemptionalism in which international law, including provisions on human rights, are seen by some as unwise and pernicious restrictions on a virtuous United States. In other words, Putin was right about the United States and its tendency to exaggerate American moral superiority when it comes to its exceptional status, although he has often been wrong about Russian policies. To be sure, the president of Russia is not the only leader to discuss human rights violations in other countries and the policy mistakes by others while pushing their own policy defects under the rug.

In our analyses, we pay persistent attention to the role of the American public opinion. Experts in this field have consistently shown that while the American mass public is not well informed about the details of world affairs, it does pay enough attention to know when U.S. foreign policy is encountering major problems. The public will occasionally vote on the basis of foreign policy issues as was the case in the 2006 congressional elections (many Democrats were elected because the voters understood that the George W. Bush policy in Iraq was in serious trouble). So while the American public is usually deferential to foreign policy elites at least for a time, voters still set the limits on what is acceptable. Those who make foreign policy know that if the foreign policy wagon lands in the ditch, the voters may become more attentive and assertive and elect those standing for a different path.

Initially and throughout the book, we are keenly interested in the question of whether contemporary polling about America and the world shows support for a special U.S. role in international politics. And has this changed since 1990 and the end of European communism? Did the events of September 11, 2001 and the attacks on the homeland by Islamic extremists shift opinions in any discernible way? What is the state of U.S. public opinion after two long and drawn out wars in Iraq and Afghanistan, both of which failed to achieve maximalist objectives? Has public opinion changed with growing awareness of major problems at home? Is there a gap between the views of the elite and the mass public on foreign policy and international questions? In other words, presidents may assert a special world role for the United States on behalf of freedom and universal rights for all, but public opinion may or may not support that role—especially when it is seen as costly—aka inconvenient. And, whatever the general public might believe, are these beliefs mostly negated by committed elites with different views?

After all, in democracies there has long been a school of thought saying that public leaders should do what they think is best for the country and not simply reflect majority views at the time. For example, polls show wide support in the American public for the United Nations, yet certain members of Congress introduce bills (usually by Republicans in the House) calling for a U.S. withdrawal from that organization. Certain elites buck public opinion because of ideology or other factors as they attempt to "lead" or "educate" citizens. So attention to public opinion has to be combined with analysis of other factors–both domestic and foreign–affecting foreign policy.

After our first substantive chapter on American political culture and public beliefs about American exceptionalism, which shows the moral superiority of the

American nation to be a myth, we then probe in further depth the U.S. record on democracy promotion in Chapter 2. If, indeed, a central component of American exceptionalism is the belief that America has a special mission, ordained by Providence or self-chosen, to lead the world toward more political freedom, does this translate into U.S. leadership for building and maintaining genuine liberal democracies? How does the United States manage its "special mission" when dealing with friendly or important autocrats? We look both at systematic programs and reactions to crises and other unexpected events. Although other consolidated liberal democracies have democracy promotion programs, we focus on policy coming out of Washington. Along the way we note that the United States has engaged in arms transfers and other kinds of mutually advantageous relationships with numerous autocratic regimes.

Despite the fact that social science cannot say definitively what guarantees liberal democracy (or majority rule with human rights protections) in any particular nation, we show increased elite agreement on what U.S. democracy promotion should entail. We show that U.S. commitment to liberal democracy is quite irregular and inconsistent. Factors such as traditional security concerns, economic advantage, and domestic special interests all cross cut this U.S. "special mission." Looking at Central Europe after 1990 and the "Arab Spring" starting in 2011, we look at how different presidents addressed the tensions between narrow national interests and liberal democratic values. The bright side is that, perhaps trapped by its own rhetoric and because of American identity, the United States usually tries to leave a situation of deep engagement more democratic than Washington found it initially, although Washington does not always succeed in this endeavor.

The liberal value of democracy promotion runs parallel to that of military intervention to protect against atrocities abroad. Our attention to "saving strangers" or humanitarian intervention in Chapter 3 is combined with our attention to the relatively new international norm of R2P—the responsibility to protect. This chapter starts off by comparing the behavior of the United States in the late twentieth century with other great powers who earlier had justified the use of force with rationalizations that they were doing "God's work" to rescue endangered peoples. Somewhat similarly, during the golden age of American humanitarian intervention that took place in the 1990s the United States implicitly and explicitly claimed that it was doing what was morally right to help people in need and promote human dignity.

Although focusing on different policies, Chapters 2 and 3 make a common point—namely, that American willingness to sacrifice for the rights of foreigners is weak and basically similar to public opinion in other Western-style democracies. Americans generally do not support democracy promotion or humanitarian intervention when costly to self-interested concerns. Note that in Britain in early 2015, public opinion supported the notion of the United Kingdom as a great power, but at the same time the public was opposed to increasing spending for a security policy that would support great power status in military affairs. The

British public wanted the image of a great power but not the spending that came with it.

In Chapter 4, we take up the subject of the U.S. record on the issue of torture. Here again we find the usual pattern, with the United States supporting the development of international norms against torture, but making sure that such norms do not restrict its own freedom of choice regarding treatment of detainees. From World War II, where the U.S. record on this issue was reasonably and relatively good, we find that in fact Washington has been moving in the wrong direction—carrying out research on torture, teaching torture techniques to others, and especially after 9/11/2001 actually authorizing and implementing torture on a fairly broad scale itself.

When it comes to the issue of torture we also find that American public opinion has also been moving in the wrong direction, with about 60 percent of Americans (and a higher percentage of Republicans) indicating that the "enhanced interrogation techniques" applied to "terror suspects" give rise to no cause for concern. The fact that some U.S. officials have termed these techniques torture has made little difference. It seems that the brutal techniques of Islamic extreme militants, attacking civilians and killing prisoners, have led to a downward spiral of negative reciprocity. While true that many governments, including democratic ones, have long engaged in torture, one can say that the situation has become worse rather than better. There is little that is exceptionally good or moral about trends in U.S. policy on this question, as the 2016 primary season demonstrates quite clearly.

Rather than trying to resist the trend toward increased brutalization of "terror suspects," certainly the George W. Bush administration contributed to the dominant trend until about 2006. We note that the Obama administration curtailed the torture techniques and sought to place terror suspects in federal courts where due process was greater than in military commissions. These moves were criticized by a variety of factions in Congress. At the same time, the Obama team did not completely rule out the use of these techniques by the CIA in the future, and it tried to avoid all prosecutions for past U.S. torture. It did this even as it pressed foreign governments like Sri Lanka to address *their* past war crimes. On the one hand, Congress did progressively restrict torture techniques both by the military and CIA in the context of no new major terror attacks on the homeland by foreign actors. On the other hand, various Republican candidates in the 2016 presidential primaries endorsed water boarding and other forms of torture as they pandered to angry citizens in order to advance their personal political objectives.

In Chapter 5, we turn to transnational corporations and human rights, again focusing on U.S. rhetoric in this area and the foreign policy record. There is no doubt that in the twenty-first century many modern corporations have tremendous wealth and power. The corporation and other private economic groups are therefore important in any scheme to improve the protection of human rights around the world. Like the state itself, the corporation is Janus-faced with the power both to advance and hinder human rights. It is for these reasons that the United Nations has facilitated the Global Compact, an effort designed to get transnational corporations to voluntarily commit to principles of social responsibility and a self-reporting system. Likewise, NGOs and social movements have fostered various techniques to try to bring various corporations into programs to protect human rights; and we discuss how the U.S. government has reinforced or taken issue with NGOs and other actors seeking more corporate responsibility.

As for U.S. foreign policy, we find some attention to this important issue, particularly during Democratic administrations, but in general we find reluctance by the U.S. government to restrict American corporate behavior abroad in the name of human rights. This general and long standing reluctance has been recently reinforced by a series of judgments by the U.S. Supreme Court. As urged particularly by the George W. Bush Administration, the pro-business and activist Roberts Court has closed off a promising development. With the Kiobel Case as central, the Roberts Court has ruled against private foreign petitioners, who were supported by human rights groups, in their effort to hold corporations legally liable for complicity in major human rights violations in South Africa, Nigeria, Argentina, and other places.

If governments are fully serious about protecting human rights around the world, they would take action to ensure that corporations did not pursue profits at the expense of human rights, especially in states unwilling or unable to eliminate gross violations. Even in liberal democratic states, however, regulating the profit motive in the name of human rights has never proven widely popular. Even domestically, labor rights, child welfare rights, and other business regulations were achieved only through much struggle. In this chapter, we will show that recently the United States has been moving in the wrong direction much of the time, closing the window on promising developments under the Alien Tort Statute which had permitted foreign nationals to sue private parties in U.S. federal courts for certain gross violations of internationally recognized human rights.

While the Roberts Court had affirmed that corporations at home were legal persons, and had provided them with rights of political speech (aka campaign contributions) and religious convictions (so as to avoid paying for insurance for women's reproductive rights), the Court has made it more difficult for private actors to be held liable in U.S. courts for complicity in (or aiding and abetting) human rights violations abroad. A situation of true American exceptionalism, namely federal universal jurisdiction for major violations of internationally recognized human rights by private actors, has been changed. This happened when human rights lawyers went after corporate misbehavior, leading to a blocking reaction by the Roberts Court that undercut some 35 years of settled law.

In Chapter 6, as we consider human rights in the twenty-first century and the probable return of a more multilateral world, we address the place of human rights in the foreign policy of the BRICs countries. Aspiring powers, sometimes called BRICs and their allies, which are presumed to have increased economic standing, seem often uninterested in, if not openly hostile to, international action to intervene against gross violations of international human rights. China and increasingly Russia are authoritarian governments and not always committed to human rights even in principle. Brazil, India, and China have all been victimized by outside interventions in the past, whether because of colonialism, imperialism, or other form of outside domination. This experience, as well as significant domestic problems, has left them hyper-sensitive to perceived neo-colonialism and, thus, their nationalisms may be more parochial than cosmopolitan. They may defer more easily to the brutal parochial nationalisms and domestic instabilities of others and may be unwilling to use their economic (and social) resources to pay for controversial (and expensive) foreign interventions as they pursue national economic development. Thus as inconsistent as U.S. foreign policy has been on universal human rights in the past, the future may be even worse in terms of protecting universal rights on a systematic basis.

Finally, in our Conclusion we address American globalism and the future of world order. It is certainly a possibility that a more multipolar world where the United States is less dominant and where other countries are rising and challenging, the U.S. position might have a salutary effect. That is to say that the United States, rather than trying to impose order via an informal U.S. empire, may wind up negotiating more durable standards. It is at least possible that one might see the implementation of R2P by diplomatic and judicial means, especially if international organizations, working with nongovernmental organizations are backed up by states. A reluctance of the United States to use military force to protect the rights of others and to act decisively against genocide, crimes against humanity (including ethnic cleansing), and major war crimes might then be accompanied by non-military efforts in the same direction.[12] The example of Kenya is instructive.

In the Kenyan case the International Criminal Court (ICC) has taken action in the wake of violence associated with campaigning and elections in 2007–2008. One result was less violence associated with elections in 2012. However, another result was the manipulation of Kenyan parochial nationalism by the indicted political leaders and the mobilization of African opinion against the Court. The defendants tried to avoid answering to the charge of having been responsible for political violence that killed and displaced sizable numbers of political opponents by stirring up opposition. Authors of R2P may have intended a focus primarily on various forms of diplomatic initiatives, and the ICC focus on Kenya may reflect action consistent with this intent, but diplomatic pressures under the principle of R2P may turn out to be as difficult to effectuate as military measures. Yet, the Kenyan case has largely collapsed at the ICC, and the prosecutor there has indicated that the indictment of the Sudanese leader al-Bashir may be the next collapse. At the end of the day, there was more diplomatic attention to violations of human rights in Kenya, and this was led by the ICC, but it also resulted in more blocking action particularly by various African political leaders. In other words, this was a recent case where actors other than the United States led the way and there was an effort to stress that the Kenyan government had the responsibility to protect the human rights of all Kenyans regardless of ethnic identity, even though this effort was undercut by various African leaders pursuing traditional self-interests.

Reflecting on American exceptionalism and American globalism in foreign policy and certainly when doing that in comparison with the BRICs in the future, it is perfectly clear that the controversies and debates about how to protect internationally recognized human rights are not likely to end anytime soon. This is especially the case as non-state actors like ISIS and Al-Shabaab increasingly threaten states and alter international events. We also have to recognize that in the influential Western democratic states, attitudes among both elite and the mass public are not reliably conducive to costly measures. This is certainly true for the United States, notwithstanding claims to American exceptionalism and to a special U.S. role in the world to advance personal freedom. But it is not at all sure that the situation will be better in the future.

Notes

1 Remarks by the President in Address to the Nation on Libya, Washington, D.C., March 28, 2011, The White House, Office of the Press Secretary. Available at: https://www.white-house.gov/the-press-office/2011/03/28/remarks-president-address-nation-libya.
2 Jeffrey M. Jones, "Americans See U.S. as Exceptional; 37% Doubt Obama Does," December 22, 2010. Available at: www.gallup.com/poll/145358/americans-excep-tional-doubt-obama.aspx.
3 Micah Zenko, "The Myth of the Indispensable Nation," November 6, 2014. Available at: http://foreignpolicy.com/2014/11/06/the-myth-of-the-indispensable-nation/.
4 But see a very different kind of analysis, more legally oriented, in Michael Ignatieff, ed., *American Exceptionalism and Human Rights* (Princeton, NJ: Princeton University Press, 2005).
5 Vladimir Putin, "A Plea for Caution from Russia," *The New York Times*, September 11, 2013. Available at: www.nytimes.com/2013/09/12/opinion/putin-plea-for-caution-from-russia-on-syria.html?_r=0.
6 Samuel Moyn, *The Last Utopia: Human Rights in History* (Cambridge, MA: Belknap for Harvard University Press, 2012). We believe this work, widely cited, is badly flawed.
7 John Gerard Ruggie, "Doctrinal Unilateralism and its Limits," in *American Foreign Policy in a Globalized World*, edited by David P. Forsythe, Patrice C. McMahon, and Andrew Wedeman (New York and London: Routledge, 2006), pp. 31–50.
8 "Primary Sources: Reagan's Farewell Speech," PBS Documentary American Experience. Available at: www.pbs.org/wgbh/americanexperience/features/primary-resources/reagan-farewell.
9 Jack Donnelly, *International Human Rights* (Boulder, CO: Westview Press, 2013) provides a good introduction.
10 Robert Gates, *Duty: Memoirs of a Secretary at War* (New York: Knopf, 2014), p. 518 and passim.
11 Jeffrey Goldberg, "The Obama Doctrine," *The Atlantic*, April 2016. Available at: www.theatlantic.com/magazine/archive/2016/04/the-obama-doctrine/471525.
12 For another positive view, see Thomas Risse, Stephen C. Ropp, and Kathryn Sikkink, eds., *The Persistent Power of Human Rights* (Cambridge: Cambridge University Press, 2013).

Further Selected Readings

Bass, G. J. *The Blood Telegram: Nixon, Kissinger, and a Forgotten Genocide*. New York: Alfred A. Knopf, 2013.

Brzezinski, Z. *Strategic Vision: America and the Crisis of Global Power*. New York: Basic Books, 2012.

Donnelly, J. *International Human Rights*. Boulder, CO: Westview Press, 2013.

Evans, G. *The Responsibility to Protect: Ending Mass Atrocity Crimes Once and for All*. Washington, D.C.: Brookings Institute Press, 2009.

Forsythe, D. P. *Human Rights in International Relations*. Cambridge: Cambridge University Press, 4th ed., 2017, forthcoming.

Forsythe, D. P., McMahon, P. C., and Wedeman, A., eds. *American Foreign Policy in a Globalized World*. New York and London: Routledge, 2006.

Gates, R. *Duty: Memoirs of a Secretary at War*. New York: Knopf, 2014.

Goldberg, J. "The Obama Doctrine," *The Atlantic*, April 2016. Available at: www.theatlantic. com/magazine/archive/2016/04/the-obama-doctrine/471525.

Hafner-Burton, E. *Making Human Rights a Reality*. Princeton, NJ: Princeton University Press, 2013.

Hopgood, S. *The Endtimes of Human Rights*. Ithaca, NY: Cornell University Press, 2013.

Ignatieff, M, ed. *American Exceptionalism and Human Rights*. Princeton, NJ: Princeton University Press, 2005.

Ikenberry, G. I. *Liberal Leviathan: The Origins, Crisis, and Transformation of the American World Order*. Princeton, NJ: Princeton University Press, 2011.

Kagan, R. *Of Paradise and Power: America and Europe in the New World Order*. New York: Vintage Books, 2004.

Mandelbaum, M. *The Case for Goliath: How America Acts as the World's Government in the 21st Century*. New York: Public Affairs, 2005.

Moyn, S. *The Last Utopia: Human Rights in History*. Cambridge, MA: Belknap for Harvard University Press, 2012.

Prestowitz, C. *Rogue Nation: American Unilateralism and the Failure of Good Intentions*. New York: Basic Books, 2003.

Renouard, J. *Human Rights in American Foreign Policy: From the 1960s to the Soviet Collapse*. Philadelphia: University of Pennsylvania Press, 2016.

Risse, T., Ropp, S. C., and Sikkink, K., eds. *The Persistent Power of Human Rights*. Cambridge: Cambridge University Press, 2013.

Ruggie, J. G. "Doctrinal Unilateralism and its Limits," in *American Foreign Policy in a Globalized World*, edited by David P. Forsythe, Patrice C. McMahon, and Andrew Wedeman. New York and London: Routledge, 2006, pp. 31–50.

Scott, S. *International Law, US Power: The United States' Quest for Legal Security*. Cambridge: Cambridge University Press, 2012.

Sikkink, K. A. *Mixed Signals: U.S. Human Rights Policy and Latin America*. Ithaca, NY: Cornell University Press, 2004.

Smith, T. *America's Mission: The United States and the Worldwide Struggle for Democracy in the Twentieth Century*. Princeton, NJ: Princeton University Press, 1994.

Walzer, M. *Thick and Thin: Moral Argument at Home and Abroad*. South Bend, IN: University of Notre Dame Press, 2006.

1

CITY ON A HILL?

American Exceptionalism Past and Present[1]

The idea of American exceptionalism, or the notion that the United States is not only qualitatively different from other states but it is morally superior, has long animated the speeches of U.S. politicians. Recently, a number of challenges both domestic and international has put this unlikely theory to the test, and the notion of American exceptionalism has clearly come up short.

Domestically, economists lament the shrinking of the middle class while sociologists document the costs of one's race in America. Upward mobility is now greater in some European states. Embarrassingly, U.S. incarceration rates are compared to some of the most undemocratic states in the world.

Internationally, its exceptional status—as champion of liberal democracy and human rights—is similarly eroding when the record is closely examined. True, the U.S. eventually intervened in Libya to help overthrow Muammar Gaddafi's dictatorship in 2011, but it did so reluctantly and only with the prodding of its allies. But it failed to follow up as tribalism engulfed the area. We know well that American intervention in Iraq (2003) led to a bungled occupation that went terribly awry. Now the Middle East faces the prospect of prolonged instability and even sometimes genocide. At the same time, a repressive Iran has been strengthened. And at least until this point, the United States has not acted decisively as President Assad in Syria has presided over more than five years of violence and an estimated death toll of over 250,000. Objectively speaking then, the end of American exceptionalism is already upon us—especially with regard to defense of human rights and humanitarian law. Particularly concerning autocracy and atrocities in the Middle East, the Obama administration reflects more fatalism than a determination that American policy can make things better.[2]

We will back up our bold claim—that the United States and its citizenry act largely as would any other country—with facts from U.S. foreign policy and throw in some domestic affairs to drive the point home. To be clear and as we stated in the previous chapter, we do not contend that U.S. foreign policy comprises an unrelenting string of negatives, but we do assert that U.S. foreign policy on human rights and humanitarian affairs—which is our main preoccupation—is mostly a matter of lofty cosmopolitan rhetoric that is then matched much of the time by parochial nationalistic behavior. Occasionally, American policy features acts of what can be considered cosmopolitanism, centered on the broader benefit for others, but its behavior, we contend, is better understood as globalism, because like many other liberal states it acts on behalf of others only when international and domestic conditions are ripe and when American power is not questioned.

On balance, the good may outweigh the bad, but our main point is that American attitudes and behavior of late are not that unusual and the United States has never been that exceptional—in the past or the present. Most other states and great powers in particular tend to see themselves in a positive light on the question of doing "good" for others while objective facts point to a more modest evaluation. Case in point, Russia's President Putin maintains that his country's involvement in Ukraine is noble, providing much needed humanitarian aid to Ukrainians and saving the country from a series of pro-Western but highly corrupt regimes. Most others in the world see Russia's behavior differently, as predatory and self-interested, based above all on a quest for domination of states in its "near abroad."

This chapter explains the origins of the myth of American exceptionalism and the reality. We then use public opinion to see if continuing claims to American exceptionalism actually resonate with public and elite opinion when confronting international questions today. We conclude by examining how appeals to American greatness shape contemporary foreign policy debates. In light of ongoing debates about America's declining position in the world, it is imperative that we examine the historical record for evidence of the inconsistency—if not complete fallacy—of the notion of American exceptionalism.

The Making of the Myth and its Critique

American exceptionalism has a long history in political rhetoric that predates the U.S. position as a world power. Indeed, this idea has had a central place in America's identity and understanding of itself since the country's founding. Sometimes called Manifest Destiny or Providential Nationalism, it is the basic notion that America is special, morally superior to others, and chosen by God to fulfill a progressive role on earth. It has taken on particular names in particular times. If one starts with Governor John Winthrop in Massachusetts and his Puritanical sermons in the 1630s, it was America as a "city on a hill," a beacon to others everywhere—and useful to sustain morale during harsh times, which included taking Indian land necessary for economic pursuits and killing many of them. For Thomas Jefferson, it was America as an "Empire of Liberty" and the "Almost Chosen," which was useful to rationalize the Louisiana Purchase via Executive action and westward expansion at the expense of still other Indians. For several later presidents, it was America as leader of the "Free World," and this idea was used to rationalize competition with the Soviet Union. All the while, the United States aligned itself with various dictators such as Salazar, Tito, Somoza, Mobutu, Mao, Ceausescu, etc. Only some of these American allies were communist, but all of them presided over decidedly unfree societies.

Recent trends—such as those during the Cold War—were summarized concisely by the historian Walter A. McDougall:

> Most of all, the idea of an America set apart by Providence and endowed with a special mission to reform (not to say redeem) the whole human race dovetailed perfectly with the political rhetoric needed to rally Americans to lead the Free World in what amounted to a holy war against "godless Communism."[3]

Never mind that some of our dictatorial de facto partners like Tito (Yugoslavia) and Ceausescu (Romania) were communist.

Most realists, including most American realists, have never believed in American exceptionalism in the sense of national moral superiority. The realist focus on state power, national interests, and state advantage leads them to acknowledge some of these inconvenient truths. Here we summarize Stephen M. Walt's top five points about the myth of American exceptionalism[4]: 1) the United States is no different from other major states in over-emphasizing the good it has done and glossing over much bad; 2) the United States has carried out ethnic cleansing, war crimes, and other major violations of human rights over time; 3) America has no special national genius; 4) the United States has certainly done some good in the world but so have many other countries and institutions, and U.S. positive contributions have usually been achieved in concert with others; and 5) the idea of having a mandate from heaven is usually a prelude to hubris and is offset by the obvious stupidities of various U.S. policy makers. We quote one section from Walt's lengthy critique of American exceptionalism:

> The United States talks a good game on human rights and international law, but it has refused to sign most human rights treaties, is not a party to the International Criminal Court, and has been all too willing to cozy up to dictators—remember our friend Hosni Mubarak—with abysmal human rights records. If that were not enough, the abuses at Abu Ghraib and the George W. Bush administration's reliance on waterboarding, extraordinary rendition, and preventive detention should shake America's belief that it

consistently acts in a morally superior fashion. Obama's decision to retain many of these policies suggests they were not a temporary aberration.[5]

Walt's analysis is accurate, and other observers, including the British author Godfrey Hodgson, conclude that the usual version of American exceptionalism is a "distorted and selective narrative of exceptional virtue."[6] Here we might recall a classic statement by a French scholar of nationalism, Ernest Renan, who remarked in 1882, that: "Forgetting, I would even go so far as to say historical error, is a crucial factor in the creation of a nation."

It is true that all nations have their national myths, built on emphasizing the positives and blocking out the negatives. Walt provides numerous domestic and foreign policy examples. Advocates for American exceptionalism almost always block out inconvenient domestic facts, such as: the prolonged practice of slavery and racial discrimination even relative to other White, Western, Christian nations; repeated practice of ethnic cleansing, persecution, and massacres of Native Americans; persistent discrimination against females similar to all other Western patriarchal nations; repeated violations of civil rights of dissidents, especially during World War I and the Cold War; arbitrary detention and violation of property rights of Japanese-Americans during World War II. More recently, American negatives center on the maintenance of a harsh form of capitalism with many pockets of extreme poverty and deprivation relative to other developed capitalist democracies; refusal to recognize economic and social rights such as access to adequate health care as fundamental human rights, the only wealthy democracy to do so. We could continue, but the point is quite clear.

With regard to the factual record both at home and abroad one has to gloss over many inconvenient negatives in order to believe in American exceptionalism. A possible counter argument is that America has been morally exceptional in recognizing its past defects and in overcoming them. After all, one version of American exceptionalism, one that came to be associated with isolationism, was that America, as a city on a hill, should work to perfect itself at home rather than to actively impose its virtues on others abroad. Hence, John Quincy Adams in 1821 spoke about "not going abroad in search of monsters to destroy." Ironically, this was at the same time that the United States proclaimed the Monroe Doctrine, endorsing U.S. hegemony in the Western Hemisphere.

Today, the argument in support of America's exceptional progress runs as follows, at least in part: America has increasingly become a multi-racial, multi-ethnic, and gender neutral society in which discrimination has been progressively reduced towards Blacks, Indians, Hispanics, women, gays, etc. While there is some truth in the view that progress has been achieved on these matters over time, clearly on some of them America continues to lag behind other Western countries. America was slower than many others to reduce racism; it still has a higher percentage of its children living in poverty compared to other wealthy democracies; it has a lower percentage of women in the national legislature than most comparable states,

TABLE 1.1 Comparison of Poverty Rates, 2009

Country	Poverty Rates
United States	23.1%
Spain	17.1%
Greece	16.0%
Italy	15.9%
Japan	14.9%
Canada	13.3%
Luxembourg	12.3%
United Kingdom	12.1%
New Zealand	11.7%
Australia	10.9%
Belgium	10.2%
France	8.8%
Germany	8.5%
Sweden	7.3%
Norway	6.1%
Netherlands	6.1%
Cyprus	6.1%
Finland	5.3%
Iceland	4.7%

Source: Data from Adamson (2012, Figure 1b), found in Elise Gould and Hilary Wething, "U.S. Poverty Rates Higher, Safety Net Weaker than in Peer Countries," Economic Policy Institute Report, Issue Brief #339, July 24, 2012. Available at: www.epi.org/publication/ib339-us-poverty-higher-safety-net-weaker.

and so on. On various indices of socio-economic progress, America is not at all exceptional—and hardly at the top.

Just two tables reinforce the point. The first, from the Economic Policy Institute, compares the United States to other wealthy democracies regarding the proportion of children who live in poverty. One can have a discussion about anything, but this table is rather self-evident: the United States is certainly not a good place for poor children. The second, from the Organisation for Economic Co-operation and Development (OECD), compares the United States to other wealthy democracies regarding the life expectancy of women in 2011.

Now the U.S. record on female life expectancy, at almost 82 years, is extremely good compared to maybe 150 middle income or poor countries, but within the club of the rich, the United States is, in fact, at the level of Poland and the Czech Republic, and 18 out of 38 countries score better than the United States. However, it still speaks volumes that the United States is below the OECD average.

TABLE 1.2 Life Expectancy, Female Pop. at Birth, 2011 (or Nearest Year)

Country	Years
Australia	84.2
Austria	83.9
Belgium	83.2
Canada	83.9
Chile	81.0
Czech Republic	81.1
Denmark	81.9
Estonia	81.3
Finland	81.8
France	85.7
Germany	83.2
Greece	83.1
Hungary	78.7
Iceland	84.1
Ireland	82.8
Israel	83.6
Italy	85.3
Japan	85.9
Korea	84.5
Luxembourg	83.6
Mexico	77.2
Netherlands	83.1
New Zealand	83.0
Norway	83.6
Poland	81.1
Portugal	84.0
Slovak Republic	79.8
Slovenia	83.3
Spain	85.4
Sweden	83.8
Switzerland	85.0
Turkey	77.1
United Kingdom	83.1
United States	**81.1**
OECD AVERAGE	82.8

Source: Data from OECD Family Database, May 2014. Available at: www.oecd.org/els/family/CO1_2_Life_expectancy_at_birth_1May2014.pdf.

Returning to our main focus on foreign policy, we are reminded of Walt's balanced, if often overlooked, analysis of American self-interested behavior abroad. To be sure, illiberal governments have a record that is much worse: Hitler's Germany, Stalin's Russia, Pol Pot's Cambodia, Mao's China, Idi Amin's Uganda, and so on. At the same time, we should not forget that it was American leadership that sent troops to address starvation in Somalia in 1992 and took the lead in winding down atrocities in Bosnia in 1995 through the application of military force and then mediation of the Dayton Peace Accords. In these cases, the United States demonstrated a certain form of liberalized realism, but an accurate and balanced analysis runs as follows across many foreign policy particulars.

Conclusion #1, the good and bad are mixed. The United States led the struggle to contain and then undermine the Soviet Union's tyrannical empire during most of 1917–1990 (except during World War II). But in the process, the Eisenhower administration overthrew an elected "leftist" government in Guatemala in 1954, and then various U.S. administrations supported the follow-on military governments there that engaged in atrocities. Perhaps 200,000 Guatemalans were killed by their own government as the United States supported the carnage—all in the name of freedom, of course. It should not be forgotten that Washington inflicted a lot of "collateral damage" in winning the Cold War—not only in Guatemala but many other places like Iran, Chile, Zaire, etc.

Conclusion #2, principled actions are combined with self-interest. After Saddam Hussein's Iraq invaded Kuwait in 1990, the United States, acting under UN mandate led the military effort to counter that aggression. The U.S. diplomatic and military actions were exemplary. But there is no doubt that a good deal of self-interest was also in play. U.S. allies depended on Kuwaiti oil, and Saddam in Kuwait posed a threat to Saudi Arabia, an important U.S. ally and trade partner. According to Secretary of State Baker, the overriding issue was American jobs at home. It was certainly not a case of Washington opting for dangerous action on the basis of international principle alone. Moreover, neither Kuwait nor Saudi Arabia had positive records on human rights or democracy, and the United States did not push them to improve as a price for protecting them. In fact, their position on women's rights makes it difficult for women in the U.S. military to be stationed in Saudi Arabia. These two states have not improved their human rights record much, even today.

Conclusion #3, atrocities are sometimes ignored with political rationalizations. In the 1930s FDR's America could have done more for German Jews persecuted by the Nazis, such as by taking in more refugees, but FDR felt the country would not sustain such initiatives. Although the United States eventually became involved in the war, helping Jews and others against Nazi atrocities, the president was unwilling before Pearl Harbor (1941) to take great political risks to protect the rights of "others" in the face of widespread American anti-Semitism. In 1971 President Nixon and his principal advisor Henry Kissinger knew about the atrocities involved in the creation of Bangladesh, but they did not want to jeopardize the opening to China—with Pakistan as a key "middle man." Pursuing self-interest meant turning a blind eye to genocide and other gross violations of human rights by Pakistani forces and their local allies. Moreover, in 1994, President Bill Clinton did not want to get deeply involved in the Rwanda genocide, fearing that Congress and the American public would not support another controversial intervention after deadly difficulties in Somalia in 1993. Avoiding risks to American soldiers cost the lives of as many as 800,000 Rwandans, primarily Tutsi.

These three conclusions and inconsistencies in American foreign policy could be expounded further on any one administration, and we do so using Eisenhower as our example. Stephen Kinzer in his fine book (2013) on the Dulles brothers, says that both Secretary of State John Foster and CIA Director Allen, believed in American exceptionalism and that the country did too during that era. He writes (p. 312):

> From their remarkable family they absorbed the belief that Providence had ordained a special global role for the United States. They were also immersed in missionary Calvinism, which holds that the world is an eternal battle-ground between saintly and demonic forces.

He continues (p. 323):

> they did it [e.g., overthrow elected foreign leaders and try to kill some of them, refuse to compromise with communists or left-center Third World leaders] because they are us. If they were shortsighted, open to violence, and blind to the subtle realities of the world, it was because those qualities help define foreign policy and the United States itself.

Kinzer continues:

> The Dulles brothers personified ideals and traits that many Americans shared during the 1950s, and still share. They did not colonize America's mind or hijack United States foreign policy. On the contrary, they embodied the national ethos. What they wanted, most Americans wanted. …
>
> Foster and Allen Dulles believed they knew what was best for all people, not just those in the United States. And they considered the United States an instrument of destiny, blessed by Providence. This gave them deep self-confidence and a sense of infinite possibility. When they treated other nations cruelly, they comforted themselves with the thought that it was all for good in the end. They felt a noble, civilizing call. Exceptionalism, or the view that the United States has a right to impose its will because it knows more, sees farther, and lives on a higher moral plane than other nations—was to them not a platitude, but the organizing principle of daily life and global politics.

In all of this, "the Dulles brothers were one with their fellow Americans. Their attitudes were rooted in the American character and they were pure products of the United States" (p. 323).

If this is indeed accurate, and some will object, then it was probably true of President Eisenhower as well, because the Dulles brothers derived their power from the president. That point aside, one should not forget the historic record and the darker side of the administration's foreign policies. The overthrow of Mohammed Mossadeq in Iran in 1953 and Jacobo Arbenz in Guatemala in 1954 were not rogue operations but were instead approved by Ike. Likewise, the plan to remove Patrice Lumumba in the Congo in 1960 was not a random endeavor by underlings but approved by the president himself. However, it is important to remind that Lumumba was the first democratically elected leader of the Congo and was quite popular throughout Africa. Lumumba was killed in 1961 by others who beat CIA operatives to the punch, but this was all done with U.S. approval.

One might argue that what drove Ike's covert and brutal use of force was just a power struggle with the Soviet Union, without the trappings of American exceptionalism. But he did not rein in the moral rigidities of particularly John Foster Dulles: like Dulles, he did not compromise with communists in Vietnam in 1954 but rather started the United States on its disastrous course there, and like Foster he also over-estimated the threat from Mossadeq in Iran, Arbenz in Guatemala, Castro in Cuba, and Lumumba in the Congo. While Eisenhower presented a more "grandfatherly image" than the Dulles brothers, Ike approved the extreme and sometimes hare-brained schemes that transpired in the 1950s—e.g., inserting para-militaries into Eastern Europe and China who were immediately rolled up. For pragmatic reasons, Ike did want to avoid World War III with all its projected destruction, but there was a moralistic and crusading dimension to Eisenhower that his likeable and "hidden hand" style obscured.

The larger point about the inconsistencies of U.S. foreign policy across time should be obvious by now. The realities of the U.S. record in the world do not sustain the narrative of superior virtue manifested by the American president, Congress, or public opinion. If we look at another slice of the historical record to drive the point home of U.S. quasi-colonialism in the direct follow-on to 1898 and the Spanish American War, the analysis is not totally dissimilar from that of British colonialism. The American record includes contesting Spanish colonialism in Cuba and granting independence to the Philippines in 1947. It also includes waterboarding, torture, and politically inspired atrocities in trying to hold the Philippines before 1947. These and other brutal actions were known at the highest levels in Washington and covered up—rationalized away. The United States was also involved in various attempts to control Cuba after the Spanish were forced out, including efforts to invade the island and assassinate Fidel Castro.

It is important to point out that American claims to exceptionalism and Manifest Destiny are not fundamentally different from British claims to a civilizing (and racist) White Man's Burden. The British colonial record includes atrocities against assertive Indians, torture against assertive Kenyans, and in general a racist and demeaning set of policies against the non-Whites under their control. At the same time, the British did spread the rule of law and notably improved administration and education. It is also the case that many former British colonies have turned out relatively well compared to Belgian, Dutch, French, German, Portuguese, and Spanish colonies. The British version of White Man's Burden is equivalent to the French self-appointed role of taking on a Civilizing Mission, even as various governments in Paris brutalized Egyptians, Algerians, Vietnamese, and others.[7] The Spanish Empire did not hesitate in slaughtering many Indians in the Western Hemisphere, precisely because it saw itself as the standard bearer of higher, Christian, Catholic civilization. The Russian Tsars and Orthodox Christians also claimed to be doing God's work as they fought to expand their power into the Crimea against Ottoman (and Islamic) forces.[8] And in all cases, inconsistencies and even atrocities followed.

It is indeed true that American exceptionalism is not so exceptional, especially when compared to other Western liberal states. Despite these facts, President Obama raised a brief media storm in September 2013 when he said that he believed in American exceptionalism the same way that Brits believed in British exceptionalism and the Greeks believed in Greek exceptionalism—viz., that all nations tend to see themselves in a positive light. This is interesting, in part, because at other times the president said something quite different. Anatol Lieven, in his fascinating book on American nationalism, nicely summarizes this point:

> From time immemorial, nations have conceived of themselves as superior and as endowed with a mission to dominate other peoples or to lead the rest of the world into paths of light. A great many nations throughout history— perhaps even the great majority—have had a sense of themselves as especially chosen by God, or destiny, for great and special tasks, and often have used remarkably similar language to describe this sense of mission. Indeed, some of the most articulate proponents of America's universal mission have been British subjects, repeating very much the same lines that their fathers and grandfathers used to employ about the British Empire.[9]

Despite this kind of objective analysis, claims to American exceptionalism continue to be made in U.S. foreign policy statements. We now turn to an examination of the more or less contemporary scene.

Recent Views and Trends

Because of space limitations we somewhat arbitrarily start with Ronald Reagan who certainly appeared to be a true believer in American exceptionalism, but he was hardly alone. In general, American presidents since Reagan, both Republican and Democrat, have regularly appealed to America's uniqueness to garner votes or to support certain positions. These quotes demonstrate how thoroughly recent presidents have embraced this rhetoric.

- Ronald Reagan:[10] "We cannot escape our destiny, nor should we try to do so. The leadership of the free world was thrust upon us two centuries ago in that little hall of Philadelphia [where the American Constitution was negotiated]. In the days following World War II, when the economic strength and power of America was all that stood between the world and the return to the dark ages, Pope Pius XII said, 'The American people have a great genius for splendid and unselfish actions. Into the hands of America God has placed the destinies of an afflicted mankind.' We are indeed, and we are today, the last best hope of man on earth."
- George H. W. Bush:[11] "This afternoon I would like to just share some of my thoughts on the past few years and on America's purpose in the world. My thesis is a simple one. Amid the triumph and the tumult of the recent past, one truth rings out more clearly than ever: America remains today what Lincoln said it was more than a century ago, 'the last best hope of man on Earth.' This is a fact, a truth made indelible by the struggles and the agonies of the 20th century."
- Bill Clinton's Secretary of State, Madeleine Albright:[12] "But if we have to use force [against Saddam in Iraq], it is because we are America. We are the indispensable nation. We stand tall and we see further than other countries into the future."
- George W. Bush:[13] "Our Founders dedicated this country to the cause of human dignity, the rights of every person, and the possibilities of every life. This conviction leads us into the world to help the afflicted and defend the peace and confound the designs of evil men."
- Barack Obama:[14] "To brush aside America's responsibility as a leader and—more profoundly—our responsibilities to our fellow human beings under such circumstances [in Muammar Gaddafi's Libya] would have been a betrayal of who we are. Some nations may be able to turn a blind eye to atrocities in other countries. The United States of America is different."

Regardless of the particulars of the situation, all recent presidents and/or their highest associates have made reference to American exceptionalism, whatever the precise words chosen—not to mention many available examples from members of Congress. Permeating the above quotes is the notion that America is unique, morally superior, and has a special mission in the world. All this rhetoric might just be political blather, semantic ritual to fill a speech, mobilize support, or rationalize a policy. The speaker might not really believe the words uttered, and in some cases they were indeed the product of a speech writer. Yet, these ideas have not only lasted for centuries, but our point is that they are used with considerable regularity, especially to justify American foreign policy.

One can recall Samuel Johnson's old adage: "Patriotism is the last refuge of the scoundrel." It bears remembering that when Joe McCarthy (R., WI) was trying to make a name for himself in the 1950s by hounding some Americans with wild charges of disloyalty, often making up allegations with total falsehoods, he claimed to be doing so as a patriot protecting American security. However, a politician's public posture is not necessarily the same as the key motivation driving behavior. U.S. presidents might be saying what someone thinks is expected of them or even desired by their constituency. We suggest that of the personalities quoted above, Reagan and George W. Bush were probably the most genuine and consistent in referring to American exceptionalism. This follows from their being seen as neo-cons, with their strong belief in American Manifest Destiny or Providential Nationalism.[15]

This conclusion we believe would be sustained by a more thorough content analysis of their speeches and other publications like memoires and diaries. Reagan reiterated his belief in American exceptionalism on many occasions. That is not in doubt. George W. Bush apparently often spoke to others about how he felt he was called by God to be president and that God was working through him with regard to Iraq, Afghanistan, and other situations.[16] Both U.S. presidents made reference to America as special in terms of values and mission, and not just in public speeches but in private and unguarded moments. Interestingly, Bush was much more religious in his personal life (at least by the time of his Presidency as a born-again Christian and recovering alcoholic) than Reagan. His father, George H. W. Bush, however, was a realist but also less overtly religious and less prone to refer to a U.S. special role in the world on moral grounds. Instead, George H. W. Bush saw the country as exceptional in power terms and argued that this power status imposed an obligation of leadership. But this is quite different from the argument of divinely blessed, moral superiority. Recognizing a malleable power position is not the same as claiming to be a chosen people.

There is much more to be said about American exceptionalism and contemporary U.S. foreign policy, but for our purposes we want to turn to whether this hoary political rhetoric, articulated by some in the legislative as well as executive branches, resonates with public and elite opinion today. That is, do America and its foreign policy elites really believe in a U.S. special role in the world today oriented to furthering individual freedom and human dignity? Whatever the accuracy of Kinzer's summary statements above about the Dulles brothers and the nature of American society in the 1950s, and in the light of the more recent statements by American leaders continuing to endorse American exceptionalism noted above, we would like to know if the situation has changed—at least for now. After the difficulties in Vietnam, Somalia, Rwanda, Iraq, Afghanistan; after the Watergate scandal by Nixon; after the Great Recession of 2008–2009, with growing awareness of partisan gridlock in Washington and the failure of the two parties to solve domestic problems, like growing inequality, poor schools and health care and massive national debt, etc., we want to know if the idea of American exceptionalism is being rethought, in whole or in part by the American public?

Initially, depending on which polls one reads, it seems that the idea of American exceptionalism holds strong in American society and that Americans are quite willing to send the military abroad to stop atrocities like genocide. Other polls, however, cast doubt on this positive interpretation. Cases from the real world also suggest that just a few casualties in a U.S. humanitarian mission are often enough to force a change in policy. Unfortunately, the polls do not ask: Are you in favor of promoting human rights or democracy abroad if it means U.S. personnel will be killed or captured?

A central point however remains perfectly clear. Neither mass nor elite opinion supports a costly crusade to advance democracy or human rights abroad. Any such alleged "special mission" lacks significant support when one gets into specifics.[17] Particular policies oriented to democracy or human rights abroad have run and will run into significant opposition if too much blood or treasure has to be expended by Americans. We should clarify terms here. By democracy, we refer to free and fair elections in which pluralistic or majority opinion controls what follows. Electoral winners exercise power. By liberal democracy, we mean genuine majority (or pluralistic) rule combined with the real practice of civil and political rights such as the operation of independent courts that function to guarantee protection for unpopular individuals, groups, and minorities. Human rights may support or constrain democracy. Some human rights endorse and facilitate majority rule, such as freedom of speech and assembly. But some human rights restrict those who win elections, preventing them from persecuting those unpopular. Some human rights are separate from the norms of democracy, such as prohibiting genocide or torture of detainees. The fundamental point is that democracy and human rights can overlap but are not the same idea. Consider the following opinion polls:

TABLE 1.3   The United States in the World

	Greatest Country	No Greater than Other Countries
Do you believe the United States has a unique character that makes it the greatest country in the world or believe every country is unique and the United States is no greater than other nations?	66%	31%

Source: Data from Dina Smeltz, "Foreign Policy in the New Millennium. Result of the 2012 Chicago Council Survey of American Public Opinion and the U.S. Foreign Policy," Chicago Council on Global Affairs, 2012. Available at: www.thechicagocouncil.org/sites/default/files/2012_CCS_Report.pdf.

TABLE 1.4 Public Support for the Use of U.S. Troops

If China invaded Taiwan	28%
If North Korea invaded South Korea	41%
If Israel were attacked by its neighbors	49%
To be part of an international peacekeeping force to enforce a peace agreement between Israel and the Palestinians	53%
To ensure the oil supply	56%
To deal with humanitarian crises	66%
To stop a government from committing genocide and killing large numbers of its own people	70%

Source: Data from Dina Smeltz, "Foreign Policy in the New Millennium. Result of the 2012 Chicago Council Survey of American Public Opinion and the U.S. Foreign Policy," Chicago Council on Global Affairs, 2012. Available at: www.thechicagocouncil.org/sites/default/files/2012_CCS_Report.pdf.

TABLE 1.5 Public Support for U.S. Intervention, December 2010

	Does	*Does Not*	*Unsure*
Do you think the United States does or does not have a special responsibility to be the **leading** nation in world affairs?	66%	31%	3%
Because of the United States' history and its Constitution, do you think the U.S. has a unique character that makes it the greatest country in the world, or don't you think so?	80%	18%	2%

Source: Data from Dina Smeltz, "Foreign Policy in the New Millennium. Result of the 2012 Chicago Council Survey of American Public Opinion and the U.S. Foreign Policy," Chicago Council on Global Affairs, 2012. Available at: www.thechicagocouncil.org/sites/default/files/2012_CCS_Report.pdf.

TABLE 1.6 Public Views on the Use of Force

Does the U.S. have a moral obligation to use force?

	Agree	Disagree	Unsure
May 2006	77%	13%	10%
July 2005	69%	21%	10%

Source: Data from Dina Smeltz, "Foreign Policy in the New Millennium. Result of the 2012 Chicago Council Survey of American Public Opinion and the U.S. Foreign Policy," Chicago Council on Global Affairs, 2012. Available at: www.thechicagocouncil.org/sites/default/files/2012_CCS_Report.pdf.

TABLE 1.7 Public Views on Promoting Democracy

Should the U.S. try to democratize other countries?

	Try	Not	Depends	Not Sure
Sept. 2013	15%	72%	7%	6%
Nov. 2011	15%	70%	9%	6%
Sept. 2008	15%	65%	9%	10%
March 2007	15%	69%	11%	6%
April 2003	29%	48%	16%	7%

Source: Data from Dina Smeltz, "Foreign Policy in the New Millennium. Result of the 2012 Chicago Council Survey of American Public Opinion and the U.S. Foreign Policy," Chicago Council on Global Affairs, 2012. Available at: www.thechicagocouncil.org/sites/default/files/2012_CCS_Report.pdf.

TABLE 1.8 Public's Policy Priorities

Should America focus on problems at home or promote democracy abroad?

	Focus on Problems at Home	Continue to Promote Democracy	Depends/ Mixed
Sept. 2013	74%	22%	3%
May 2005	54%	33%	11%

Source: Data from Dina Smeltz, "Foreign Policy in the New Millennium. Result of the 2012 Chicago Council Survey of American Public Opinion and the U.S. Foreign Policy," Chicago Council on Global Affairs, 2012. Available at: www.thechicagocouncil.org/sites/default/files/2012_CCS_Report.pdf.

TABLE 1.9 Public Views on Democracy Promotion Abroad

Should the United State promote democracy in other countries?

	Should	Should Not	Unsure
March 2011	32%	64%	4%

Source: Data from Dina Smeltz, "Foreign Policy in the New Millennium. Result of the 2012 Chicago Council Survey of American Public Opinion and the U.S. Foreign Policy," Chicago Council on Global Affairs, 2012. Available at: www.thechicagocouncil.org/sites/default/files/2012_CCS_Report.pdf.

TABLE 1.10 Public Views on American Responsibility for Global Democracy

Does the U.S. have a responsibility to promote democracy?

	Does Not	Does	Depends	Unsure
Feb. 2011	28%	63%	4%	5%
July 2009	31%	60%	2%	7%

Source: Data from Dina Smeltz, "Foreign Policy in the New Millennium. Result of the 2012 Chicago Council Survey of American Public Opinion and the U.S. Foreign Policy," Chicago Council on Global Affairs, 2012. Available at: www.thechicagocouncil.org/sites/default/files/ 2012_CCS_Report.pdf.

TABLE 1.11 Comparing Top Policy Priorities

	General Public	Council on Foreign Relations (CFR) Members
Protecting U.S. from terrorist attacks	83%	76%
Protecting jobs of American workers	81%	29%
Preventing spread of WMDs	73%	47%
Reducing dependence on imported energy sources	61%	17%
Combating international drug trafficking	57%	11%
Strengthening the United Nations	48%	17%
Dealing w/ global climate change	37%	57%
Promoting and defending human rights in other countries	33%	19%
Helping improve living standards in developing nations	23%	25%
Promoting democracy in other nations	18%	12%

Source: Data from Dina Smeltz, "Foreign Policy in the New Millennium. Result of the 2012 Chicago Council Survey of American Public Opinion and the U.S. Foreign Policy," Chicago Council on Global Affairs, 2012. Available at: www.thechicagocouncil.org/sites/default/files/2012_ CCS_Report.pdf.

In this last poll above, it is interesting that the public *sometimes* expresses *somewhat* more support for protecting human rights abroad than for advancing democracy in other countries. This could be because protecting human rights includes such ideas as protecting against genocide and other atrocities. Interestingly, the public seems more interested in human rights than Council on Foreign Relations members. This could be because Council members are deeply focused on national security and economic issues.

The larger point from many of the other poll results noted above is that citizen interest in human rights and/or democracy greatly lags behind other more self-interested options such as protecting against terrorist attacks or protecting jobs of American workers. This is not an aberration in 2013 but a pattern that has shown up for a long time in most survey research of Americans, whether elite or mass. Claims that America has a special role to advance democracy and/or human rights simply do not find great support in public opinion when questions are asked with specificity. If a general question is asked about belief in American exceptionalism with no costs attached, and not in relation to various policy goals, then a favorable response may indeed be found. It seems that the general public still believes in the myth of American exceptionalism if questions remain vague and general. The more specific and relative one gets, the less support for the idea is found. One might say that Americans believe in U.S. foreign policy that should be cosmopolitan, doing good for others, but in practice they want a foreign policy built on narrow, nativist nationalism reflecting self-interest.

The persistent facts about citizens' relatively low concern about democracy and/or human rights abroad in relation to other *specific* foreign policy goals do not mean that a president or other high foreign policy official will necessarily terminate democracy promotion programs or ignore democracy or human rights issues. High officials may not always feel constrained by citizens' opinions. It is one thing to check a box on an opinion survey, but it is something else to vote on the basis of foreign policy and/or be highly active on foreign issues. George W. Bush and his advisors may have seen elections in Iraq as a necessary event for the withdrawal of many U.S. military forces, whatever public opinion might think. The polls indicate clearly why citizens did not care so much that the United States did not take action to block genocide in Rwanda in 1994. In fact, Samantha Power, an Obama administration official, back in her academic career, reminded us in her book *A Problem from Hell* (2002) that the United States has never responded vigorously to situations of genocide, whether in 1917 (Ottoman Armenia) or 1942 (Nazi Germany) or 1994 (Rwanda) or whenever. Certainly public opinion is not going to compel the government to block such atrocities.

Most of these poll results help us understand why Clinton used bombing at relatively high altitudes when he (and NATO) decided to use force presumably to counteract ethnic cleansing by Serb authorities in Kosovo in 1999, and why Obama likewise opted for air strikes rather than boots on the ground in Libya to protect (rebel) civilians from Gaddafi in 2011. The public was not likely to tolerate American casualties in a humanitarian mission devoid of major self-interest. The point no doubt was clear after 1993 when the U.S. military took casualties in its humanitarian mission in Somalia. Congressional and public opinion led to a rapid shift in policy and the fairly rapid withdrawal of most U.S. forces.

The idea that America is morally superior to other nations in being willing to sacrifice for democracy and human rights abroad simply does not hold water. That said, America is probably not worse than other liberal democracies in this regard; both Belgium and the Netherlands abandoned their humanitarian missions in

Bosnia (1995) and Rwanda (1994) respectively when their soldiers were killed. French public support for humanitarian policies in the Central African Republic in 2013–2014 also declined when difficulties were encountered and the loss of French military lives occurred.

In other words, U.S. leaders like Obama or former Secretary of State Condoleezza Rice may make nice speeches about promoting democracy in the Arab world, but when push came to shove in places like Egypt during the Arab Spring, Washington was reluctant to cut its ties with friendly autocrats and their military backers. It is not surprising that Obama's deference to the Egyptian military coup of 2013, which deposed the elected Morsi of the Muslim Brotherhood, did not give rise to a backlash in American public opinion. Polls about specific

TABLE 1.12 Partisan Gaps over Long-Range Policy Priorities

Foreign policy priorities rated as more important by Republicans

	Republican	Democrat	Independent	R-D Diff
Reducing illegal immigration	62%	38%	49%	+24%
Protecting U.S. from Terrorism	93%	81%	78%	+12%

Foreign policy priorities on which Rep and Dem generally agree

	Republican	Democrat	Independent	R-D Diff
Reducing dependence on imported energy	64%	59%	60%	+5%
Combating international drug trafficking	59%	60%	52%	-1%
Preventing spread of WMD	76%	78%	68%	-2%
Protecting American jobs	81%	84%	80%	-3%

Foreign policy priorities rated as more important by Dems

	Republican	Democrat	Independent	R-D Diff
Promoting democracy abroad	16%	27%	13%	−11%
Promoting human rights abroad	27%	41%	30%	−14%
Improving living standards in developing nations	13%	32%	23%	−19%
Strengthening the UN	25%	50%	35%	−20%
Dealing with global climate change	16%	57%	35%	−41%

Source: Data from Dina Smeltz, "Foreign Policy in the New Millennium. Result of the 2012 Chicago Council Survey of American Public Opinion and the U.S. Foreign Policy," Chicago Council on Global Affairs, 2012. Available at: www.thechicagocouncil.org/sites/default/files/2012_CCS_Report.pdf.

TABLE 1.13 Public Views on Conflict Resolution

Should the U.S. lead in trying to solve conflicts?

	Should	Should Not	Unsure
Sept. 2013	34%	62%	5%
May 2013	35%	58%	6%
April 2003	48%	43%	9%
Sept. 2002	45%	49%	6%

Source: Data from Dina Smeltz, "Foreign Policy in the New Millennium. Result of the 2012 Chicago Council Survey of American Public Opinion and the U.S. Foreign Policy," Chicago Council on Global Affairs, 2012. Available at: www.thechicagocouncil.org/sites/default/files/2012_CCS_Report.pdf.

TABLE 1.14 Public Views on Isolationism

Do you agree that the U.S. should "mind its own business"?

Date	Agree
1964	20%
1976	43%
1995	41%
2002	30%
2013	52%

Source: Data from Dina Smeltz, "Foreign Policy in the New Millennium. Result of the 2012 Chicago Council Survey of American Public Opinion and the U.S. Foreign Policy," Chicago Council on Global Affairs, 2012. Available at: www.thechicagocouncil.org/sites/default/files/2012_CCS_Report.pdf.

options or comparisons give no reason to expect such a backlash. With this said, there are still partisan differences on these matters, with Democrats being more interested in democracy and human rights in the world, and also strengthening the United Nations, than Republicans, as the cited polls confirm (with some slight statistical variation).

Several polls show that circa 2013 the American public wishes to scale back U.S. international involvement, emphasize multilateral endeavors or burden sharing in foreign policy, and pay more attention to domestic problems. These views do not indicate isolationism à la the 1930s but rather a retrenchment away from an extensive internationalism and unilateralism.

Such polls might fit with a more inward-looking conception of American exceptionalism already noted—namely that the United States should be a city

TABLE 1.15 Public Views on American Leadership

U.S. Leadership should seek…

	Sept. 1993	*Sept. 1997*	*(Early) Sept. 2001*	*Oct. 2005*	*Nov. 2009*	*Nov. 2013*
Single world leadership	10%	12%	13%	12%	14%	12%
Shared leadership role	81%	73%	75%	74%	70%	72%
Be most active	27%	22%	25%	25%	19%	20%
Be as active as others	52%	50%	49%	47%	48%	51%
No leadership role	7%	11%	8%	10%	11%	12%
Don't know	2%	4%	4%	4%	6%	4%

Source: Data from Dina Smeltz, "Foreign Policy in the New Millennium. Result of the 2012 Chicago Council Survey of American Public Opinion and the U.S. Foreign Policy," Chicago Council on Global Affairs, 2012. Available at: www.thechicagocouncil.org/sites/default/files/2012_CCS_Report.pdf.

on a hill and moral beacon to all by trying to perfect American society at home, rather than going abroad in search of evil "monsters to destroy." The downside of such a conception is that this then leaves situations like Darfur in Sudan or Syria under Assad without adequate attention by the state with the power to make some difference. Given the reach of its military power, the size of its economy, and its diplomatic-legal position in the UN Security Council, the United States often remains the indispensable nation—whether it likes it or not. At least at this point in time, in terms of being well positioned to have an impact if it wishes to try, there is no other country like the United States.

A compromise or half-way option for a more restrained Washington, mindful of domestic defects, is to pursue active diplomacy and multilateralism but without major economic or military investments in those situations. The central problem is that diplomacy that does not reflect economic and military realities on the ground usually does not succeed. This was evident in the Obama–Kerry approach to the humanitarian disaster in Syria in early 2013. Active diplomacy did not alter the disaster, because the military facts on the ground had not changed. This can be compared with its successful negotiations to end to the Bosnian war at Dayton (1995), which occurred after the United States organized and armed a Bosnian-Croat military force that checked Serb militias and altered the military balance of power on the ground.

We thus cannot ignore the fact that a return to an internationally more passive approach to American exceptionalism carries potential downsides for those abroad victimized by violations of human rights and humanitarian law. Trying to perfect American society at home does not save the Iraqi Yazidis from the depredations of ISIS. Certainly, a multilateral approach has much to recommend it, where economic and/or military burdens are shared, but multilateralism requires the cooperation of key partners. It is also usually more time consuming and it may ultimately result in more bloodshed and human rights abuses. It also tends to undermine the notion of America as uniquely gifted and morally superior, willing to sacrifice to save others. That could be a good thing.

Conclusion

U.S. policy in Somalia (after 1993, disengagement after loss of American lives), Rwanda (in 1994, ignoring genocide), Kosovo (in 1999, intervening but without ground troops), and elsewhere (like Libya in 2011, intervening but without ground troops or major commitment to that state's stability after Gaddafi) confirms the more guarded findings of several reliable polls. And contrary to what U.S. politicians may say, American public opinion does not rank the rights and well-being of foreigners high in their specific priorities. The case studies and specific questions in polls used in this chapter make it painfully clear that the United States displays no special virtue in sacrificing for "others," regardless of how fervently Ronald Reagan and others may believe in the myth of American exceptionalism as moral superiority. Above all, whatever the various polls say, the facts of U.S. diplomatic and domestic history do not support a record of American moral exceptionalism in many concrete situations.

It seems that many in the United States do, indeed, believe in the idea of American exceptionalism. To be sure this notion is an important part of the country's historical narrative and national identity. Some may even endorse a U.S. foreign policy that is directed at good for others and thus cosmopolitan in its outlook. At the same time, the public clearly prioritizes a foreign policy that is based on parochial nationalism and national self-interest. Given the somewhat delusional and schizophrenic American public, it is not surprising that most American foreign policy leaders would make some rhetorical appeal to American exceptionalism. It is popular to do so in the abstract. More important is the fact that some American presidents at particular points in history have genuinely tried to do good for others within the constraints of an American public whose majority is fundamentally nativist and oriented to self-interest.

Hence, Clinton's policy on Kosovo (high-altitude bombing to stop ethnic cleansing), George W. Bush's policy on Darfur (allowing referral of atrocities to the International Criminal Court), or Obama's policy on Libya (bombing to block the massacre of civilians) has been as follows: do something but do not trigger a backlash because of costs to the nation. At the same time, Clinton ignored the Rwandan genocide, Bush's policies triggered another humanitarian disaster because of a failure to plan adequately for the occupation of Iraq, and most recently Obama has tried to stay disengaged from the Syrian civil war which has created a massive humanitarian disaster.

Most presidents seem to know that although Americans like the notion of American exceptionalism, they also know that Americans do not like to undertake the spending of blood and treasure in a cosmopolitan crusade to protect the rights and well-being of foreigners. If the latter goal is actually pursued, it has to be done on the cheap; otherwise, the people will not support it and the popularity of policy makers will suffer.

Notes

1 The authors thank Courtney Hillebrecht and Morton Winston for comments on earlier drafts of this chapter.
2 See Jeffrey Goldberg, "The Obama Doctrine," *The Atlantic*, April 2016. Available at: www.theatlantic.com/magazine/archive/2016/04/the-obama-doctrine/471525.
3 Walter A. McDougall, "The Unlikely History of American Exceptionalism," *The American Interest*, Spring (March/April 2013), 7–13.
4 Stephen M. Walt, "The Myth of American Exceptionalism," October 11, 2011. Available at: www.foreignpolicy.com/articles/2011/10/11/the_myth_of_american_exceptionalism.
5 Ibid.
6 Godfrey Hodgson, *The Myth of American Exceptionalism* (New Haven, CT: Yale University Press, 2009).
7 Paul Strathern, *Napoleon in Egypt* (New York: Bantam Books for Random House, 2007).
8 Orlando Figes, *The Crimean War: A History* (New York: Metropolitan Books, 2010), p. 133.
9 Anatol Lieven, *America Right or Wrong: An Anatomy of American Nationalism* (Oxford: Oxford University Press, 2004), p. 33.
10 Ronald Reagan, "The Shining City Upon a Hill" (speech, Washington, D.C., January 25, 1974), Origin of Nations. Available at: www.originofnations.org/books,%20 papers/quotes%20etc/Reagan_The%20Shining%20City%20Upon%20A%20Hill%20 speech.htm.
11 George H. W. Bush, "Remarks at Texas A&M University" (speech, College Station, TX), December 15, 1992. Texas A&M. Available at: http://millercenter.org/president/ speeches/speech-3432.
12 Madeline Albright, "Transcript: Albright Interview on NBC-TV February 19," February 19, 1998. Available at: http://fas.org/news/iraq/1998/02/19/98021907_tpo. html.
13 George W. Bush, "Text of President Bush's 2003 State of the Union Address" (speech, Washington, D.C., January 28, 2003), *Washington Post*. Available at: www.washington-post.com/wp-srv/onpolitics/transcripts/bushtext_012803.html.
14 Barack Obama, "Remarks on Libya, America Cannot Stand Aside" (speech, Washington, D.C., March 29, 2011), *Washington Post*. Available at: www.washingtonpost.com/ blogs/plum-line/post/did-obamas-libya-speech-%09%09%09finally-kill-american-exceptionalism-zombie/2011/03/04/AFPJTluB_blog.html.
15 There is no agreed upon definition of neo-conservatism (Forsythe, 2011: 29–37). Kissinger, by all accounts a realist, considered Reagan to be a Wilsonian liberal because of his optimism about progressive change and his belief in American exceptionalism (Kissinger, 1994: 771–773 and passim). It is not unusual for analysts to disagree about how to label most policy makers. We do not wish to get sidetracked by those debates about who best represents what theory of international relations or school of foreign policy.
16 Jim Wallis, "Dangerous Religion—Bush's Theology of Empire," December 19, 2003. Available at: www.informationclearinghouse.info/article5402.htm.
17 Tony Smith, *America's Mission: The Worldwide Struggle for Democracy* (Princeton, NJ: Princeton University Press, 2012).

Further Selected Readings

Albright, M. "Transcript: Albright Interview on NBC-TV February 19," February 19, 1998. Available at: www.fas.org/news/iraq/1998/02/19/98021907_tpo.html.

Bass, G. *The Blood Telegram: Nixon, Kissinger, and a Forgotten Genocide*. New York: Alfred A. Knopf, 2013.

Barnett, M. *Witness to a Genocide: The United Nations and Rwanda*. Ithaca, NY: Cornell University Press, 2002.

Breitman, R. and Lichtman, A. J. *FDR and the Jews*. Cambridge, MA: Belknap Press for Harvard University Press, 2013.

Bush, G. H. "Remarks at Texas A&M University" (speech, College Station, TX), December 15, 1992. Texas A&M. Available at: http://millercenter.org/president/speeches/detail/3432.

Bush, G. W. Remarks in State of the Union address, America's role from start was to do good and "confound desires of evil men." January 28, 2003. Available at: www.washingtonpost.com/wp-srv/onpolitics/transcripts/bushtext_012803.html.

Ferguson, N. *Empire: The Rise and Demise of the British World Order and the Lessons for Global Power*. London: Allen Lane, for Penguin Books, 2002.

Figes, O. *The Crimean War: A History*. New York: Metropolitan Books, for Henry Holt Publishers, 2010.

Forsythe, D. P. *The Politics of Prisoner Abuse: The United States and Enemy Prisoners after 9/11*. Cambridge: Cambridge University Press, 2011.

Gitlin, T. and Leibovitz, L. *The Chosen Peoples: America, Israel, and the Ordeals of Divine Election*. New York: Simon & Schuster, 2010.

Hodgson, G. *The Myth of American Exceptionalism*. New Haven, CT: Yale University Press, 2009.

Ignatieff, M., ed. *American Exceptionalism*. Princeton, NJ: Princeton University Press, 2005.

Jones, G. *Honor in the Dust: Theodore Roosevelt, War in the Philippines, and the Rise and Fall of America's Imperial Dream*. New York: New American Library, 2012.

Kinsella, H. M. *The Image Before the Weapon: A Critical History of the Distinction Between Combatant and Civilian*. Ithaca, NY: Cornell University Press, 2011.

Kinzer, S. *The Brothers: John Foster Dulles, Allen Dulles, and their Secret World War*. New York: Times Books for Henry Holt Publishers, 2013.

Kissinger, Henry. *Diplomacy*. New York: Simon & Schuster, 1994.

Lieven, A. *America Right or Wrong: An Anatomy of American Nationalism*. New York and Oxford: Oxford University Press, 2004.

Lipset, S. *American Exceptionalism: A Double-Edged Sword*. New York: Norton, 1996.

McDougall, W. A. "The Unlikely History of American Exceptionalism," *The American Interest*, vol. 8, no. 4, February 2013, 7–13.

Madsen, D. L. *American Exceptionalism*. Edinburgh: Edinburgh University Press, 1998.

Mandelbaum, M. *The Case of Goliath: How American Acts as the World's Government in the 21st Century*. New York: Public Affairs, 2005.

Murray, C. *American Exceptionalism: An Experiment in History*. Washington, D.C.: AEI, 2013.

Obama, B. "Remarks on Libya, America Cannot Stand Aside" (speech, Washington, D.C.), March 29, 2011. *Washington Post*. Available at: www.washingtonpost.com/blogs/plum-line/post/did-obamas-libya-speech-finally-kill-american-exceptionalism-zombie/2011/03/04/AFPJTluB_blog.html.

Power, S. *A Problem from Hell: America and the Age of Genocide*. New York: Basic Books for the Perseus Book Group, 2002.

Reagan, R. Quote on American exceptionalism. 1974. Available at: www.intellectualtakeout. org/content/ronald-reagan-quotes-america-city-upon-hill.

Renan, E. "What is a Nation," in *Becoming National: A Reader*, edited by Geoff Eley and Ronald Suny. New York and Oxford: Oxford University Press, 1996, pp. 41–55.

Strathern, P. *Napoleon in Egypt*. New York: Bantam Books for Random House, 2007.

Walt, S. M. "The Myth of American Exceptionalism," *Foreign Policy Magazine* online, October 11, 2011. Available at: www.foreignpolicy.com/articles/2011/10/11/the_myth_of_american_exceptionalism.

2

PROMOTING DEMOCRACY AFTER THE COLD WAR

Mission Contained

Democracy promotion has a long history in U.S. foreign policy that alternately surfaces and submerges depending on the context and America's power. But after the Cold War and especially after 9/11, this policy took a different, more aggressive turn. At the beginning of the 1990s, President George H. W. Bush spoke cautiously about the new world order and America's leadership. By 1993, President Clinton proclaimed that "Our overriding purpose must be to expand and strengthen the world community of market-based democracies."[1] The popularity of democracy promotion was not due solely to a change in leadership, nor was it the result of a surge in cosmopolitanism among the population. Democracy promotion instead became a central part of Clinton's foreign policy because it could. As an integral part of America's national identity, the president acknowledged that with the Soviet Union's collapse and the absence of challengers, the United States had an unprecedented opportunity to link power with purpose.

After 9/11, U.S. foreign policy found a more urgent mission: fighting terrorism. The promotion of democracy did not disappear, but instead it lost what Tony Smith calls its "fortunate vagueness," or its ability to emerge and disappear without much notice, and became what President George W. Bush declared "the calling of our time."[2] Confident that the United States could make the world safe for democracy, the Bush administration camouflaged the country's strategic interests and divided the world into those "who are with us" and those "who are against us." Using lofty rhetoric about America's duty and desire to extend the blessings of democratic liberalism around the world, the Bush administration relied on military force to coerce and cajole recalcitrant governments in the name of democracy promotion. Unique international circumstances after 9/11, combined with a too-rosy view of assumed U.S. power, produced a new imperial mission. The effect of this assumption was not good for democracy promotion or American credibility.[3]

This chapter will examine democracy promotion in the post–Cold War era with a focus on how the Bush administration's so-called freedom agenda took the country down a different and dangerous path. Democracy promotion includes a range of policies, institutions, and mechanisms, but it generally implies financial support or in-kind assistance for the creation of certain institutions (such as free and fair elections); groups in civil society (specifically advocacy organizations and an independent media); and rule of law. It may involve an array of political actions as diverse as diplomatic pressure, the tying of foreign aid to certain conditions or outcomes, sanctions, as well as the use of force. By comparing different administrations in the 1990s and 2000s, we find more similarities than political party or rhetoric might suggest, in part because national interest is not a given but is, in fact, a social construct. Thus, with every president (with the exception of Obama), democracy promotion rhetoric grew stronger while the actual record of promoting democracy was always mixed. After 9/11, however, an inconsistent promise became an intentional strategy not only to promote "freedom" but to advance national interests and secure American primacy.

We also address the role of the public and why these ideas remained so strong among different administrations. We show that the public's support of integrating the defense of democracy into U.S. foreign policy is lukewarm at best. Some Americans may genuinely care about democracy in other countries, but when this foreign policy goal is compared to other interests, Americans consistently prefer that the government focus on stability abroad, but they are still far more concerned about security and economic matters within their borders.

Historical Roots and Political Legacies

Woodrow Wilson after World War I was the first American president to formally link the promotion of democracy abroad to U.S. foreign policy goals— hence the term Wilsonianism or liberal democratic internationalism to describe American efforts to make the world safe for democracy. The roots of this policy, however, go much deeper and can be traced back to the Founding Fathers and their beliefs in the country's presumed exceptional nature. Early on, presidents and pundits regularly linked the colonies' call for freedom with the causes of all mankind. Equating America's aspirations with universal values not only made the young country supposedly a model for others to emulate, but it provided the United States with a unique national purpose: to help the rest of the world become free.

For many years, America's ideas about democracy in other countries were a passive endeavor circumscribed by the young country's relatively weak power position. President Jefferson, for example, believed that the United States would never be truly safe until European autocracies had disappeared. But since the United States was weak, the best it could do was to act as a beacon for the rest of the world, expanding its territory in North America and increasing its military power to protect American interests. All of this was said to be the creation of "an empire of liberty." But the United States did not involve itself, for example, in the push for more democracy across Europe in 1848.

It was only after the Spanish-American war (1898) and during President McKinley's administration that a more activist agenda was adopted. Since neither annexation nor occupation were acceptable choices in Cuba and the Philippines, President McKinley, reluctantly and after asking for divine guidance (!), decided to intervene in these countries and establish presumably democratic governments— with the intention of leaving quickly. The challenges of imposing democracy from the outside proved more difficult than expected, and the United States became bogged down in rebellions and revolts—most notably in the Philippines. In Cuba, it opted to turn the government over to a corrupt and autocratic regime that served American interests. But in both cases, the United States acted as other great powers do, believing that its wisdom and greatness sanctioned American control over non-European peoples.

Presumably, the United States did not learn much from its first experiences with a more activist democracy agenda, because many times since in Germany and Japan after World War II and in Afghanistan and Iraq more recently, the United States has adopted the idea that it could "fight them, beat them and make them democrats."[4] The United States did succeed in Germany and Japan, but only through occupation, significant investments, and staying the course for many years. More often than not, the United States has failed in its efforts to impose democracy on others, and it suffered high costs in the process. This is especially the case when it has tried to do so at the point of a bayonet.

President Wilson was unique in that he not only linked democracy in other major countries directly to American security, but he essentially redefined what it meant for the country to be a world power. Believing that the European balance of power politics was dangerous and obsolete but certain that some form of world order was necessary, Wilson intentionally tried to put the United States at the center as a new way of stabilizing the world. Despite appearances, Wilson was no altruist, nor did he believe in national self-determination for all peoples. But by redefining the idea of national interest for the United States and linking it with global interests institutionalized in the League of Nations, he intention- ally linked America's security with universal needs and a more peaceful world. Theoretically, liberal democratic internationalism would make the world safe for democracy. It also made it easier for the United States to advance its own inter- ests and hegemonic position through diplomacy and economics. Yet, the Senate, as is well known, did not choose to follow Wilson's more activist plans when it failed to ratify the Versailles Treaty of 1919 containing the League of Nations Covenant.

After World War II, Wilson's original desire to link America's interests with global stability was more fully implemented, thanks in large part to President Truman's combination of realism and liberalism. International stability, democracy, human rights, and economic progress was supposed to be institutionalized via the United Nations, whose Security Council was to be dominated by the great powers and had the authority to even override other parts of international law if necessary (as per UN Charter Article 103). At the same time, in trying to advance its own interests and (liberal) values, the United States endorsed other global and regional organizations that tied democratic principles to membership.

During the Cold War (1947–1989) most American presidents at least talked about some version of democracy and the "free world," even as Washington often aligned with autocrats as long as they were sufficiently anti-communist or anti-Moscow. Some presidents (like Johnson and Nixon) tended to discount democracy promotion rhetoric, believing that such talk would undermine the country's more important national interests.[5] But even for presidents like Truman, Kennedy, and Reagan who more actively defended its place in U.S. foreign policy, the differences in their actions were not always that significant. President Carter may have been an exception in terms of his personal commitment to democracy and human rights, but like every other American president he too had to struggle with the pull of parochial nationalism and need to balance our ideals with more tangible national concerns. Regardless of the intensity of the rhetoric, democracy promotion as a policy and practice was selective and inconsistent and no U.S. president elevated democracy promotion to a place where it interfered with competition with the Soviet Union. In fact, it regularly aligned itself with autocrats, dictators, and even communists (such as Tito in Yugoslavia) as long as they opposed the Soviet Union.

In 1961 President Kennedy created the United States Agency for International Development (USAID). Promoting democracy through economic development was both a moral obligation and a way to counter communism and other extremist movements that upset global stability and U.S. interests. President Kennedy formally institutionalized this thinking by establishing the Agency for International Development. At least in theory, USAID helped meet U.S. political and economic moral obligations as a leader and good neighbor.

More than two decades later, President Reagan expanded the country's repertoire of foreign policy instruments, calling on Congress to create the National Endowment for Democracy (NED) to both fulfill America's values mission and intensify the country's anti-communist agenda. Because of these efforts, democracy promotion has been a bipartisan feature of U.S. foreign policy for many decades. However, regardless of the president and what each might have said about national interests and concern for democracy promotion, they all balanced U.S. interest in democracy with other competing concerns. President Reagan in particular is known for the strong rhetoric he used about America's moral duty to protect freedom and the free world from communism. But his behavior, like other presidents, included close alignments with dictators—in Reagan's case in Argentina and Zaire (now the Democratic Republic of Congo), to cite just two examples. The Iran-Contra scandal (1985–1987) exposed the hypocrisy of his supposed democracy agenda as his administration was criticized for collusion with autocratic Iran in order to provide arms to the contra militia in Central America in violation of a statute adopted by Congress.

Eventually, a certain consensus did emerge under Reagan's leadership, from the early line of accepting anti-communist dictators as necessary allies to a growing willingness to support democracy against tyrants. Throughout the 1980s as the Cold War weakened, the United States urged many of its autocratic allies in Latin America and East Asia toward democracy, facilitated the departure of General Augusto Pinochet as Chile's leader (largely, though, because it was believed that if Pinochet stayed in power it would provoke instability), and pushed Taiwan, South Korea, and the Philippines in the direction of electoral democracy.

It was during George H. W. Bush's administration (1989–1992) that the Soviet Union collapsed and the Cold War came to a sudden but peaceful end. The United States was the world's sole superpower, able to direct, if not dominate, international politics. Given these unique international circumstances and its preponderance of power, was the United States finally able to fulfill its democratic promises? Was it successful, moreover, in encouraging more countries to become democratic? To be sure, democracy promotion was increasingly mentioned as an important part of U.S. policy by both Republican and Democratic presidents. Money for democracy promotion abroad also increased steadily, with significant funding, at least initially, going to communist Eastern Europe. But although the senior Bush was not as predisposed to crusading rhetoric as his predecessor, his responses to communism's demise were largely aimed at trying to create a world order based on democracy, capitalism, and American leadership.

More pragmatic than principled, the first Bush administration moved away from Reagan's ideological rigidity, but he still backed up commitment to democracy with money, military might, and different, more flexible strategies. To help the countries in Central and Eastern Europe transition away from communism for example the Bush administration established the Support for East European Democracy (SEED) act to encourage political and economic change. And in places like the Philippines, Panama, El Salvador, and Nicaragua, where the Reagan administration had supported the government and prolonged violence by supporting right-wing extremists who ran death squads, attacked civilians, and committed other human rights violations, Bush opted for more pragmatic, flexible policies that relied on diplomacy.

President Bush was a pragmatic realistic. He understood the limits of American power but also the problems that would result if the United States relied too heavily on democracy promotion—even if it was largely rhetoric. The Gulf War in 1990 in response to Iraq's invasion of Kuwait was both the highpoint of Bush's more activist foreign policy and the beginning of its decline, as Bush appreciated well the costs and risks that were always involved in using military force.

American power, especially its military superiority, remained strong, but new threats were emerging and the Bush administration made it clear that democracy promotion or any other interest in advancing democratic values would be limited to certain countries in a very circumscribed way. Context and American power vis-à-vis the targeted country made all the difference. This is why in the summer of 1989 when Chinese students demanded democratic freedoms but were met with bloody repression, the Bush government condemned the communist government but it did little else. Privately, the president even went so far as to say that he wanted a resumption of normal relations with China, after a pro forma period of symbolic protest. Even in Europe, as violence ripped the Yugoslav state apart, strategic national interests as traditionally and narrowly defined won out as the Bush administration tried to avoid the country's unfolding civil war.

William Clinton campaigned on the promise that a historical moment had arrived. The Cold War's end provided an unprecedented opportunity to build a world order congenial to American interests and identity. The presumed unipolar moment meant that the United States had both the capacity and the leadership to become the world's indispensable power by using its military and economic resources to promote democracy and protect human rights. From Baghdad to Beijing, President Clinton promised, the United States would fight tyranny, because it "protects our interests and security and ... reflects values that are both American and universal."[6]

Once in office and after setbacks in controlling local politics in Somalia and Haiti, the Clinton administration was less vocal about the urgency of defending American values and human rights. Democracy promotion did not in fact become a top priority for the Clinton administration, but was instead one of several important national concerns. Realizing the challenge of matching deeds with words and the need to respond to crises, U.S. strategy shifted, making democracy promotion more pluralistic by enlisting nongovernmental organizations (NGOs) to become part of the mission. Democratic aid grew exponentially but rather than take on the task alone the Clinton administration emphasized enlarging and institutionalizing the democratic community of market democracies. Despite what he once said, like all other presidents Clinton was selective in terms of where democracy promotion was a priority. Where democratic changes were under way, as in formerly communist Europe and Latin America, democracy promotion played a more central role in U.S. policy. In Europe, though, policies worked through a combination of praise and criticism, using multilateral institutions like NATO and the Partnership for Peace program to leverage democratic change. In Latin America the course was a bit different, but the United States still relied on familiar strategies, promoting free trade first and then political changes.

In other regions, the promotion of democracy was uneven or nonexistent. In the Middle East and many Asian countries where either the United States perceived its position to be weaker or where American strategic interests pointed in a different direction, democracy promotion was downplayed or suppressed completely. Although the Clinton administration was generally successful in creating multilateral coalitions, it was unable to garner a lot of Western support to pressure China on its human rights policies or in favor of democracy there. In China, as in Saudi Arabia and Egypt, the Clinton administration failed to integrate democratic concerns effectively with economic and security interests, weakening the credibility of America's leadership in this area. Despite Clinton's initial enthusiasm, his record of promoting democracy was uneven at best. However, the trend of promising a lot and delivering little continued under George W. Bush's administration.

The Effects of 9/11

According to George W. Bush,

> America's story is of a new world that became a friend and liberator of the old, the story of a slaveholding society that became a servant of freedom, the story of a power that went into the world to protect but not possess, to defend but not conquer.[7]

Supposedly, this is why President Bush, when he was first elected, was unenthusiastic about the United States becoming the world's policeman. Early on, democracy promotion in the form of nation building was not embraced and there was an intentional, if brief, suggestion that the United States would focus narrowly on strategic national concerns. To inspire trust and respect in America's leadership, President Bush promised that the United States would act humbly and with restraint.

At the same time, Bush's first inaugural address, as well as other comments he made, exposed the new president's interest in American exceptionalism and the fate of all people in the world. The terrorist attacks on September 11, 2001 produced major changes within the United States, including a whole host of new institutions to protect the homeland. In foreign affairs, changes were just as evident, and promises to act humbly and build trust were abandoned as the country's security and the war on terror became overriding concerns. As we now know, President Bush had surrounded himself with neo-conservatives or neocons who never saw the United States or foreign affairs through a realist prism. The attacks on U.S. soil, thus, allowed more aggressive thinkers to convince the president of the need to use hard power to secure the United States and create a new world order.

President Bush did not give up the idea of defending democracy and freedom in the world; on the contrary, he embraced it as a central tenet of his foreign policy. To weaken Islamic extremism and defend the country from another attack, the Bush administration adopted a "neo-Wilsonian ideology." The policy contained familiar ideas about democracy and freedom for people all over the world, but it was enhanced with messianic notions about America's religious duty and scientific certitude. As Tony Smith critically observes, after 9/11 the country of imperial possibilities finally had a doctrine of imposing responsibility and a new imperial mission.[8]

Unique circumstances and the hope of unchallenged power allowed the Bush government to adopt ambitious ideas for promoting democracy, prosperity, and world peace. And it was prepared to use military force to carry out them out. The National Security Strategy of 2002, the so-called Bush Doctrine, made the case for both why and how the United States would secure itself and the world. The doctrine contained four central elements: a belief in the importance of a state's domestic regime in determining its foreign policy; the perception that great threats must be defeated by new and vigorous policies (such as preventive war); a willingness to act unilaterally when necessary; and an overriding belief that peace and stability in the world required American primacy.

Under the Bush administration it was no longer just in America's interest to defend liberty and promote democracy in other countries, but it maintained that these policies were morally right and universally embraced by people everywhere in the world. As President Bush explained:

> Our Nation's cause has always been larger than our Nation's defense. We fight, as we always fight, for a just peace—a peace that favors liberty. We will defend the peace against the threats from terrorists and tyrants. We will preserve the peace by building good relations among the great powers. And we will extend the peace by encouraging free and open societies on every continent.[9]

This tale of a new moral crusade was believed by few and disliked by most. For much of the world U.S. democracy promotion had become a code for regime change and efforts to ensure American primacy.

The first targets of Bush's aggressive democracy promotion agenda were Afghanistan (2001) and Iraq (2003). The history of U.S. interventions in these countries differed in important ways, but in both countries the Bush administration tried to legitimize military actions with the language of democracy and freedom. The administration maintained that the liberation and democratization of these countries would not only succeed but they would inspire democratic revolutions all around the world. Bush was certainly not the first American president to cloak security interests in democracy promotion rhetoric, but the suddenness and forcefulness of his policies stood out as did his faith in the ability of the United States to transform societies and to convert a hostile world into a peaceful one. In his 2005 State of the Union address Bush confidently reminded the world that

> By now it should be clear that decades of excusing and accommodating tyranny in the pursuit of stability have only led to instability and tragedy ... It

should be clear that the advance of democracy leads to peace, because governments that respect the rights of their people also respect the rights of their neighbors.[10]

The United States spent billions of dollars on its freedom agenda and the Middle East was ground zero for these policies. Afghanistan and Iraq provided excellent testing ground for its two-pronged strategy to fight terrorism and promote democracy. Funding for democracy promotion and human rights increased accordingly from about $500 million in 2000 to almost $1.5 billion in 2008. In addition, the Bush administration initiated a high-profile public diplomacy campaign to convince the world and Muslims in particular of America's honorable intentions. It also established and generously financed democracy promotion programs like the Greater Middle East Initiative (GMEI) and the Middle East Partnership Initiative (MEPI) which supported local efforts at political reform, women's rights, a free media, and specific institutions research. Despite some good intentions and significant amounts of investment, the efforts were not very successful.[11] Some suggest this was true because the administration's policies in the region were inconsistent and contradictory. The supposed liberation of Iraq was nothing short of a mess, almost from the beginning. Instead of working with Iraqis to help rebuild the county, the Coalitional Provisional Authority walled itself off, living in a compound of swimming pools and luxury. Instead of throwing flowers at the feet of "liberating" U.S. soldiers, as some had promised, by late summer 2003 there was violent insurgency in many parts of the country. In Afghanistan, U.S. misadventures were having a similar effect. In hindsight most agree that the Bush administration's freedom agenda actually made things worse in the Middle East.

The other problems with U.S. policies in the Middle East were just as obvious. The fact is the United States had different and contradictory goals in the region, and how it interpreted its democracy mission varied by country. The radical strand of its democracy agenda insisted on political democracy (using military force if necessary). This more radical strand targeted countries like Iran and Syria that were opposed to American influence in the region. Meanwhile, the more conservative strand of the administration's policies emphasized democratic elections and socioeconomic issues but sought gradualism, aiming to protect rather than undermine undemocratic allies and power structures. Gradual conservative policies were thus applied to autocratic countries like Saudi Arabia and Egypt that happened to be two of America's closest allies in the region. Rather than emphasize political reform in these countries it supported the opening up of markets and free trade, adopting an economics-first strategy. Thus, depending on the country, domestic conditions, and America's relative power vis-à-vis the targeted country, policies only selectively focused on political and democratic change but instead emphasized free trade and creating markets. In Morocco, for example, some $6 million was given in return for opening its markets to American corporations, while $1 million was allocated to help Saudi Arabia, Yemen, and Algeria join the World Trade Organization.[12]

More than a decade of investments and policies did not produce anything like democracy in most of the Middle East. In fact, American misadventures in Afghanistan and Iraq left the entire region more unstable, undemocratic, and conflict-prone. Part of the reason was that the United States continued to cultivate, if not strengthen its relationships with autocratic allies in the region and elsewhere, believing these countries could help the United States contain terrorism and ensure stability. Egypt is a case in point. Although the Bush administration promised to spread democracy throughout the region, its alliance with Mubarak and the nearly $2 billion in annual military and economic aid did not change under President Bush.

In explaining the country's historical relationship to Egypt all references to democracy and human rights were noticeably absent and instead the administration emphasized Egypt's strategic importance for peace in the Middle East, the war on terror, and the ongoing wars in Afghanistan and Iraq. Democracy promotion was, thus, submerged despite Mubarak's authoritarian grip on power and lack of freedom in the country. Although some in Egypt welcomed the administration's focus on democracy promotion, the Bush administration's heavy hand in the region, to say nothing of its invasions of Afghanistan and Iraq, played into the hands of those who had long distrusted the United States, believing that democracy promotion was part of America's broader imperial project in the Middle East.

Based on its actions and continued support for the Mubarak government, but also its close relations with governments in Pakistan, Saudi Arabia, and the Gulf States, it was clear to many that democracy promotion was little more than window dressing to pursue U.S. security and economic interests in the region. More important than democracy were allies that could assist with the wars in Afghanistan and Iraq and fight terrorist extremists. The Bush administration worked hard to create "a coalition of the willing" or a group of countries from all over the world that would help protect the United States and the world from the so-called Axis of Evil—states and non-state actors that supported terrorism and were intent on disrupting world order. In particular, the United States needed the diplomatic and military support of great powers and countries that bordered Afghanistan and Iraq.

It did not matter, therefore, that Saudi Arabia was a dictatorship that blatantly dismissed women's rights. It also was not much of a concern that China flagrantly abused human rights or that free speech and other freedoms were deteriorating in Russia under Vladimir Putin. The Bush administration's obsession with national security and American primacy meant that it was not only willing to work with undemocratic allies but it even hinted that it wanted to get rid of democratically elected politicians (like Hugo Chavez, President of Venezuela) who openly defied the United States. For a time the Bush administration's pretense at liberal internationalist policy, in reality a pathology of hubristic power, was without limits.

In Africa, where the United States had much more power, the Bush administration adopted a less militaristic but equally activist strategy, creating the Millennium Challenge Account (MCA) and introducing politically conditioned aid. Conditionality had been used in the past but the MCA was unique because of its size and the flexibility it provided states in determining how aid was spent. Although its primary goal was economic development, one of its strategic objectives was decreasing poverty by enhancing personal freedom and fostering democratic development. Despite its benefits, it should not be forgotten that this policy too was a unilateral American initiative that bypassed UN and allied development efforts. Thus, while the Bush administration pursued different, less coercive strategies in Africa, it nevertheless imposed its liberal ideas on these countries without consulting or cooperating with others.

It is too early to say whether MCA has had a decisive effect on democratizing Africa. Although it did not produce a wave of democratization throughout the continent, important political improvements occurred. Some evidence suggests these positive political changes were due to the reform catalyzing capacity of the MCA or "The MCA Effect" on certain African countries.[13] The "effect" however is most commonly referenced in association with economic changes, as 24 countries cited the prospect of receiving funds from the MCA as the primary reason for implementing economic reforms.

Balancing democracy promotion with strategic national security concerns was not easy or that successful. After setbacks and reversals the Bush administration turned to a one-size-fits-all approach to promote democracy. This included a call for elections, opening markets following the prescriptions of neoliberal economics and pushing for free trade, with the goal of generating gradual and stable transformations to market democracies.[14] When Bush left office his most prominent foreign policy project—the global promotion of democracy, with the goal of ending tyranny in the world—was plagued with crisis and criticism.[15] His administration's unique strand of Wilsonianism with a vengeance proved problematic not only for the state of democracy in the world but for democracy promotion as an idea and practice in U.S. foreign policy. It produced a hell of good intentions in the Middle East in particular.

Overcoming Bush's Legacy

More than anything else, President Obama wanted to shake off the legacy of the Bush administration and restore credibility to the country as a reliable, non-imperial partner in international relations. Thus, unlike all of the other presidents in the post-Cold War era, Obama did not explicitly mention democracy promotion in his first inaugural address. Instead, he emphasized humility, restraint, and the importance of being an example to the world. Cosmopolitan ideals associated with democracy and human rights did not disappear completely, but the Obama administration promised a more practical foreign policy based on the firm conviction that democracy could not be imposed from the outside and democratization was neither sure nor rapid. The failure of Bush's policies, alongside what many saw as a decline in U.S. power and different ideas on American leadership meant that, at least initially for the Obama administration, democracy promotion was contained, becoming once again a more passive foreign policy idea.

President Obama's top foreign policy officials like Secretary of State Hillary Clinton similarly adopted measured rhetoric, voicing their skepticism of military intervention while emphasizing America's responsibility in the world but promising that the United States would use multilateral institutions and partnerships. In her speeches Secretary Clinton talked regularly about the three D's in U.S. foreign policy but they were defense, diplomacy, and development.[16] Explicit and forceful attempts to defend and promote democracy abroad were noticeably absent, especially in the first years of the Obama presidency. In fact, when the Secretary of State visited China for the first time, more than one observer was surprised that Clinton did not pay more attention to human rights, including those that pertained to democracy. Instead, the administration emphasized the important role of development and human dignity as ways of both countering Islamic extremism and enabling a stable modernization to take place. From time to time President Obama mentioned American exceptionalism and the country's unique role in the world, but gone were the missionary fervor and certitude that colored the language of the Bush administration.

Obama did talk more about democracy promotion in 2009 while in Cairo, but his tone and emphasis were noticeably different from his predecessor. In this speech and in others that followed, President Obama explained that while he believed democracy was essential for reflecting the will of the people, it could not be imposed on a country. He said this explicitly in his Havana speech in 2016 during his historic trip to Cuba. Moreover, while the Bush administration clearly saw an important role for military force in promoting democratic ideas, privileging unilateralism over efforts to bring together coalitions, President Obama promised that his administration would use different strategies and tools to help countries that supported universal principals of democracy. He promised Egyptians in 2009 that the United States would not rely on its military in the region, planning to invest billions via foreign assistance in Pakistan, Afghanistan, Egypt, and elsewhere to build schools and hospitals, roads and businesses, and to provide hundreds of millions to help those who have been displaced.[17] Despite this rhetoric, and Obama's general desire to avoid further military ventures in the Middle East, by the end of his administration the president had authorized further military action in both Iraq and Syria, mainly directed against ISIS after it had killed Americans in the region and claimed credit for terrorist attacks on U.S. allies in Europe.

Some have criticized the Obama administration for downgrading democracy too much in its foreign policy. It is true that no new policy infrastructure has been developed on the same scale as under the senior Bush, Clinton, or the second

Bush administrations. There were no major new legislative initiatives and no institutional expansion of democracy promotion within the government agencies.[18] At the same time, the Obama administration vociferously defended its efforts to promote democracy, maintaining a sizable budget despite Republican efforts to cut it.

More serious criticisms have centered on the administration's reactions (or lack thereof) to major democratization crises. For example, in 2009 when protests over fraudulent elections were brutally repressed by the Iranian government during Iran's Green Movement, the Obama administration barely responded. Presumably, it did little because it did not want to damage ongoing discussions over the country's nuclear activities. It was also probably sensitive to tainting Iranian progressives with an open endorsement of their activities, since this would have given Iranian hardliners a further excuse to crack down—which the Iranian government eventually did anyway. In the same month, the administration initially denounced the coup d'état in Honduras that pushed elected President Zaleya from office, but a few months later it dropped its sanctions and recognized the new Honduran government. During this time the Organization of American States (OAS) was working hard to restore democracy in Honduras but was essentially undercut by the United States and its embrace of the government. Although U.S. policy was driven by congressional conservative interests which were sensitive to business concerns, the White House and President Obama did not care enough about events to determinedly fight for democratic principles. U.S. recognition of the new government undermined both U.S. rhetoric in favor of democracy and the OAS principle opposing any interruption of electoral democracy.

By the end of the summer, fraudulent elections in Afghanistan produced little reaction from the Obama administration, even though the United States had a substantial influence in the country. But here as in other countries where the administration was confronted by major democratization crises and setbacks as in Niger, Sri Lanka, Kyrgyzstan, Guinea, and Belarus, U.S. actions were less than satisfying and democracy seemed to have little place in U.S. policy. In Afghanistan and Iraq the administration has stopped talking about these countries as cases of post-conflict democratic nation-building. It still spends a large share of its democracy budget on them, but to little effect. The Obama administration wanted to reduce involvement in the complicated Middle East while "pivoting" to Asia. This meant downgrading democracy promotion in places like Afghanistan and Iraq.

Since 2011 the Arab Spring has forced the Obama administration to confront democracy promotion in a more direct way. While it took a few months to respond, in May 2011 President Obama announced what he called "a bold new approach to foreign policy" and U.S. relations with the Middle East. Attributing the revolutions in the Middle East to a denial of dignity and a lack of political and economic self-determination, he committed his government to more actively supporting democracy in the region. At the same time, he promised that the United States would continue to "keep our commitments to friends and partners." In other words like the Bush administration before him, the United States would use the Arab Spring as an opportunity to try to change the region, in theory by supporting political change, human rights, and economic reforms. Since U.S. strategy today is held together by some of the same ideas of the Bush administration, emphasizing economic reform and gradualism, some believe that the Obama administration is making many of the same mistakes as the previous administration.

It might be easy to link U.S. democracy promotion efforts to the Arab Spring, but research suggests that U.S. democracy promotion assistance and the United States did not, in fact, play a significant role in encouraging anti-government protests in any of the Arab countries. We do know that the Obama administration ignored many of the pro-democracy movements and, at times, it demonstrated that it was more concerned with security interests and gradualism than it was in recognizing grassroots democratic impulses.

More telling has been the U.S. position in the post-Mubarak period. In Egypt as in the other pro-Western countries of the region, foreign military aid continued to be greater than aid for democracy promotion—even as the latter amount increased relative to the past. And at first the United States decided not to place conditions on its $1.3 billion of annual military funding, despite the Egyptian military's coup against the elected Morsi of the Muslim Brotherhood. The army's practice of using emergency laws, mass arrests, violent breaking up of protests, torture, and harassment of opposition did not provoke a strong Obama response. As the military's repression escalated, the State Department continued to remain silent on events, noting only that the United States deplored violence.

In many ways the Obama administration has continued with "business as usual," not only working with undemocratic actors as in Saudi Arabia and Bahrain, but at times suggesting that it would support groups that promote the status quo rather than aiding unstable but more democratic power sharing arrangements. To encourage autocratic adversaries to reform and liberalize, a dual-track engagement strategy, which works with regimes and their citizens, has been central to the Obama administration's conception of democracy diplomacy. This means improving government-to-government relations, using this dialogue to advance human rights while at the same time engaging civil society and peaceful political opposition and encouraging U.S. nongovernmental actors to do the same. This strategy is based on the belief that changes in government-to-government relations will create permissive conditions for civil society to operate and for more extensive people to-people exchanges.[19] It is still to be seen whether dual-track engagement makes much of a difference in places like China, Russia, and Iran where this strategy has been most consistently pursued, much less in the Middle East. In Egypt under military rule, pro-democracy foreign NGOs have been barred or expelled or harassed—as has also been the case in India and Russia.

In some countries it seems that U.S. democracy promotion efforts have only made things worse, or failed to make things better. In Jordan, for example, where U.S. officials have regularly applauded the government for its liberalizing reforms, the country was for a time, at best, a slightly liberalized autocracy despite more money from the U.S. government for democracy promotion. In 1993 the American NGO Freedom House scored Jordan a three on political liberties and three on civil liberties. (A score of one is best and six is worst.) This was the highest "freedom" scores of any Arab country at the time. In 2011 and after the United States started to pay more attention to democracy promotion, Jordan scored a six on political liberties and a five on civil liberties, indicating that it had authoritarian status. Or, in the words of Freedom House, Jordan had moved from "partly free" to "unfree."

So-called democracy initiatives after 2001 provided assistance to civil society organizations, but since these organizations had to work closely with the government they did not in fact "give voice" to the interests of the people but instead disconnected politics from peoples' lives.[20] We also cannot forget that during this period Jordan was hosting large numbers of Syrian refugees, which the United States no doubt appreciated. Jordan also cooperated with the United States and its "enhanced interrogation" technics of terrorist suspects. And in January 2011, when some 5,000 people rallied to protest the policies of the government and called for the resignation of Prime Minister Rifai, the United States responded by increasing cash transfers to the Jordanian government. President Obama reportedly called King Abdullah II to reassure him of U.S. support.

President Obama, while sometimes speaking out in favor of democracy, as he did during his historic trip to Cuba, certainly did not make that theme the centerpiece of his foreign policy. Instead of harking back to the past and the role of the United States historically, he regularly talked about the future and how globalization had changed the world. In particular the proliferation of threats and non-state actors has made the country vulnerable despite its military power. The United States no longer had the luxury of thinking about a single country or threat. And since power is dispersed and decentralized the United States must be ready to respond to many states and non-state actors that can harm the United States and its allies.

Under Obama, U.S. foreign policy goals have not changed fundamentally, but the president's perception of the world, of globalization and American leadership, means that the United States needs to use different strategies. It needs to cooperate more and do more listening rather than assuming or imposing American leadership. At the same time, Obama is clearly not a die-hard cosmopolitan or singularly minded idealist. He has been very assertive regarding the use of unilateral drone strikes, he has increased special operations on the ground in Iraq and maybe Syria, and he regularly admits to being sometimes a realist, as Jeffrey Goldberg's April 2016 article in *The Atlantic* magazine makes plain.[21] Obama understands the messy world that we live in and the need for nuance in his position, explaining:

I am also an idealist insofar as I believe that we should be promoting values, like democracy and human rights … because not only do they serve our interests … but because it makes the world a better place … [but] "you could call me a realist in believing we can't, at any given moment, relieve all the world's misery … We've got to be hardheaded … and pick and choose our spots. … There are going to be times where our security interests conflict with our concerns about human rights."[22]

The Role of Public Opinion

In the abstract the American public may like the notion of promoting democracy in other countries. But when asked directly about what should be the country's foreign policy priorities, public opinion is clear at least on one point: democracy promotion is not a top priority. It is not even near the top. When Americans were asked at different points in time, starting in 1993 and ending in 2011, to prioritize the country's foreign policies, democracy promotion was regularly at the bottom of a long list of national concerns.

At the top of the list was protecting the country from terrorist attacks, protecting American workers, and stopping the spread of weapons of mass destruction (WMDs). In other words when asked to rank American goals, narrow realist concerns associated with security were on top while cosmopolitan issues like promoting human rights and democracy and improving living standards in poor countries were not. More recent surveys from 2013 confirm that these trends have continued and are linked to perceptions that the country's power is declining and that it should focus more on domestic affairs.

TABLE 2.1 Priorities and Democracy Promotion

% saying each is top priority	1993	1997	2001	2005	2009
Protect against terror attacks	–	–	80%	86%	85%
Protect jobs of American workers	85%	77%	77%	84%	85%
Stop spread of WMD	69%	70%	78%	75%	74%
Reduce dependence on imported energy	–	–	–	67%	64%
Reduce illegal immigration	–	42%	–	51%	46%
Deal with global climate change	–	–	44%	43%	40%
Strengthen the United Nations	41%	30%	42%	40%	37%
Promote human rights abroad	22%	27%	29%	37%	29%
Improve living standards in poor countries	19%	23%	25%	31%	26%
Promote democracy abroad	22%	22%	29%	24%	21%

Source: Data from "America's Place in the World" Surveys, The Pew Research Center, February 4, 2011. Available at: www.pewresearch.org/2011/02/04/historically-public-has-given-low-priority-to-promoting-democracy-overseas.

TABLE 2.2 Consistent Long-Term Foreign Policy Goals

% saying each is top priority	Sept. 1997	Early Sept. 2001	Oct. 2005	Nov. 2009	Nov. 2013
Protect against terror attacks	–	80%	86%	85%	83%
Protect jobs of American workers	77%	77%	84%	85%	81%
Stop spread of WMD	70%	78%	75%	74%	73%
Reduce dependence on imported energy	–	–	67%	64%	61%
Combat international drug trafficking	67%	64%	59%	56%	57%
Reduce illegal immigration	42%	–	51%	56%	57%
Deal with global climate change	50%	44%	43%	40%	37%
Strengthen the United Nations	30%	42%	40%	37%	37%
Promote human rights abroad	27%	29%	37%	29%	33%
Improve living standards in poor countries	23%	25%	31%	26%	23%
Promote democracy abroad	22%	29%	24%	21%	18%

Source: Data from "America's Place in the World" Surveys, The Pew Research Center, February 4, 2011. Available at: www.people-press.org/2013/12/03/section-3-long-range-foreign-policy-goals.

As with American presidents, the public's party affiliation does not affect support for this foreign policy. In 2009, for example, only 25 percent of Republicans, 22 percent of Democrats, and 15 percent of independents indicated that democracy promotion was a top priority.[23] For some Americans democracy promotion is not only regarded as a good in and of itself, but it is seen as a policy that can advance strategic and security concerns. Almost 40 percent of Americans for example responded that they believed that the promotion of democracy in Middle Eastern countries was "very important" to reducing terrorism. At the same time, 41 percent believed just the opposite and that not getting involved in other countries' problems would reduce terrorism in the future.[24]

Recent polls also indicate that faith in the transformative power of this foreign policy tool is waning, particularly in certain parts of the world. Although foreign policy elites polled in 2013 were somewhat optimistic about the prospects for democracy in places like China (52 percent) and Iran (50 percent), they were considerably less enthusiastic about the democratic futures of Egypt, Saudi Arabia, or Russia. Similarly the American people have less confidence in the possibilities for democracy—and for American foreign policy—to transform the world, especially in the Middle East. This is why more than half of Americans (63 percent) indicated that they favored stable governments in some countries, even if there was less democracy in the region, over democratic governments and less stability.

TABLE 2.3 U.S. Priorities in the Middle East

For the Middle East, is democracy or stability more important?

	Total	Republican	Democrat	Independent
Democratic governments even if less stability	28%	25%	39%	23%
Stable governments even if less democracy in the region	63%	67%	53%	69%
Don't know	9%	8%	8%	8%

Source: Data from "America's Place in the World" Surveys, The Pew Research Center, February 4, 2011. Available at: www.people-press.org/2013/12/03/public-sees-u-s-power-declining-as-support-for-global-engagement-slips/12-3-2013-47.

TABLE 2.4 Priorities Are at Home

Should the U.S. mind its own business internationally and let other countries get along the best they can on their own?

	Agree	Disagree
1964	20%	69%
1974	43%	45%
1984	36%	52%
1994	41%	48%
2004	35%	54%
2013	52%	38%

Should we not think so much in international terms but concentrate more on national problems and building up our own strengths and prosperity at home?

	Agree	Disagree
1964	54%	32%
1974	73%	25%
1984	60%	33%
1994	78%	28%
2004	65%	32%
2013	80%	16%

Source: Data from "Public Sees U.S. Power Declining as Support for Global Engagement Slips," "America's Place in the World" Surveys, The Pew Research Center, December 3, 2013. Available at: www.people-press.org/2013/12/03/public-sees-u-s-power-declining-as-support-for-global-engagement-slips/12-3-2013-20.

TABLE 2.5 Balancing Civil Liberties and Security

What concerns you more about the government's anti-terrorism programs?

	Not gone far enough to protect the country	Gone too far in restricting personal liberties
2004	49%	29%
2007	55%	26%
2010	58%	27%
2013	44%	39%

Source: Data from "Public Sees U.S. Power Declining as Support for Global Engagement Slips," "America's Place in the World" Surveys, The Pew Research Center, December 3, 2013. Available at: www.people-press.org/2013/12/03/public-sees-u-s-power-declining-as-support-for-global-engagement-slips/12-3-2013-34.

These views correspond with the public's belief in the declining power of the United States and its leadership ability in the world. In fact, for the first time since World War II more than half of Americans polled believed that rather than trying to solve the world's problems or get involved in other countries' affairs, it was time for the United States to mind its own business and focus on domestic concerns.

It is clear that the American public wants the government to focus on protecting the country from terrorist attacks, but large numbers of Americans are concerned that the government's anti-terrorism programs may have gone too far and are actually hurting democracy at home. When asked about the government's efforts to fight terrorism in 2013, some 44 percent of those polled indicated that they were concerned that the war on terrorism restricted civil liberties in the United States.[25] Yet, almost the same percentage (39 percent) said that they were still more concerned that anti-terrorist measures did not go far enough to protect the country's security.

Thus, public support for democracy promotion is not only weak but it is split over whether or not the United States has gone far enough to protect the country—even if it is dangerous for democracy at home.

Conclusion

For all of the differences between George W. Bush and Barack Obama (and other presidents in the post-Cold War period), they shared the belief that the United States is exceptional and the world both wants and needs American leadership.[26] For George W. Bush, these beliefs played out as a crusade, inspired and approved by God, to make the world safe for democracy through the unilateral use of force. For Obama, American exceptionalism means doing good in the world by assuming responsibility in certain crises while also sharing the burden with other countries. As he puts it, "One of the reasons I am so focused on taking action multilaterally where our direct interests are not at stake is that multilateralism regulates hubris."[27] President Obama never abandoned democracy promotion altogether, reintroducing it into his foreign policy agenda, albeit in a far more contained, multilateral manner. This is because Obama knows that democracy promotion is deeply engrained in the country's national identity as the leader of the Free World. Thus, even when America's actions are selective and inconsistent, a central characteristic of its nationalism is the ambition to liberate and enlighten the world by endowing it with human rights and democracy.

There are important differences among presidents in the post-Cold War era in terms of the intensity of their rhetoric, the strategies they used to carry out their goals, but also their understanding of American leadership. Unlike the Bush administration's missionary incantations about America's moral duty and divine right, Obama has been unapologetically pragmatic in terms of how he approaches foreign policy, scaling back grandiose rhetoric and assuming a more reserved stance on the promotion of democracy in other countries. It remains nonetheless an important part of how the United States engages in the world. As the National Security Strategy explains, the purpose of America's engagement abroad and democracy promotion within it is to

> strengthen the regional partners we need to help us stop conflicts and counter global criminal networks; … advance democracy and human rights; and ultimately position ourselves to better address key global challenges by growing the ranks of prosperous, capable, and democratic states that can be our partners in the decades ahead.[28]

Democracy promotion in the next administration will no doubt look different. It might not be about regaining political credibility and moral humility, but it will, no doubt, claim to be a policy to advance American interests. Indeed, beyond the question of its centrality in U.S. policy is the perennial question of its effectiveness. Although the U.S. government naturally tends to claim success in its efforts, noting for example in one report that 36 out of 57 countries that were recipients of U.S. democracy assistance from 1980 to 1995 successfully democratized, most academic research on the topic is more skeptical.[29] Targeting of aid may improve the chances of success, but even in places like Central and Eastern Europe where the United States was fairly consistent and generous in its support for democracy, most research credits other organizations like the European Union, NATO, the Council of Europe—rather than the United States—or any single actor for its role in promoting democracy and stability. Yet, even in countries like Poland and Hungary that eagerly embraced democracy and the United States in the early 1990s seem to be losing ground as conservative, right-wing governments have come to power.

For centuries, democracy promotion has emerged and submerged depending on the context and American power. This is not likely to change any time soon. Rhetoric is likely to remain strong while support will be selective and inconsistent. When democracy promotion must compete with other more important security and economic interests, it will likely fade away, as it has in the past. But democracy promotion will not disappear entirely because it is part of America's identity and its exceptional character and because Americans continue to believe that its interests are universal, democracy is inevitable, and more democracies make the world a more peaceful place.

Notes

1 Quoted in Mark Peceny, *Democracy at the Point of Bayonets* (University Park, PA: Penn State, 1999), p. 159.
2 Quoted in David Price, "Global Democracy Promotion: Seven Lessons for the New Administration," *The Washington Quarterly*, 32:1, January 2009, 159–170.
3 Tony Smith, *A Pact with the Devil: Washington's Bid for World Supremacy and the Betrayal of the American Problem* (New York: Routledge, 2007), p. 4.
4 Bruce Russett, "Bushwacking the Democratic Peace," *International Studies Perspectives*, 5, 2005, 396.
5 For more on the differences in American presidents see Smith, *A Pact with the Devil*, chapter 3.
6 This was a quote from Anthony Lake taken from Peceny, *Democracy at the Point of Bayonets*, p. 159.
7 Inaugural Address, January 20, 2001. Available at: www.presidency.ucsb.edu/ws/?pid=25853.
8 Smith, *A Pact with the Devil*, pp. 323–359.
9 "The National Security Strategy of the United States of America," The White House. Available at: www.informationclearinghouse.info/article2320.htm.
10 Russett, "Bushwacking the Democratic Peace," 396.
11 See Tamara Cofman Wittes and Andrew Masloski, *Democracy Promotion under Obama: Lessons from the Middle East Partnership Initiative* (Saban Center for Middle East Policy at the Brookings Institution, 2009).
12 Barbara Ann J. Rieffer and Kristan Mercer, "U.S. Democracy Promotion: The Clinton and Bush Administrations," *Global Society*, 19:4, 2005, 400.
13 Cited in Stephen D. Collins, "Can America Finance Freedom? Assessing US Democracy Promotion Via Economic Statecraft," *Foreign Policy Analysis*, 5:4, 2009, 374.
14 Oz Hassan, "The United States After Unipolarity: American Democracy Promotion and the 'Arab Spring'," LSE IDEAS report, 2011, pp. 46–47.
15 See Annika E. Poppe, "Whether to, Obama? U.S. Democracy Promotion after the Cold War" (*Peace Research Institute Report [PRIF]*, 2010).
16 Ibid, p. 27.
17 Remarks by the President at Cairo University. Available at: www.whitehouse.gov/the-press-office/remarks-president-cairo-university-6-04-09.
18 Nicolas Bouchet, "The Democracy Tradition in US Foreign Policy and the Obama Presidency," *International Affairs*, 89:1, 2013, 47.
19 Ibid, 49.
20 For more on this in Jordan see Ashley Barnes, "Creating Democrats: Testing the Arab Spring" (*Middle East Policy Council Report*, 2013).

21 See Jeffrey Goldberg, "The Obama Doctrine," *The Atlantic*, April 2016. Available at: www.theatlantic.com/magazine/archive/2016/04/the-obama-doctrine/471525.
22 Ibid.
23 "Historically, Public Has Given Low Priority to Promoting Democracy," Pew Global Attitudes Survey, February 2011. Available at: www.pewresearch.org/2011/02/04/historically-public-has-given-low-priority-to-promoting-democracy-overseas.
24 Ibid.
25 "Public Sees U.S. Power Declining as Support for Global Engagement Slips America's Place in the World 2013," Pew Global Attitudes Survey, December 2013. Available at: www.people-press.org/2013/12/03/section-4-the-threat-of-terrorism-and-civil-liberties.
26 James M. Lindsay, "George W. Bush, Barack Obama and the Future of U.S. Leadership," *International Affairs*, 87:4, 2011, 765.
27 See Goldberg, "The Obama Doctrine."
28 Bouchet, "The Democracy Tradition," 43–44.
29 For more on this see James M. Scott and Carie A. Steele, "Sponsoring Democracy: The United States and Democracy Aid to the Developing World, 1988–2001," *International Studies Quarterly*, 55, 2011, 47–69.

Further Selected Readings

Barnes, A. "Creating Democrats: Testing the Arab Spring," *Middle East Policy Council Report*, 2013.

Bouchet, N. "The Democracy Tradition in US Foreign Policy and the Obama Presidency," *International Affairs*, vol. 89, no. 1, 2013, 39–51.

Carothers, T. *Aiding Democracy Abroad: The Learning Curve*. Washington, D.C.: Carnegie Endowment, 2011.

Chandrasekram, R. *Imperial Life in The Emerald City: Inside Iraq's Green Zone*. New York: Vintage Books, 2007.

Fukuyama, F. *America at the Crossroads: Democracy, Power, and the Neoconservative Legacy*. New Haven, CT: Yale University Press, 2007.

Goldberg, J. "The Obama Doctrine," *The Atlantic*, April 2016. Available at: www.theatlantic.com/magazine/archive/2016/04/the-obama-doctrine/471525.

Goldsmith, A. "Making the World Safe for Partial Democracy? Questioning the Premises of Democracy Promotion," *International Security*, vol. 33, no. 2, 2008, 120–147.

Hill, M. A. "Exploring USIAD's Democracy Promotion in Bosnia and Afghanistan: A 'Cookie-cutter Approach' "? *Democratization*, vol. 17, no. 1, 2010, 98–124.

Jervis. R. *American Foreign Policy in a New Era*. New York: Routledge, 2005.

Jones, S. *The Graveyard of Empires: America's War in Afghanistan*. New York: Vintage Books, 2009.

Lindsay, J. L. "George W. Bush, Barack Obama and the Future of U.S. Leadership," *International Affairs*, vol. 87, no. 4, 2011, 765–779.

Ninkovich, F. *The Wilsonian Century: U.S. Foreign Policy*. Chicago: University of Chicago Press, 1999.

Peceny, M. *Democracy at the Point of Bayonets*. University Park, PA: Penn State University Press, 1999.

Poppe, A. E. "Whether to, Obama? U.S. Democracy Promotion after the Cold War," *Peace Research Institute Report (PRIF)*, 2010.

Price, D. "Global Democracy Promotion: Seven Lessons for the New Administration," *The Washington Quarterly*, vol. 32, no. 1, January 2009, 159–170.

Rieffer, B. and Mercer, K. "U.S. Democracy Promotion: The Clinton and Bush Administrations," *Global Society*, vol. 19, no. 4, October 2005, 385–408.

Russett, B. "Bushwacking the Democratic Peace," *International Studies Perspectives*, vol. 6, no. 4, 2005, 395–408.

Santini, H. and Hassan, O. "Transatlantic Democracy Promotion and the Arab Spring," *The International Spectator*, vol. 47, no. 3, 2012, 65–82.

Scott, J. M. and Steele, C. A. "Sponsoring Democracy: The United States and Democracy Aid to the Developing World, 1988–2001," *International Studies Quarterly*, vol. 55, 2011, 47–69.

Smith, T. *A Pact with the Devil: Washington's Bid for World Supremacy and the Betrayal of the American Problem*. New York: Routledge, 2007.

Smith, T. *America's Mission: The United States and the Worldwide Struggle for Democracy*. Princeton, NJ: Princeton University Press, 2012.

Wittes, T. C. and Masloski. A. *Democracy Promotion under Obama: Lessons from the Middle East Partnership Initiative*. Saban Center for Middle East Policy at the Brookings Institution, 2009.

Zielonka, J. and Pravda, A., eds. *Democratic Consolidation in Eastern Europe*, Vol. 2: International and Transnational Factors. Oxford: Oxford University Press, 2001.

3

SAVING STRANGERS

Humanitarian Intervention and the Responsibility to Protect (R2P)[1]

When it comes to the use of military force to help citizens in other countries, U.S. policy is inconsistent at best. The United States will use military power to "save strangers," but it has to be done when there is minimal cost. Policy-making elites understand this and are thus prudent about risky involvements perceived as devoid of national self-interest. This is the case even when atrocities are committed. The recent case of Syria and U.S. reluctance to take action against Assad's regime, despite the thousands killed and the humanitarian disaster it has provoked, demonstrates clearly the pull of parochial nationalism. When costs are high, it is easy for Americans to overlook, if not totally forget, their supposed unique mission to make the world freer and safer for all.

In this chapter, we probe the concept of humanitarian intervention, discussing the related idea of the Responsibility to Protect (R2P). Many public opinion surveys have also addressed the issue of humanitarian intervention and we use these surveys as evidence of background conditions. We conclude by reinforcing the central argument of our previous chapter about America's rather "unexceptional" but not altogether surprising self-interested behavior. We find little evidence that the United States generally chooses to act on behalf of others—unless it simultaneously attends to its own national interests. A good way to understand America's occasional acts to save others is through the lens of mixed motivations, risk calculation, as well as certain ideals. In the last analysis, we believe that although the idea of a Responsibility to Protect, that emphasizes early diplomatic action to curtail atrocities abroad, has much to recommend it, even this cosmopolitan notion will be difficult to implement in a world that manifests many illiberal governments and armed non-state actors, not to mention the continuing pull of parochial nationalism in states.

In other words, it is encouraging indeed that states adopted the principle of R2P in 2005. The fact remains however that norms do not implement themselves; some powerful state has to take the lead in turning principle into practice. The evidence presented here demonstrates that the United States has only led in this way spasmodically, within definite limits, and with very mixed results. When specific and complicated situations arise, narrow national interest—often influenced by public opinion—still tends to temper any activist version of cosmopolitan ideals directed at saving strangers.

From God's Instrument to Conflicted Great Power

The United States is certainly not the first country to use military force but justify its use with reference to saving others. Many European humanitarian interventions in the nineteenth and twentieth centuries were driven largely by narrow nationalism and the pursuit of national self-interest, despite the rhetoric of saving religious or ethnic brethren. More often than not, the primary goal of these interventions was to expand the national power of a European state and to weaken the Ottoman Empire (where Christian and/or Slavic communities were sometimes at risk) and thus enhance a country's own position in the world. And on a few occasions, public opinion in Britain pushed the government into military action that foreign policy professionals believed was counter-productive to British self-interest, but this situation arose infrequently. The most prominent example of a powerful public opinion causing a great power to change course in foreign policy toward a redefinition and more cosmopolitan conception of the national interest was the Quaker-led movement against the trans–Atlantic slave trade and then against slavery itself in the late nineteenth century. This new British human rights policy was enforced mostly, but not always, by the British navy.

At the height of its power, the British government often and quite passionately justified military interventions with rhetoric about humanitarianism and its unique concern for others. Public opinion helped drive the point home, supporting, for example, some British policies in Africa. The public and particularly religious organizations were crucial to attracting the attention of both the British and American governments to push for changes in Africa, particularly in Sudan in the 1870s. Like the American rhetoric that came later, British missionaries maintained that privileged Americans and Britons were no better off eternally than the millions groveling in ignorance. In other words, Christians in the United States and United Kingdom had a religious obligation to intervene in the affairs of another country. For both elites and masses, European colonialism—whether it was British, French, Russian, Dutch, Spanish, or Portuguese—along with the military force that went with it, was rationalized as doing God's work to "enlighten" more primitive non-Western peoples. Thus, the United States was not the first to put the rhetoric of so-called "Providential Nationalism" at the service of brutal military intervention and forceful control in foreign lands.

This history of self-styled humanitarian intervention by the powerful Northern states against the weak, and more generally the tendency by colonialists to rationalize their expansive (and sometimes brutal) foreign policies as doing the Lord's work, has definitely given humanitarian intervention a bad odor, particularly in the global South today. Unfortunately, U.S. foreign policy did little to change this. As the United States began its uncertain trek toward great power, even superpower, status, it followed the European well-traveled path of using cosmopolitan and often religious rhetoric to advance perceived national, self-interested goals. This can be demonstrated by one example in particular, the Spanish-American War in 1898 with follow-on developments in the Philippines.

At the time of the Spanish-American War, capturing foreign territory (and the people living there) was what great powers did. This was as true for Germany after Bismarck and for the United States during Teddy Roosevelt's era—despite America's revolutionary and anti-colonial tendencies. Although American politicians maintained that the war with Spain was "begun with the highest motives," its more banal, national interests could not be hidden.[2] A highly nationalist press, so-called "yellow journalism," as well as public opinion pushed the McKinley administration into the war against Spain. President McKinley then rationalized military action as the will of God to Christianize the Filipinos (it didn't seem to matter that they were already largely Catholic!). When Filipinos resisted the U.S. occupation, the United States resorted to torture and other atrocities to subdue the resistance. All this however was covered up and explained away in Washington, where policy makers sought to avoid the contradiction between claiming God's blessing while destroying villages and waterboarding detainees. It was a similar contradiction that was to reappear in places like Vietnam after 1966 and Iraq after 2003. The United States granted independence to the Philippines in 1947, almost a half-century after ousting the Spanish when colonialism was becoming a spent force in world affairs.

At the same time, the United States has often rebuffed opportunities to act on behalf of cosmopolitan ideals, as was the case when the question of creating an American protectorate over Armenia after World War I was raised. At that time Woodrow Wilson, having earlier rejected pleas to intervene on behalf of Christian Armenians being victimized by Turkish leaders of the Ottoman Empire, proposed to Congress in 1920 that it authorize an American protectorate for Armenia. Wilson explicitly argued that the United States had no ulterior, self-interested motives, but rather as a Christian nation it was trying to protect a Christian people. The Senate rejected his proposal and instead opted for more self-interested isolationism focused on domestic priorities. Wilson's appeal for a relatively cosmopolitan foreign policy oriented toward doing good—at least providing protection to one community (the Armenian), instead fell on deaf ears in the Senate.

During the Cold War, the subject under discussion here did not change in any fundamental way and the inconsistencies remained, if they did not intensify. Cosmopolitan rhetoric in favor of humanitarian intervention was usually accompanied by calculation of national self-interest. This was clearly evident in 1965 when the United States under Lyndon Johnson intervened in the Dominican Republic, allegedly to protect lives and property. In reality, the move was to defeat a rebel movement that might have made the Dominican Republic a second (leftist) Cuba. Thus, claims about use of force to protect civilians masked an intervention designed to affect the distribution of power in Dominican politics. The U.S. intervention went a long way to shore up conservative, pro-American, pro-business factions despite their lack of democratic legitimacy. And a leftist-tinged opposition movement was curtailed.

This brief historical review reinforces a foundational point developed in the previous chapter—namely, that American exceptionalism is not so exceptional at all. Although we provide just a few examples, American diplomatic history is replete with periods of expansion and periods of retrenchment as the notion of American exceptionalism is entangled by competing applications: to lead with active internationalism for the good of the world, or to perfect American society at home in order to serve as passive beacon and "city on a hill." Washington also acts as most countries do: largely on behalf of parochial nationalism, but with the rhetoric of broader cosmopolitan goals.

To repeat, most great powers have acted similarly, putting a moral sheen on their power maneuvers while claiming the high moral ground as they went about the dirty business of using force to colonize or otherwise control foreign peoples and weaken adversaries. Sometimes the press and public opinion pushed leaders where they did not initially want to go, but more often than not elites themselves sought support and legitimacy by relying on cosmopolitan rhetoric and claiming to be acting for the welfare, if not the rights, of others.

As we will see, a basic principle of true humanitarian intervention and for implementing the principle of R2P is that outside involvement in a situation must show a reasonable prospect of progress at reasonable cost. Intervention must be both doable and relatively low risk. These constraints help explain American behavior during the Cold War. Since the United States could not respond directly to the Soviet Union's human rights abuses at home or its military crackdowns in Eastern Europe (Poland in 1956, Hungary in 1956, or Czechoslovakia in 1968 to name a few examples) without significant damage to itself, it worked indirectly and invoked cosmopolitan ideas for effect.

In 1974, for example, Congress passed the Jackson-Vanik Amendment, supposedly to help Jews emigrate from the Soviet Union and its fellow communist allies, denying Most Favored Nation (MFN) trading status to such states until reasonable Jewish emigration obtained. This peaceful and seemingly cosmopolitan undertaking, contesting the repressive nature of European communism, was certainly safer than military confrontation. It had the additional benefit of appealing to American exceptionalism and the fiction that the United States was leading the human rights charge and largely interested in promoting freedom around the world.

The targeted communist regimes claimed foreign "intervention" in their domestic affairs, but of course the legislation was not military intervention. One should not forget that this bit of cosmopolitan legislation served other purposes as well. One of the authors, namely Senator "Scoop" Jackson of Washington state, was determined to undermine the Nixon–Kissinger policy of détente with the Soviet Union and wanted a more assertive and confrontational approach. One of the first "neo-cons" in American politics, Scoop Jackson was soon to be followed by Ronald Reagan and others, who sought to inject their own version of morality into U.S. foreign policy. In the neo-con view that asserts that the United States needs to do good things with its power, it was argued that the Nixon–Kissinger more realist approach was insufficiently moral and too accommodating of great power relations. Again, the rhetoric of doing good for others, in this instance via attention to repressed European Jews, masked other national objectives—in this case, more political confrontation with the Soviet Union.

Again, we remind that this frequent blend of cosmopolitan rhetoric with self-interested motivations is not at all unique to the United States. In the Nigerian civil war (1967–1970), for example, France recognized Biafra, claiming genocidal policies on the part of the central (federal) government in Lagos. But at the same time France was seeking to carve out its own zone of influence in Africa, wanting to offset British and American support for Lagos. In any event, France greatly overstated the prospect of genocide in that civil war. Biafran leaders were cruelly using Ibo civilian suffering in the Eastern or Delta region to mobilize foreign support for their separatist cause. In fact there was no genocide after the federal victory, and Ibos along with other dissident groups were peacefully reintegrated into Nigerian society.

There was also the Vietnamese intervention in 1979 to dislodge the Khmer Rouge regime in Cambodia—one of the most vicious regimes in world history. One would not expect a purely humanitarian intervention from Hanoi, which had waged a long and brutal war for control of the south of Vietnam, and indeed the intervention into Cambodia was not. Although communist agrarian fanatics killed off about a quarter of the Cambodian nation, the Khmer Rouge was aligned with communist China and thus seen as a national security threat to the Vietnamese. As for the United States, cosmopolitan rhetoric was painfully absent when it came to Cambodia and the atrocities and human rights abuses there. At first, the United States ignored the Cambodian genocide and then it, unbelievably, supported the rump Khmer Rouge diplomatically.

The U.S. government did not know everything that was happening on the ground in Cambodia, but as early as 1975 U.S. politicians were providing detailed and well-documented accounts of the killing and chaos. Despite numerous reports of nearly a million slaughtered, the United States stood by and did nothing, consumed by domestic problems (the Watergate scandal) and tired of Southeast Asia after Vietnam. Only in 1978 did President Carter publically recognize the atrocities, claiming that "America cannot avoid the responsibility to speak out in condemnation of the Cambodian government, the worst violator of human rights in the world today."[3] Nonetheless, representatives of the Khmer Rouge continued to occupy the Cambodian seat at the United Nations for another 11 years with U.S. support, because it did not want to award the seat to the new Cambodian government led by Hun Sen and backed by communist Vietnam.

In the cases of France regarding Nigeria, Vietnam regarding Cambodia, and the United States regarding Cambodia, one can easily see that the rhetoric supposedly to save innocent strangers instead reflected parochial, nationalistic behavior. To be sure, some genuine good may have been done in these cases, but the fact remains that in none of these cases did pure altruism drive policy. And absent attempts to advance narrow nationalistic goals, these countries' foreign policies would have been different. In the case of the United States, as with other countries, the issue of mixed motives has always been a reality and there is little evidence that this will change.

The Golden Age of Humanitarian Intervention

The Cold War's end contributed to many situations of suffering, human rights abuses, and mass atrocities. But the early 1990s were also a period when the United States had unparalleled military and economic resources. Its resources were unrivaled and even its soft power (or its positive reputation) was so great that many forecasted a fundamental transformation in world politics. At least for a while, no state seemed to want to "balance" against the United States; rather, they seemed to want to "bandwagon" and thus join U.S.-led coalitions. The unipolar moment in history had seemingly arrived where the United States could bring together power with purpose. U.S. putative power, or its reputed power based on such things as tabulated resources, explains why this decade was initially projected by many to be the golden age for humanitarian intervention. The apparent triumph of not just U.S. power but also "Western" values led Francis Fukuyama in the early 1990s to write about "the end of history" and the last political man. In his view, since the West had won the Cold War, there could be no more debate about institutions or ideology: democratic capitalism, based on human rights, was the only viable path forward.

After 1991 and the final collapse of European communism, the United States carried out several high-profile military interventions, presumably under the auspices of cosmopolitan humanitarian ideals and for the broader benefit of others. These were undertaken despite the so-called Weinberger rules or the Powell doctrine. That is, smarting from the defeat in the Vietnam War which ended in 1975, the U.S. military under then Secretary of Defense Caspar Weinberger and later the key advisor Colin Powell argued that U.S. use of military force should be limited to situations where vital national security interests were at stake, with clearly defined objectives, and with a clear exit strategy. But after 1991 and given the apparent absence of an effective countervailing power, the George H. W.

Bush administration intervened in Somalia in late 1992 and then the Bill Clinton administration intervened in the Balkan Wars during 1995–1999. These two cases tell us much about the conditions for humanitarian intervention, its appeal but also its limitations.

Clearly, the senior Bush rejected Weinberger and Powell recommendations. President Bush even argued that in some cases the use of the military might be best—even when the interests are important but not necessarily vital to U.S. national security.[4] The 1992 intervention in Somalia, which came almost a year after the UN Security council authorization and was supported by Powell, is often identified as the clearest case of purely humanitarian intervention. Yet, U.S. involvement cannot be explained by cosmopolitanism urgings alone. Certain ideals may have propelled the United States to act, but here as elsewhere when the United States uses its military, many factors, including a calculation of cost and the role of public opinion, must be considered to understand the full picture. In early 1992, with half of Somalia's population at risk of starvation, the U.S. Joint Chiefs of Staff argued against action in Somalia, and later the administration argued that it was a "bottomless pit" and the United States had no interests there. "Even within Africa, Angola and Mozambique are more important" than Somalia, the Joint Chiefs advised the president.[5]

However, in the same year Andrew Natsios, the director of the Office of Foreign Disaster Assistance (OFDA) in the U.S. Agency for International Development (USAID), made the case for involvement in Somalia, declaring that the famine was the greatest humanitarian emergency in the world. Natsios' appeal, however, fell on deaf ears, attracting little interest from the White House or the American people. The deployment of more than 3,500 UN peacekeepers early in 1992 that proceeded without U.S. direct participation but with its diplomatic support, unfortunately, did little to help and the crisis in Somalia only intensified.

The United States did eventually act later that year, but only after high-profile media coverage *and* the presidential elections. Quietly, the administration had secured the green light from various Somali warlords, and President Bush authorized a deployment of about 25,000 U.S. military personnel to provide armed protection for Red Cross humanitarian relief—thus protecting civilians from starvation. It must be stressed that the U.S. effort in Somalia was not directed at affecting competing political actors in the failed state. The U.S. military deployment in Somalia was instead put at the service of a Red Cross supply system that was being subjected to attacks by bandits. In a context in which the Bush administration had no clear macro-strategy for dealing with the world after the Cold War, the media's coverage and other factors clearly mattered in the decision to deploy.

A push from some factions in Congress also contributed to President Bush taking action. According to Bush's then Secretary of State, Lawrence Eagleburger, "television had a great deal to do with President Bush's decision to go in ... pictures of these starving kids and substantial pressure from the Congress" pushed the president to believe that he could "not leave office with 50,000 people starving that he could have saved."[6] To Congress that December, the president stressed that the U.S. mission would be limited and would prepare the way for the UN.[7] He also reiterated that this was a humanitarian mission where no strategic interests were at stake for the United States.

Administration officials and the American public were upset by the unfolding crisis, but it is important to remember that Somalia was seen and discussed as being a relatively risk-free, low-cost, and short-term operation. Action in Somalia was also contrasted regularly with the other more complicated foreign policy crises of the day, specifically the disintegration of the Yugoslav federation and the war in Bosnia. Viewed in this comparative light, saving Somalis seemed both safer and simpler than entanglement in the Balkans. Not only did cosmopolitan values favor American involvement in Somalia, but so did some public opinion and much of the broader international community. That is to say, the UN Security Council gave the green light for the U.S. military deployment, and the perception was that U.S. actions would open the door for the United Nations to take over. There is no evidence in this case that the United States had any hidden geostrategic interests, and its involvement in Somalia comes closest to pure cosmopolitanism at work. But these moral impulses prevailed only because of sustained media coverage, and when balanced against the costs and risks of doing something there instead of the Balkans. In other words, as with actions on behalf of democracy, humanitarian intervention was shaped by context and American power.

U.S. intervention in Somalia may have been rooted to a significant degree in a cosmopolitan concern for others, but it also marked a turning of the tide against such endeavors. This is particularly true when it came to "boots on the ground" or specific strategies for when the United States was willing help others. As the first Bush administration gave way to the Clinton administration, U.S. and UN goals expanded in Somalia whereas resources were gradually drawn down. All outside political parties moved toward coercive state building and not just the secure delivery of humanitarian relief. When U.S. forces attempted the capture of the leaders of a recalcitrant warlord faction in Mogadishu, the resulting firefight cost the lives of 18 military personnel and the wounding of many more. Some of the American dead were abused, a fact broadcast widely by television cameras. This, in turn, caused much of the American public and Congress to promptly turn against the operation. As we suggested, once the operation started to drag on and become complicated by politics, the Clinton team reduced and then eventually withdrew the American military contingent.

Complications in Somalia weakened cosmopolitan concerns even more in the United States, allowing the Clinton administration to stand by while almost a million Rwandans were killed in 1994. America's willingness to again be a bystander to genocide occurred despite ample media coverage of the slaughter of Tutsis and moderate Hutu by militant Hutu. Media coverage did not generate action, because the Clinton administration and high UN officials like Kofi Annan, then head of the UN Peacekeeping Department, were firmly set against significant intervention, fearing for the future of UN security operations after the Somalia controversy. Other important actors like Belgium, which had military forces in the UN security force, also favored withdrawal after some of their troops were killed and mutilated.

The Clinton administration, appreciating that there was little public or congressional demand for intervention and a great deal to be lost from ill-conceived or ill-advised military interventions, developed the argument that Rwandan deaths were not the result of genocide. Instead, the horror in Rwanda was "only" a regrettable result of one of Africa's innumerable civil wars—about which little could realistically be done. Because of the implications for the use of military force, U.S. officials were instructed not to use the "G" word. At the end of the day, the constellation of factors that galvanized action for Somalia in 1992 did not work the same way regarding Rwanda in 1994.[8] Part of that difference also stemmed from Washington's growing concern with developments in the Western Balkans which were seen as of more strategic importance.

In the early 1990s, the George H. W. Bush administration, led by a mostly realist president not prone to moral crusades, adopted a restrained position in the Western Balkans, as the republics of Slovenia, Croatia, and Bosnia seceded from the Yugoslav federation. With the CIA predicting a blood bath if Yugoslavia broke up, early U.S. policy under the senior Bush was to support the continuation of that state. With events outrunning this policy, Washington avoided deep involvement in the growing violence. Early on, Secretary of State James Baker opined that the United States had no important interests at stake, or in his Texas version, Washington "had no dog in that fight." U.S. passivity on Bosnia under the senior Bush can be contrasted with his exceptionalist rhetoric when running for president in 1998:

> Then-Vice President Bush [said], while running against Michael Dukakis: "My opponent ... sees America as another pleasant country on the U.N. roll call, somewhere between Albania and Zimbabwe. I see America as the leader—a unique nation with a special role in the world."[9]

By the time of the Clinton administration in 1993, it was clear that neither Europe nor the United Nations had been effective in controlling the violence in the disintegrating Yugoslav state. The media had much to report on as the Serb government and the Serbs within Bosnia continued to target Bosnian Muslims and Croats. Stories of ethnic cleansings, the systematic rape of women, and concentration camps, while initially dismissed, were increasingly hard to ignore. Yet, the "Somalia syndrome" was still in play, and President Clinton avoided unilateral intervention by U.S. military forces. Instead, Washington supported: 1) a new Bosnian-Croat armed force to check Serb gains on the ground; 2) increased attacks on Serb positions through the United Nations; and 3) intense diplomacy by Richard Holbrooke which produced the 1995 Dayton accords. All of this put an end to the Bosnian War of 1992–1995. U.S. active diplomacy, linked to some use of force, was crucial. But Somalia-like costs, specifically the loss of American lives, were avoided.

In time, the Clinton administration's leadership did end the violence in Bosnia—even absent vital threats to U.S. national security. In this case, public and congressional opinion was permissive, but only as long as the price of action was judged reasonable. The president, moreover, regularly reminded the country of America's exceptional position. At an address explaining the peace accords that would end the violence in Bosnia, Clinton explained that

> Because of our dedication, America's ideals—liberty, democracy, and peace—are more and more the aspirations of people everywhere in the world. It is the power of our ideas, even more than our size, our wealth, and our military might, that makes America a uniquely trusted nation.[10]

At the same time, Clinton realized that after the Battle of Mogadishu, a policy of deep involvement in another troubled country would not be popular for long. As in Somalia, it would not take much for domestic support to erode underneath and then the United States would have to change its Bosnian policy.

As in the past, the government's rationale for involvement in Bosnia (and later in Kosovo in 1999) was a combination of concern for the people in the Balkans and national self-interest. This is why President Clinton presented four distinct reasons for American intervention in Bosnia, with humanitarian concerns coming only *after*: 1) avoiding a broader European war; 2) lending credibility to NATO; and 3) concern over the flow of refugees coming from the country which stressed America's allies. In this case as well, U.S. policy was shaped considerably by the media and public opinion, with a discernable turning point in U.S. policy coming after reports revealed Serb concentration camps and attacks on innocent civilians. Still, the Clinton administration's perception was that if there were high costs for the United States, particularly in the form of casualties for the U.S. military, this would turn domestic support into opposition, as had happened in Somalia.

By 1999, the Clinton team was again feeling domestic pressure to act in the Balkans, as violence spilled into Kosovo, an autonomous province of Serbia. A majority of the inhabitants, ethnic Albanians, demanded independence. The Serb leader in Belgrade, Slobodan Milosevic, replied with ethnic cleansing and other human rights violations on behalf of the Serb minority in the province. Local Albanian militias were not free from charges of human rights violations, not to mention criminal behavior, but for the combination of reasons indicated above, and with Russia blocking multilateral action through the UN Security Council, the Clinton administration opted for a high-profile NATO intervention to help the Albanians in Kosovo. An 11-week bombing campaign, Russian quiet diplomacy, but also the threat of a ground invasion persuaded Milosevic to finally capitulate and accept loss of Belgrade's control over Kosovo.

On the one hand, media coverage of Serb deportations of ethnic Albanians mobilized demands for increased U.S. involvement. The Serbs packing ethnic Albanians on trains in forced ethnic cleansing, broadcasted by television, was reminiscent of Germany and the Jews in the 1930s and 1940s. On the other hand, Clinton's fear of domestic opinion turning against his policy and his presidency caused the NATO bombing to be conducted at high altitude to reduce the chances of planes shot down and pilots taken prisoner. (One pilot was shot down but escaped capture.) It should be noted however that high-altitude bombing increased the chances of targeting mistakes and increased collateral damage to innocent civilians. There was also the controversy of trying to do good by bombing so-called "dual use" targets that included television stations and bridges.

Clinton's policy on Kosovo did lead to "winning ugly," as the protracted and controversial air campaign produced the desired short-term results. NATO held together and controlled the situation, and Serb persecution of Kosovar Albanians was curtailed. The usual mixed motives were evaluated differently by different analysts. So-called "humanitarian hawks" were satisfied while critics argued that the NATO bombing was imperial and unnecessary, ignored Albanian violations of human rights, but also set a precedent for Russia's later detachment of Crimea from Ukraine. Although one of the enduring consequences of the NATO bombing of Serbia was a renewed debate about humanitarian intervention and the emergence of the principle of R2P, it demonstrated the challenges and contradictions of using the military for humanitarian ideals. Without a doubt "humanitarian war" is an oxymoron.

The Shift to the Responsibility to Protect

NATO bombing of Serbia in 1999 without UN Security Council authorization led the Canadian government to establish a panel of eminent persons to consider events and make recommendations for the future of humanitarian intervention. The Independent Commission on Intervention and State Sovereignty (ICISS), comprised of both scholars and practitioners, wrestled with the central question of how to protect civilians against atrocities occurring within a "sovereign" state rather than in a traditional international war—the latter already being legally regulated by international humanitarian law (or the law of armed conflict). Yet, in the Kosovo case, the Serbian government would not admit that it faced even an internal war. The same had been true for the British government with regard to the "troubles" of Northern Ireland and the same was to prove true for the Assad government in Syria when faced by opposition forces in 2011 and thereafter. Governments facing forceful internal opposition and/or separatist movements are prone to claim terrorism or domestic instability, in order to avoid international scrutiny, regulation, or involvement.

To shorten a longer and much more complicated story, the 1999 bombing of Serbia and the Canadian-sponsored ICISS led to a 2005 statement by heads of state at the United Nations that has been termed the Responsibility to Protect (R2P) principle. Based on two short paragraphs in a much longer document detailing guiding principles for the proper conduct of international relations, this diplomatic statement tried to shift the discussion from state intervention to state responsibility. Under the R2P principle, the sovereign state had the primary responsibility to ensure that genocide, crimes against humanity, ethnic cleansing (which is legally subsumed under crimes against humanity), and major war crimes did not occur. In this view, state sovereignty is not an absolute and unlimited right for a government to do as it wishes; it is relative and conditional on following international law. If a state is "unwilling or unable" to prevent the named four atrocities, then outside parties have not only a right but also a responsibility to respond.

The latter phrasing papers over much controversy. International law permits states to use force either in self-defense or when authorized by the UN Security Council. The 2005 R2P language leaves unresolved the old question of use of force by states when not acting in self-defense and when not approved by the Security Council—as was the case regarding NATO and Kosovo. Be that as it may, the authors of R2P such as former foreign minister Gareth Evans of Australia argued that the main intent of R2P language was the responsibility of the international community to help sovereign states govern in a responsible way. This arguably meant primarily assistance to governments, helping them to avoid policies that might lead to situations of violence out of which might spring the four named types of atrocities. Evans and others of a similar mind thus tried to move the international discussion away from use of forceful intervention to something supported by broad consensus—namely, aid in the responsible exercise of sovereign power. But a central problem still remained. What about the Kosovo-type situation in which the UN Security Council was blocked by internal disagreement, atrocities were occurring, and concerned outside parties could not reasonably claim action in self-defense?

These issues did not arise in the U.S. attack on Afghanistan in late 2001 in response to the Al-Qaeda attacks on New York and Washington, since Washington claimed self-defense—which met with universal support. But in the U.S. invasion of Iraq in 2003, where the main argument of the Bush administration was preemptive or anticipatory self-defense, there was widespread opposition. Given the weaknesses of the self-defense argument in relation to Saddam Hussein's supposed weapons of mass destruction, the Bush team then tried to focus on Saddam's human rights violations and bring into play the idea of a humanitarian intervention. This argument also provoked much disagreement at home and abroad, many seeing U.S. policy as a war of choice and not necessity.

Even a number of democratic allies and friends of the United States opposed the Iraqi invasion—which proved to be long, costly, disruptive, ineffective, and replete with atrocities. In the final analysis, by the time the United States withdrew military forces from Iraq in 2011, about two-thirds of sampled Americans thought the Iraq invasion had been a bad idea. And although the Bush team had invoked arguments about protecting Iraqis from gross human rights violations, not many bought this argument as the real motivation for the invasion. The use of force in Iraq was widely viewed as yet another intervention by a few states from the Global North, which was strongly opposed by much of the Global South as well as others like France and Germany. And it once again gave claims to supposedly humanitarian intervention a bad name—not to mention the controversial claim of preemptive self-defense when there was no clear and imminent threat.

There were several situations in which a discourse on R2P has come into play, but U.S. support and involvement in terms of providing troops to implement this policy has been minimal at best. For example, the United States had almost no role in invoking R2P after typhoon Nargis hit Myanmar in 2008, and the isolationist junta there proved slow in allowing international relief to reach the storm's victims. Particularly France, which had military vessels off the Myanmar coast, and which much earlier had been central to a discussion of a right of humanitarian "interference," utilized the language of R2P to initiate a debate on forceful intervention. Involved in the debate was a discussion of whether failure to allow adequate humanitarian relief after a natural disaster could be considered a crime against humanity. The controversy faded, as did appeals to R2P, when the junta gradually opened the country to improved international assistance.

It was even possible to see a kind of judicial R2P at work in Kenya. The 2007 presidential elections resulted in much ethnic violence. The International Criminal Court, on its own initiative, launched an investigation into matters, Kenya having ratified the treaty comprising the Court's statute. With the ICC conducting its preliminary investigation, violence declined in the 2013 elections. Thus international oversight seemed to have a beneficial effect on the situation, which is what Evans and other authors of R2P had in mind in constructing a policy that might prevent atrocities. However, when the Court came in with indictments against the sitting president and his top deputy because of previous behavior linked to 2007, the defendants were successful in mobilizing domestic and regional opposition to the Court. They were successful in a political sense in presenting the Court to their supporters as a manifestation of neo-colonialism.

The United States and Britain had endorsed the ICC's proceedings (even though the United States had never accepted the Court's jurisdiction and authority). While the Court, being a judicial body, did not use the language of R2P in its various proceedings, one could see developments as a kind of judicial diplomacy directed at reducing crimes against humanity within a state, thus preempting any discussion on the need for forceful intervention. In fact, there was no state pressing the case for military intervention in Kenya. At the time of writing, court proceedings had collapsed in the Kenya affair, due primarily to lack of cooperation from Kenyan authorities.

The clearest example of R2P at work was in Libya in 2011, as active opposition mounted against the dictator Muammar Kaddafi. When he publically declared his intention to exterminate his opponents, this played into the hands of states like Britain and France which took the lead in calling for some type of forceful international response. The United States under the Obama administration, even though reluctant to get involved militarily again in the Middle East and wanting to "pivot to Asia," nevertheless agreed to "lead from behind." This meant, in effect, that the United States initiated a limited military action as long as states like Britain and France, and a few Arab countries, would put their fighter pilots in harm's way. The Obama team not only used the language of American exceptionalism to build domestic support but also the logic of R2P in getting UN Security Council approval for use of force.

In this context, and with Kaddafi being a pariah without major international friends, the UN Security Council authorized a no-fly zone over Libya designed to protect civilians from governmental atrocity by way of international military action that would hamper Kaddafi's push toward Bengazi—the eastern city that was the center of early opposition. The implementing Western and Arab states then turned this UN authorization into something it was not, namely the pursuit of regime change instead of the more limited humanitarian objective of protecting civilians. Kaddafi was eventually captured and killed and his supporters weakened, but particularly Russia and China were intensely unhappy by the Western use of Security Council resolutions as cover to pursue regime change. It was also a fact that once Western countries had done their part, Libya disintegrated into violent instability as various militias competed for control. The United States and other Western states, however, largely disengaged from follow-on reconstruction and peacebuilding, not wanting to make a costly and long-term commitment there. As Libya fell into chaos, politicians in Washington focused on partisan wrangling about responsibility for the deaths of four U.S. diplomats. And Congressional Republicans showed almost no interest in the question of R2P and concern for Libyan civilians but instead focused on showing the alleged mistakes of Secretary of State Hillary Clinton.

An Unexceptional Public

It is well established that when it comes to the specifics of international relations, the American public is often out of the loop, disinterested, and uninformed. As Ole Holsti, a foremost scholar of American public opinion put it, for a long time and to a distressing extent the American people know little and generally care less about foreign affairs. This is not always the case and Americans sometimes follow the general outlines of some foreign developments, especially when it comes to security and military matters. And they often express their opinions, regardless of how uninformed they might be. With regard to the American public's support for saving strangers, we repeat what we have said in Chapter 1: mass public opinion is volatile and incoherent, particularly when it comes to the use of force abroad and possible humanitarian intervention.

Generally, this is how events unfold, though the specifics may change depending on the country and other domestic and international events at the time. In the abstract, Americans tend to hold altruistic and cosmopolitan values, but when specific and complicated situations arise when force might be necessary, the public becomes more cautious and self-regarding. Recent surveys moreover indicate that as American power changes in the world and domestic problems grow, the public becomes less interested in international issues. The following considers the complex and constraining role of public opinion on using force to save others. It demonstrates that similar to elite policy makers, the public often finds comfort in the general notion of helping or saving citizens in other countries, but it only supports these actions under limited conditions and for a short time. In fact, there is little evidence of anything exceptional in how Americans view the problems of others or their willingness to help.

One poll from 2006, for example, indicated that when asked about whether the United States should "look beyond its own self-interest and do what's best for the world as a whole," a large majority (71 percent) agreed.[11] Other polls that query general attitudes about what the United States "ought to do" in different hypothetical situations show responses that are both compassionate and generous in their concern for the welfare of strangers. Yet, time and time again, when the public is asked about using military force in a specific situation, imposing solutions on others or changing regimes, public attitudes are not genuinely supportive of the use of force. Based on a review of many polls, it is clear that while Americans may say that they care about the human rights of others and democracy in other countries, this does not necessarily mean that Americans think that certain actions are warranted, specifically that the use of military force is appropriate.

Despite what the public might say about its concern for the world or the welfare of others, it most forcefully supported the use of military abroad in Afghanistan in 2001, when this action was linked directly to American security. However, if immediate, national interests are not at stake, the American public, like its leaders, tends to snub broader, altruistic notions about saving others.

Earlier we suggested that U.S. intervention in Somalia came closest to fitting the definition of humanitarian intervention. If our argument is correct that the public tends to be more concerned with parochial nationalism than cosmopolitan ideals but will allow the president some "room to maneuver"—but only if the costs are perceived to be low and the gains high—Somalia is a case worth more attention. There are not many polls taken before the United States became involved in Somalia, but those that came right after the pictures of dead American soldiers being dragged through the streets of Mogadishu flashed across the nation's TV screens on October 5, 1993, reveal a complex reaction. More than 70 percent of those sampled wanted the United States to reduce its involvement in Somalia, with 43 percent favoring gradual rather than immediate disengagement. Only slightly more than a quarter (27 percent) indicated they were prepared to stay the course longer than six months. Other polls and analysis of U.S. involvement in

TABLE 3.1 Approval of U.S. Military Actions, 2011

Country/Region	Dates	% approve	% disapprove
Libya	March 2011	47%	37%
Iraq	March 2003	76%	20%
Afghanistan	October 2001	90%	5%
Kosovo/The Balkans	April–May 1999	51%	45%
Afghanistan and Sudan	August 1998	66%	19%
Haiti	September 1994	54%	45%
Somalia	June 1993	65%	23%
Iraq	January 1993	83%	9%
Libya	April 1986	86%	21%
Grenada	October 1983	53%	34%

Source: Data from Jeffrey Jones, "American Approve of Military Action Against Libya," March 22, 2011. Available at: www.gallup.com/poll/146738/americans-approve-military-action-against-libya.aspx.

Somalia showed that while there was undeniable concern for saving Somalis from starvation, a strong majority of respondents recognized that involvement should be limited, agreeing that "now that people are eating, our job is done and it is time to bring out boys home."[12]

It is also true that during the crisis in Somalia in fall 1993, there was a strong push by large numbers of members of Congress to quickly change course and reduce danger to U.S. personnel. Some interpret American opinions on Somalia as a demonstration of an emerging globalist sentiment in the United States. We see this differently, as confirmation that once things turn costly and a theoretical situation becomes real and deadly, the public is ready to hand off responsibilities to others. In other words, as costs and risks increase, domestic support ebbs.

As for Bosnia at approximately the same time (the early 1990s), different polls indicated that most Americans were initially opposed to getting involved in what was packaged by the George H. W. Bush administration as a complex, age-old ethnic problem. Not only had the Bush administration argued for steering clear of this complicated affair, as we have already noted, but the first year of the Clinton administration was characterized not only by general confusion in foreign policy but also forced preoccupation with Somalia. Attitudes and policy toward Bosnia did shift, but this started to happen after the February 1994 Serb attacks on a Sarajevo marketplace, which was widely covered by the media. In polls taken in that year, sampled Americans began to react more positively to the use of military force to curtail Serb atrocities.

It is still important to note that although almost half of the Americans polled indicated that they were worried about "becoming bogged down" in Bosnia (as it had been in Vietnam), almost 70 percent still concurred with the argument that because "Serbia is making direct attacks on Bosnia as well as sending weapons to the Serbian rebels, members of the UN should defend the Bosnian government."[13] It was only at the end of 1994 and after other atrocities that the Clinton administration developed a more coherent policy in dealing with the unfolding crisis in the Balkans.

However, there was always the expectation on the part of the Clinton administration that the crisis in the Balkans would be addressed in a multilateral way and that international intervention needed to include European countries. Polls taken in the United States in the second half of the 1990s demonstrate an appreciation of and support for international organizations like the United Nations and NATO to help stop the Serbs but also to advance U.S. interests in the region. An April 1995 poll for example found that 66 percent of Americans agreed that

> when innocent civilians are suffering or being killed, and a UN peace operation is organized to try to address the problem, in most cases the United States should be willing to contribute some troops, whether or not it serves the national interest.[14]

By the middle of the 1990s a majority of Americans believed that despite American involvement in other places in the world, the country had a moral obligation to intervene when genocide or gross human rights violations were taking place. These cosmopolitan values are consistent with the more recent polls we provided in Chapter 2 in which 70 percent of Americans polled indicated that the United States should use force to stop a government from committing genocide and killing large numbers of its own people (see Table 1.4). Yet, because the questions are written in a hypothetical, abstract way, this neither says that the public was demanding that the government act nor that it even approved of specific actions.

The Clinton administration was sensitive to Vietnam's long shadow and how easily the tide turned in Somalia once American lives were lost and the situation became more complicated. It also expected that various factions in Congress— e.g., the opposing party and those who wanted to focus on domestic problems— would seize upon any shortfalls in the Clinton approach to demand a change in policy. Thus, although President Clinton and Richard Holbrooke exercised decisive leadership in ending the Bosnian war by the end of 1995, they did so without placing any American military personnel overtly on the ground. The administration hoped to repeat this in Kosovo in 1999 once it decided that Milosevic's behavior there demanded American attention and military force. Opinion polls on Kosovo provide further indication of some cosmopolitan ideals, but again this conflict was packaged as being low-risk and part of a broader Balkans campaign that directly affected American and NATO credibility in the region. Various polls taken in the spring of 1999 found that although Americans wanted to leave ground forces on the table as an option in case bombing failed to make Milosevic stop the ethnic cleansing, large majorities did not support the use of ground forces.

Support for involvement in Kosovo arose primarily from humanitarian concerns and the belief that genocide was occurring, and almost three-quarters of Americans found this a convincing reason for American involvement. A strong majority also felt that once NATO and the United States started to do something in this part of Serbia, they were under a moral imperative to follow through with the effort. A Gallup poll taken in March 1999 for example found 58 percent of Americans felt that "the U.S. has a moral obligation" to intervene. ABC polls taken a month later were even higher. Other justifications were made for intervening in Kosovo, like fears of a wider war and protecting the credibility of the United States and NATO, but humanitarian concerns at least at this point in time fared better than these other reasons. In fact, even arguments made about U.S. national interest were not as compelling as humanitarian ones. In 1999 and after some success in Bosnia, Americans remained relatively supportive of helping others, especially to stop genocide. But again these efforts were always packaged by advocates as low-cost and low-risk endeavors that would only be carried out within a multilateral framework.

The American public's support for cosmopolitan ideas does not appear to be limited to certain regions or countries. Surveys thus suggest that Americans believe that the United States should "do the right thing," regardless of continent or country, and while this supports R2P and efforts to avoid atrocities, this is still different than support for military intervention. In September 1999 for example more than half of the Americans polled (56 percent) chose a cosmopolitan response, favoring humanitarianism when asked the following:

> Which is closer to your view of the proper role of the U.S. in the world? …
> The U.S. sometimes needs to get involved in regional conflicts that do not
> directly threaten U.S. interests, because we are often the only country able to
> maintain world peace and prevent humanitarian disasters such as Kosovo and
> East Timor, OR The U.S. should only act to protect our own national interests because it is not our responsibility to keep peace around the world?[15]

Another survey taken in 1999 posed a different question about the moral obligation to use military force to stop genocide in different regions and in all the regions, and again majorities indicated that the United States has an obligation to intervene, whether it is in Europe (60 percent), Asia (58 percent), or Africa (58 percent), affirming that the responsibility to intervene was not tied that closely to either certain populations or national interest. Yet, they are all hypothetical and devoid of context or a looming crisis.

Questions about moral obligation and genocide also evoke different responses than questions that asked about Americans regime change and trying to democratize countries. In fact, as we argued elsewhere, in Chapter 2, depending on when the question is asked large majorities of Americans in several polls indicated that the United States should not promote democracy in other countries and that it does not have a responsibility to do so. Thus, when it comes to public opinion and moral responsibility and the use of force, genocide is viewed quietly differently than democracy promotion.

Opinion polls often conflict or contradict but generally our perspective on public opinion and humanitarian intervention is three-fold. First, how questions are worded plays a role in how supportive Americans are in using military force abroad. Generally surveys suggest that Americans are less willing to use force when they must do so alone—the UN's involvement is seen as important. Second, we also note that public opinion on this issue is inconsistent at best and sensitive

TABLE 3.2 The United States and the World, Problems and Priorities

The most important problem facing the country...	
War/foreign policy/terrorism	41%
Economic issues	26%
Other issues	26%
The U.S. is...	
Less respected	67%
Major problem	24%
Minor problem/no problem/DK	24%
More respected	10%
No change	20%
Don't know	3%
Foreign policy should be based mostly on...	
U.S. interests	37%
Take other allies' interest into account	49%
Both/neither	8%
Don't know	6%
The Bush administration ...	
Tries hard for diplomacy	33%
Too quick to use force	49%
Don't know	8%
Top U.S. foreign policy priority to (be)...	
Follow moral principles	72%
Cautious	66%
Decisive	62%
Practical	58%
Compassionate	54%
Flexible	40%
Follow religious principles	33%
Idealistic	25%
Forceful	23%

Source: Data from "Foreign Policy Attitudes Driven by 9/11 and Iraq," The Pew Research Center August 18, 2004. Available at: www.people-press.org/2004/08/18/foreign-policy-attitudes-now-driven-by-911-and-iraq.

to a variety of other factors both domestic and international. In the abstract, more than 70 percent of Americans indicated that a top priority for foreign policy should be following moral principles.

Yet, there is a difference between abstract and specific situations, which we indicated in the previous chapter. When specific situations arise that put our principles and ideals to the test, cosmopolitan enthusiasm often erodes and the public becomes as reticent as elites when it comes to putting Americans in harm's way.

Well into the twenty-first century, Americans remained generally supportive of an activist foreign policy that was presented as altruistic and concerned with the welfare of others. However, concern and even support for early diplomatic action, as promoted by R2P to avoid atrocities, does not necessarily translate into actions and the use of force. In a September 2004 speech before the United Nations, Secretary of State Colin Powell concluded that genocide, or at least horrific genocidal acts, were occurring in Darfur. Although his statement did not legally commit the U.S. government to intervention, it definitely put American exceptionalism to the test. A poll taken in December 2004 indicated almost three-quarters of Americans believed that the United Nations should step in with military force in Darfur, and more than half (60 percent) indicated that the United States should be willing to contribute some troops.[16] Despite strong signs of cosmopolitan values among both elites and the public, the U.S. government did not act and support for involvement in Darfur declined quickly. As Steven Kull, director of the Program on International Policy Attitudes (PIPA), observed, even if it was fleeting, the public's support for involvement in Darfur was important.

> What is quite striking here is that even as the United States is tied down in Iraq and suffering daily casualties, a majority of Americans would support contributing troops to a multilateral operation in Darfur … Indeed, multiple polls have found that many Americans believe that if severe human rights abuses are occurring, especially genocide, the UN should have the right to intervene and the United States should be willing to contribute troops.[17]

A July 2005 poll also confirmed that that almost 70 percent of those asked agreed that "the U.S. and other Western powers have a moral obligation to use military force if necessary, to prevent one group of people from committing genocide against another," nearly the same level found when the question was asked in March 2001.[18]

Ultimately, the United States did not play a leading role in Darfur, failing to turn cosmopolitan rhetoric into decisive action. The campaign undertaken by Britain and the United States to cobble together a multilateral force to stop the atrocities was also unsuccessful and their efforts diluted, because by this point the George W. Bush administration had thoroughly used and abused the notion of humanitarian intervention. Instead, an AU-UN force was eventually deployed in Darfur, but it lacked the troops and political support to be fully successful. Alexander Bellamy argues that American involvement in Iraq was largely blamed for the global crisis in humanitarianism and the inability of the R2P norm to take effect in Darfur, wrecking "the case for humanitarian wars."[19] Bush did allow a UN Security Council resolution to pass that referred the Darfur situation to the International Criminal Court, but diplomatic action (in this case also indecisive) is different from putting one's nationals in harm's way for the rights of others.

Perhaps surprisingly, U.S. prolonged and inconclusive involvement in Iraq (and Afghanistan) did not mean the end of humanitarian intervention or support for R2P, as we saw with regard to Libya in 2011. However, it did signal a brake on the leadership abilities of both the United States and Britain. This was also evident in public wariness about U.S. ground forces in the Syrian civil and war and in debates about contesting ISIS in 2014. Similar to other cases of humanitarian intervention, Darfur reiterates important lessons related to the media's coverage, domestic interest groups, and public opinion. Even more crucially, it demonstrates that international crises never occur in a vacuum. While U.S. leaders or the public may, in theory, agree that the United States has an obligation to take meaningful action in certain situations and especially when genocide is happening, words are not deeds. In 2016, both the Obama administration and the Congress declared that the Islamic State group in Iraq and Syria had committed genocide. No new and decisive action followed.

Conclusion

Given periodic references to the notions of humanitarian intervention and R2P, all states, including the United States, face the question of whether they will actually use military force to stop or prevent atrocities in other countries. As we demonstrated in this chapter, neither the politics nor the rhetoric of this matter are that different for the United States compared to other countries past or present with capable militaries. Although many great powers have rhetorically taken the moral high ground, asserting that they are exceptional when it comes to helping others, the facts suggest mostly otherwise. Liberal democracies like Britain, France, Australia, etc. face similar challenges related to media coverage, domestic supporters and critics, military capability, multilateral factors, and so forth.

It also seems to be the case that in all liberal democracies, mass public opinion rarely leads but instead follows; its reactions to policies undertaken sets the outer limits of what a country can sustain. In liberal democracies with the capability to use force abroad, publics in all countries grow restless when foreign adventures become long or costly (as subjectively perceived and defined) and when national interests are not apparent. When French military personnel suffered casualties in Mali and the Central African Republic in 2014, or Belgian soldiers in a UN force were killed and mutilated in Rwanda in 1994, or a Dutch soldier in a UN deployment was killed in Bosnia in 1995, democratic publics reacted similarly and they were all less supportive of saving others. A central lesson from Mogadishu in 1993 is still relevant.

For the United States in the twenty-first century, it is likely that the past will be a powerful predictor of when it will act in response to a humanitarian crisis abroad. Some quantitative research on U.S. intervention argues that the United States is more likely to use force for humanitarian reasons than for security reasons like terrorism, but these studies cannot account for how the conflicts are packaged or perceptions of risk and loss. Thus, it could still be the case that the United States uses force for "humanitarian reasons," because leaders perceive this to be easier and cheaper while using force for security purposes might engender a stronger and more threatening reaction.

U.S. responses or lack thereof to events in Syria and Libya après Kaddafi suggest that more research is indeed warranted and that intervention abroad is shaped by shifting domestic priorities—not to mention the complexity of the situation in the targeted country. Moreover, all recent studies of U.S. intervention agree that there has never been a mass public movement pushing the government to use its military to help with the suffering of others abroad (excepting the domestic push for starting the Spanish-American War). There is no evidence forecasting that there will be one any time soon. Yet, an argument about humanitarian intervention sustained by public opinion is also not total fiction either.

More than two decades after the Cold War's end and with diverse challenges coming from China, Russia, and the Middle East, the reality is that neither the American government nor its people have a coherent or well-defined perspective on when the United States should use its military for humanitarian purposes. Academics too are divided over whether it is actually possible to separate national security concerns from cosmopolitan humanitarian claims.

What is consistent and agreed upon is that increasingly Americans want shared leadership and do not want the United States to act alone—even for humanitarian reasons. For a short time after September 11, 2001, Americans had a go-it-alone mentality but surveys taken just a few years later found that a large majority of Americans indicated that the United States should coordinate its power together with other countries according to shared ideas that are best for the world as a whole.

In 2013 not only did Americans want to work with others and share global responsibilities, but they were becoming skeptical of global engagement more generally (aside from concerns with international terrorism) and they did not believe that their country had either the power or the prestige to engage effectively in international affairs, especially when it came to the use of military force. This meant that Americans were turning somewhat inward, focusing more on more narrowly defined national interests (again with the exception of international terrorism). What we noted in Chapter 2 is confirmed in Table 3.2: when asked about long-range foreign policy priorities, Americans are more likely to prioritize protecting the United States from terrorist attacks and job security over promoting and protecting human rights or promoting democracy abroad.[20]

To be sure, Americans do not want isolationist policies, nor are they ready to pass on leadership to another country, but they are more interested in sharing leadership, working with the United Nations and trying to take into account its allies' views. Shared leadership, like the idea of a Responsibility to Protect, has many benefits and it might even suggest growing cosmopolitan values. Yet, shared leadership is difficult to implement in a world that manifests so many illiberal governments and armed non-state actors, as well as the regular pull of parochial nationalism in the United States. Such attitudes are also not good for the future of genuine humanitarian intervention. American exceptionalism and concern for saving others have always been more rhetoric than reality. But it is still the case that the United States has done a great deal of good, both alone and with others to help those suffering from political violence and leading effective coalitions to save strangers. It is this leadership, however flawed, that many in the world will someday miss.

Notes

1 We appreciate the comments from Matt Eberthart on this chapter.
2 Mike Sewell, "Humanitarian Intervention, Democracy, and Imperialism: The American War with Spain, 1898, and After," in *Humanitarian Intervention: A History*, edited by B. Simms and D. J. B. Trim (Cambridge: Cambridge University Press, 2011), p. 303.
3 For more on this and U.S. behavior in Cambodia, see Samantha Power, *"A Problem from Hell": America and the Age of Genocide* (New York: Basic Books, 2002), p. 131.
4 Richard N. Haas, *Intervention: The Use of American Military Force in the Post-Cold War World* (Washington, D.C.: Brookings Institution Press, 1999), p. 16.
5 Andrea Talentino, *Military Intervention After the Cold War* (Columbus, OH: Ohio State University Press, 2005), p. 113.
6 Nicholas J. Wheeler, *Saving Strangers: Humanitarian Intervention in International Society* (Oxford: Oxford University Press, 2000), pp. 179–180.
7 Haas, *Intervention*, p. 44.
8 Talentino, *Military Intervention After the Cold War*, p. 115.
9 This source, *Forbes* magazine, ran this story as part of an attack on Barack Obama for not speaking out enough in favor of American exceptionalism. The author declared his belief in American exceptionalism.
10 Address to the Nation on the Implementation of the Peace Agreement of Bosnia-Herzegovina, November 27, 1995. Available at: www.presidency.ucsb.edu/ws/index.php?pid=50808&st=exceptional&st1=.
11 See "US Role in the World: Altruism, the Global Interest and the National Interest," World Public Opinion. Available at: www.americans-world.org/digest/overview/us_role/nat_interest.cfm.
12 See Kull, "What New Isolationism? Wrong, Pundits. We Still Feel a Global Duty, even in Somalia," *The Washington Post*, October 24, 1993.
13 Steven Kull and Charlie Ramsay, "Public Seeks Sense of Purpose in US Bosnia Policy: Approval for Airstrikes Rose When Need Was Explained," *The Christian Science Monitor*, February 18, 1994.
14 See "US Role in the World."
15 Ibid.

16 See "Americans on the Darfur Crisis," PIPA/Knowledge Networks Poll, December 21–26, 2004.
17 Ibid.
18 See "America and the World," "Foreign Policy Attitudes Driven by 9/11," Pew Global Attitudes Surveys, 2004.
19 Alexander Bellamy, "Responsibility to Protect or Trojan Horse? The Crisis in Darfur and Humanitarian Intervention after Iraq," *Ethics and International Affairs*, 19:2, 2005, 38.
20 See "Public Sees U.S. Power Declining as Support for Global Engagement Slips," "America's Place in the World" Surveys, The Pew Research Center, December 3, 2013. Available at: www.people-press.org/2013/12/03/public-sees-u-s-power-declining-as-support-for-global-engagement-slips/12-3-2013-20.

Further Selected Readings

Abiew, F. K. *The Evolution of the Doctrine of Humanitarian Intervention*. Cambridge, MA: Kluwer Law International, 1999.

Address to the Nation on the Implementation of the Peace Agreement of Bosnia-Herzegovina, November 27, 1995. Available at: www.presidency.ucsb.edu/ws/index.php?pid=50808&st=exceptional&st1=.

"America and the World," "Foreign Policy Attitudes Driven by 9/11," Pew Global Attitudes Surveys, 2004.

"American Exceptionalism—And an 'Exceptional' President," Mallory Factor, *Forbes online*, August 31, 2010. Available at: www.forbes.com/2010/08/31/barack-obama-exceptionalism-america-opinions-columnists-mallory-factor.html.

"Americans on the Darfur Crisis," PIPA/Knowledge Networks Poll, December 21–26, 2004.

Amnéus, D. "Responsibility to Protect: Emerging Rules on Humanitarian Intervention," *Global Society*, vol. 26, no. 2, 2012, 241–276.

Badescu, C. and Bergholm, L. "The Responsibility to Protect and the Conflict in Darfur: The Big Let-Down," *Security Dialogue*, vol. 40, no. 3, 2009, 287–309.

Badescu, C. G. *Humanitarian Intervention and the Responsibility to Protect: Security and Human Rights*. London: Routledge, 2012.

Bass, G. *Freedom's Battle: The Origins of Humanitarian Intervention*. New York: Alfred A. Knopf, 2008.

Bellamy, A. J. "Responsibility to Protect or Trojan Horse? The Crisis in Darfur and Humanitarian Intervention after Iraq," *Ethics and International Affairs*, vol. 19, no. 2, 2005, 31–54.

Bellamy, A. J. *Responsibility to Protect: The Global Effort to End Mass Atrocities*. Cambridge, MA: Polity Press, 2009.

Bellamy, A. J. *Global Politics and the Responsibility to Protect: From Words to Deeds*. New York: Routledge, 2011.

Bellamy, A. J. and Williams, P. D. "The New Politics of Protection? Côte d'Ivoire, Libya and the Responsibility to Protect," *International Affairs*, vol. 87, no. 4, 2011, 825–850.

Carey, H. F. "The Third U.S. Intervention and Haiti's Paramilitary Predicament," *Journal of Haitian Studies*, vol. 11, no. 1, 2005, 88–111.

Carey, H. F. "U.S. Domestic Politics and the Emerging Humanitarian Prevention Policy: Haiti, Bosnia, and Kosovo," *World Affairs*, vol. 164, no. 2, 2001, 72–82.

Chesterman, S. *Just War or Just Peace? Humanitarian Intervention and International Law.* Oxford: Oxford University Press, 2001.

Choi, S. "What Determines US Humanitarian Intervention?" *Conflict Management and Political Science*, vol. 30, no. 2, April 2013, 121–139.

Choi, S. and James, P. "Why Does the United States Intervene Abroad? Democracy, Human Rights Violations, and Terrorism," *Journal of Conflict Resolution*, 2014, 1–28.

"The Darfur Crisis: African and American Public Opinion," PIPA report, June 29, 2005. Available at: www.worldpublicopinion.org/pipa/pdf/jun05/Darfur_Jun05_rpt.pdf.

de Waal, A. "Darfur and the Failure of the Responsibility to Protect," *International Affairs*, vol. 83, no. 6, 2007, 1039–1054.

Draper, T. *The Dominican Revolt: A Case Study in American Policy.* New York: Commentary, 1968.

Evans, G. "The Responsibility to Protect: An Idea Whose Time Has Come ... and Gone?" *International Relations*, vol. 22, no. 3, 2008, 283–298.

Evans, G. *The Responsibility to Protect: Ending Mass Atrocity Crimes Once and For All.* Washington, D.C.: Brookings, 2008.

Evans, G. and Sahnoun, M. "The Responsibility to Protect," *Foreign Affairs*, vol. 81, no. 6, 2002, 99–110.

Finnemore, M. "Constructing Norms of Humanitarian Intervention." In *The Culture of National Security*, edited by Peter Katzenstein. New York: Columbia University Press, 1996, pp. 153–185.

Finnemore, M. *The Purpose of Intervention: Changing Beliefs about the Use of Force.* Ithaca, NY: Cornell University Press, 2003.

Fukuyama, F. *The End of History and the Last Man.* New York: Simon & Schuster, 1992.

Hamilton, R. J. "The Responsibility to Protect: From Document to Doctrine—But What of Implementation?" *Harvard Human Rights Journal*, vol. 19, 2006, 289–297.

Hehir, A. and Murray, R., eds. *Libya, the Responsibility to Protect, and the Future of Humanitarian Intervention.* New York: Palgrave Macmillan, 2013.

Hildebrandt, T., Hillebrecht, C., Holm, P. M., and Pevehouse, J. "The Domestic Politics of Humanitarian Intervention: Public Opinion, Partisanship, and Ideology," *Foreign Policy Analysis*, vol. 9, no. 3, 2013, 243–266.

Holzgrefe, J. L. and Keohane, R. O., eds. *Humanitarian Intervention: Ethical, Legal, and Political Dilemmas.* Cambridge: Cambridge University Press, 2003.

Kinsella, H. M. *The Image Before the Weapon.* Ithaca, NY: Cornell University Press, 2011.

Kull, S. "What New Isolationism? Wrong, Pundits. We Still Feel a Global Duty, even in Somalia," *The Washington Post*, October 24, 1993.

Kull, S. and Ramsay, C. "Public Seeks Sense of Purpose in US Bosnia Policy: Approval for Airstrikes Rose When Need Was Explained," *The Christian Science Monitor*, February 18, 1994.

Kuperman, A. J. *The Limits of Humanitarian Intervention: Genocide in Rwanda.* Washington, D.C.: The Brookings Institution, 2001.

Livingston, S. and Eachus, T. "Humanitarian Crises and U.S. Foreign Policy: Somalia and the CNN Effect Reconsidered," *Political Communication*, vol. 12, no. 4, 1995, 413–429.

MacFarlane, N. S., Thielking, C. J., and Weiss, T. G. " 'The Responsibility to Protect': Is Anyone Interested in Humanitarian Intervention?" *Third World Quarterly*, 25, no. 5, 2004, 977–992.

MacQueen, N. *Humanitarian Intervention and the United Nations.* Edinburgh: Edinburgh University Press, 2011.

Mead, W. R. *Special Providence: American Foreign Policy and How it Changed the World.* New York: Routledge, 2002.

Pattison, J. *Humanitarian Intervention and the Responsibility to Protect: Who Should Intervene?* Oxford: Oxford University Press, 2010.

Payaslian, S. *United States Policy Toward the Armenian Question and the Armenian Genocide.* London and New York: Palgrave Macmillan, 2005.

Rabe, S. G. "The Johnson Doctrine," *Presidential Studies Quarterly*, vol. 36, no. 2, 2006, 48–58.

Roberts, A. "Humanitarian War: Military Intervention and Human Rights," *International Affairs*, vol. 69, no. 3, 1993, 429–449.

Seung-Whan, C. "What Determines US Humanitarian Intervention?" *Conflict Management and Peace Science*, vol. 30, no. 2, 2013, 121–139.

Sewell, M. "Humanitarian Intervention, Democracy, and Imperialism: The American War with Spain, 1898, and After," in *Humanitarian Intervention: A History*, edited by B. Simms and D. J. B. Trim. Cambridge: Cambridge University Press, 2011.

Simms, B. and D. J. B. Trim, eds. *Humanitarian Intervention: A History.* Cambridge: Cambridge University Press, 2011.

"Study of US Public Attitudes: Americans on Kosovo," Program on International Public Affairs, May 27, 1999. Available at: www.pipa.org/OnlineReports/Kosovo/Kosovo_May99/Kosovo_May99_rpt.pdf.

Talentino, A. *Military Intervention After the Cold War.* Columbus: Ohio State University Press, 2005.

"US Role in the World: Altruism, the Global Interest and the National Interest," World Public Opinion. Available at: www.americans-world.org/digest/overview/us_role/nat_interest.cfm.

Walsh, J. "Civilian Protection in Libya: Putting Coercion and Controversy Back into RtoP," *Ethic and International Affairs*, vol. 25, no. 3, 2011, 255–262.

Weiss, T. G. "The Sunset of Humanitarian Intervention? The Responsibility to Protect in a Unipolar Era," *Security Dialogue*, vol. 35, no. 2, 2004, 35–153.

Weiss, T. G. *Humanitarian Intervention.* Cambridge, MA: Polity Press, 2007.

Weiss, T. G. "RtoP Alive and Well after Libya," *Ethics and International Affairs,* vol. 25, no. 3, 2011, 287–292.

Wheeler, N. *Saving Strangers: Humanitarian Intervention in International Society.* Oxford: Oxford University Press, 2000.

Williams, P. D. and Bellamy, A. J. "The Responsibility to Protect and the Crisis in Darfur," *Security Dialogue*, vol. 36, no. 1, 2005, 27–47.

4

U.S. DETENTION AND INTERROGATION POLICIES AFTER 9/11/2001

A Tortured Evolution

The subject of U.S. treatment of "enemy prisoners" after the terrorist attacks of September 11, 2001 casts serious doubt on any claim that the U.S. record on this particular public policy is one of exceptional virtue. Despite diplomacy helping to construct international standards designed to protect prisoners in peace and war, Washington has engaged in the abuse of prisoners similar to many other democracies. Britain in dealing with Northern Ireland and Israel dealing mainly with Palestinians come to mind. To be sure, the United States treated enemy prisoners better than some other states in history. Several notorious comparisons can be noted: the Soviet and Nazi treatment of each other's prisoners in World War II; the Japanese treatment of allied prisoners in that same war; and the Chinese and North Korean treatment of American P.O.W.s during the Korean War.[1] To be sure, the United States has not been the worst offender in this area; at the same time, it has engaged in torture and other cruel acts—despite its claims to moral superiority and concern for the rights of all.

This chapter will show that early on during the so-called global war on terrorism, the George W. Bush administration adopted policies resulting in abusive detention and interrogation that sometimes amounted to cruel, humiliating, and degrading treatment (cruelty, for short), and sometimes even to torture. The abuse resulted primarily from carefully chosen policies, not simply from a few rogue individuals down the chain of command. We also make clear that the Barack Obama administration, while adopting certain ameliorative changes, refused to pursue prosecutions for these past policies. It was also uninterested in a fact-finding or truth commission that might deter repeat violations in the future.

We will also address the complex subject of the public's views on torture since that is an underlying factor that can support or oppose elite decisions and push for cosmopolitan values. Two points will be stressed: 1) Republicans are more sympathetic to torture policies than Democrats, and 2) while the public as a whole may passively oppose this or that torture technique, it has not compelled elected officials to renounce past torture policies with a view to more humane policies in the future.

America's torture record is due, in part, to the perceived unique and threatening conditions after 9/11, especially because our enemies, to some extent, were not known. We suggest that especially when liberal democracies are faced with asymmetrical warfare, featuring shadowy attacks on civilians and other manifestations of total war thinking, traditional humanitarian law restraints are weakened. The laws of war that were intended to protect prisoners of war, as found for example in 1949 Geneva Convention number three (the P.O.W. convention), had always relied heavily on reciprocity. Absent that reciprocity, humanitarian restraints were more difficult to apply. Human rights law, in particular the 1987 UN convention against torture, fared no better during the Bush administration.

After 9/11 the United States, at least for a time, was part of the downward spiral away from a humanitarian quarantine for enemy prisoners. Washington did not exhibit exceptional moral virtue by bucking this negative trend but rather contributed to it. Based on what was heard from some of the Republican candidates during the 2016 presidential primary, there is also a reasonable expectation that in the future a Republican administration, backed by a segment of a conservative legislative and public opinion, would behave in a similar way to the Bush administration during 2001–2006. Many of the Republican candidates in the prolonged run-up to the 2016 presidential election endorsed waterboarding and other examples of torture in responding to the atrocious behavior of the al-Qaeda network and the Islamic State. One might argue that trends were politically understandable, but it is difficult to reasonably conclude that on a national basis American exceptionalism was or is alive and well in the matter of treatment of enemy prisoners.

The Political and Legal History

The effort to guarantee humanitarian protections for fighters who are no longer active by reason of wounds, capture, or surrender has a long history.[2] The basic norm, articulated by many over many years (for example by Jean Jacques Rousseau in the early 1700s) was that those fighters out of the fight (hors de combat) reverted to being just an individual and merited a humanitarian quarantine for the duration of the conflict. The 1864 Geneva Convention that neutralized the war wounded and those who cared for them is seen by some as the start of the modern laws of war. It was drafted by the International Committee of the Red Cross (ICRC) for approval at a diplomatic conference hosted by Switzerland. The United States was not among the first states to consent to this treaty, but did so later in 1881. By 1929, there was a Geneva Convention (GC) on prisoners of war in international armed conflict, based largely on experiences in World War I. The United States accepted this Geneva Convention in 1932.

After World War II, Washington was quite active in negotiations leading to the 1949 Geneva Conventions. Geneva Convention number three was an extensive treaty covering prisoners of war. Its Article 3 covered detainees in non-international armed conflict (or internal war, also known as civil war). The 1949 Geneva Convention number 4 protected detained civilians in international war and follow-on occupation. The United States accepted these legal provisions in 1955.

Importantly, Washington was heavily engaged in negotiations leading to the 1977 Additional Protocols I and II, which represented further development of the 1949 law—the first on international and the second on internal armed conflict. However, the many provisions on detainee protections were not immediately accepted by the United States, as Washington rejected both Protocols. Similar to a few other democracies like Israel and Turkey, Washington claimed that the Protocols were politicized, subjective, and unworkable. Other democracies, including most NATO members, accepted the Protocols and their norms that once again prohibited cruelty and torture. However, the U.S. position is more complex regarding the possibility that some provisions of the Protocols mandating prisoner protections may have become legally binding as part of customary international law rather than treaty law. Although the subject is too complex for coverage here, others have dealt with it extensively.[3]

Like all other states, Washington accepts in the abstract that war should be regulated by international humanitarian law (aka the laws of war, or the law of armed conflict), with regard to both international and internal armed conflict. But general endorsement is not the same as the serious application in particular contexts. In fact, the United States has adopted many measures that undermine international law intended to protect human dignity—whether by humanitarian law in war or human rights law more generally.

In terms of international human rights law, there was the belated U.S. ratification of the 1948 Genocide Convention in 1988. The Ronald Reagan administration submitted this treaty to the Senate for approval in 1988 as part of a maneuver to offset criticism of the president for having visited a German cemetery at Bitburg containing the graves of Nazi war criminals. A reservation to this treaty blocked automatic referral to the World Court (ICJ) in the case of unresolved disputes about genocide. There is also the 1966 International Covenant on Civil and Political Rights (ICCPR) which prohibits torture and cruel treatment at all times, with no provisions for derogation (aka exception) from such core norms, even during times of national emergency threatening the life of the nation. The United States ratified the ICCPR in 1991, but with controversial reservations that basically gutted the treaty as an applicable legal instrument in U.S. courts.

There is also the 1987 Convention Against Torture negotiated at the United Nations, which prohibits torture and cruel treatment at any time and for any reason. The Reagan team submitted numerous reservations to the treaty. These were widely criticized as incompatible with the central purpose of the treaty. At the time of ratification in 1994, the Senate appended a smaller number of controversial reservations which again undermined the treaty. One of these held that not all infliction of severe pain was prohibited, but only such pain that was the result of an intention to inflict it. If one intended to gather security information and happened to produce severe pain as a by-product, this was not prohibited.

Especially concerning the United States and international human rights law, one can easily see that the United States wanted to be on record as favoring such norms, but it did not want to really be bound by them. Despite the façade of multilateral cooperation on human rights, Washington continued its strong tradition of unilateralism on this subject. There is nothing morally exceptional about using international human rights law for public relations exercises while making sure international norms are not enforceable in U.S. jurisdiction.[4] In fact, American behavior has been closer to exemptionalism instead of exceptionalism. Rather than exercising moral leadership in this domain, the United States has made sure to exempt itself from the law's restraints.

It is perilous to make sweeping generalizations about U.S. fidelity to the 1949 Geneva Conventions and other instruments of international humanitarian law. (One does not need to attempt that exercise with regard to international human rights law regarding prisoner protections, since Washington has seen to it that these legal provisions were not really in full legal force in the United States.) But as a matter of intermittent observation about the United States and taking International Humanitarian Law (IHL) seriously, the following can be said.

First, at least parts of the U.S. government take IHL seriously with regard to its application. While war crimes exist in all wars, the U.S. record with regard to P.O.W. protections in World War II, especially regarding Germany where reciprocity prevailed (both being bound by the 1929 P.O.W. Convention), was reasonably good, even if it was not perfect. True, for example, after Nazi soldiers shot some U.S. P.O.W.s at the Battle of the Bulge in Belgium, there were U.S. reprisals against German P.O.W.s. It is also the case that the United States did hide some German high-value detainees (e.g., submarine commanders) from ICRC visits for a time in northern Virginia in secret camps. However, detention and interrogation there fell far short of cruelty and torture (but not so for some Germans held in British secret internment places). One might also say that the U.S. record regarding P.O.W. affairs was also relatively good in the Korean War—certainly better than the record compiled by the Chinese and North Koreans on the other side. We comment more on this last situation below.

Second, the U.S. record is different in irregular wars, particularly wars of an internal or mixed nature. This was evident as early as the aftermath of the Spanish-American war in the Philippines (1898)—as we note in passing in our chapter on democracy promotion. When certain Filipinos resisted the American presence with an armed uprising, the U.S. commanders in the field responded with brutal policies that included torture such as waterboarding. Press reports of American harsh tactics were mostly covered up and explained away in Washington. Certainly the record of the United States' presence in the Philippines prior to its independence does not support any notion of American exceptionalism with regard to prisoner affairs. For a time, U.S. interrogation policies in the Philippines were quite brutal.[5]

Likewise, in the American phase of the war in Vietnam (1954–1975), where one found harsh tactics by Hanoi which included the torture of American pilots shot down and interned in the north, the American response was certainly not a textbook example of commitment to IHL standards. In a context in which there was debate about which parts of IHL applied, the United States did enter into certain agreements with the ICRC regarding prisoner affairs (based on similar ICRC agreements in the war in French Algeria) and did lean on its allies in Saigon from time to time to reduce the cruelty and torture being practiced by those authorities.

Basically, the U.S. official position was to treat captured guerrilla fighters out of uniform as if they were prisoners of war. But in that internationalized internal war with much terrorism and guerrilla warfare, and absent reciprocity on prisoner matters, there was much American brutality of those detained by U.S. security personnel. U.S. torture and massacres were part of that unhappy record, as in the CIA's Phoenix Program of torture and political murder. If the U.S. treatment of prisoners was better than that compiled by North Vietnamese regulars and the National Liberation Front, the Vietnam War—like the Algerian War—was known for terror and torture on a broad scale.[6]

Finally, in this very brief section, while making summary comments about the record of the U.S. military and its civilian leadership, we should highlight the growing role of the Central Intelligence Agency (CIA). As a result of Chinese and North Korean mistreatment of U.S. P.O.W.s during the Korean War of 1950–1953, and the apparent ability of these enemies to get American P.O.W.s to make false and incriminating statements about such things as Americans using germ warfare, Washington began to research torture tactics. This was done in secret, utilizing mainly the CIA—although some military personnel were assigned to the CIA project. Handing secret torture research to the CIA was strategic and calculated. It increased the prospects for plausible denial and it avoided mainly the uniformed military officials who believed strongly in military honor. There was also the matter of avoiding close congressional oversight. The main objective was initially defensive: to learn about the effects of Chinese and North Korean policies to better prepare U.S. military personnel in resisting such efforts.

However, the CIA program eventually morphed in a different direction, in the sense that the CIA (and the Pentagon) begin to teach and oversee torture tactics for certain allies, particularly in Vietnam and the Western Hemisphere. Thus, the United States outsourced its secret torture program to allies in a number of Latin American dictatorships during the Cold War, and also to security personnel in

Saigon, in order to help them repress primarily left-wing challengers. In short, the United States moved from wanting to train U.S. military personnel in how to resist torture by unprincipled enemies to employing torture itself in order to obtain information and coerce deference.[7]

To make a long and disturbing story short, the United States prior to 9/11 was teaching and practicing torture abroad—secretly, here and there, with plausible denial by top civilian leaders. The military was sometimes implicated, but it was the CIA which had been given the early lead in this approved program. It was to this program and this experience that the George W. Bush administration turned after 9/11 for the so-called Enhanced Interrogation Techniques (EHTs). During the Cold War, the United States tried mostly to supervise torture administered mainly by others, especially in Latin America. After 9/11, torture became U.S. public policy, approved in writing at the top, and was implemented frequently by Americans themselves, including uniformed military personnel.[8]

9/11 and the Decision to Torture

The shock of 9/11, which entailed the killing of some three thousand persons, mainly civilian, in New York and Washington (one hijacked plane crashed in Pennsylvania), had a profound impact on officials in the George W. Bush administration like Vice President Dick Cheney. Those killed were approximately twice the number killed in 1941 in the Japanese surprise attack on Pearl Harbor, and they were the first significant number of "political" deaths in the U.S. mainland since the war of 1812 with Britain. One result was Cheney's determination to prevent any similar attacks by almost any means necessary, regardless of traditional values or international laws prohibiting torture. Put differently, in his view 9/11 ushered in a new era and the United States would have to go to the "dark side" to protect itself.[9]

Cheney was a skilled and experienced operator in Washington, serving in the administration of a new president who did not always involve himself in the details of policy making. Cheney and his staff were assertive in making sure that White House and Justice Department lawyers arrived at the desired permissive memos, enabling harsh detention and interrogation of terror suspects and indeed of many enemy militants. The various civilian lawyers involved worked closely to enable CIA personnel who were already harshly interrogating certain prisoners. At the Pentagon, Secretary of Defense Donald Rumsfeld and his immediate civilian staff were also in favor of discarding inconvenient notions of military honor and military law. Those in the Bush administration who might be seen as moderates on detention and interrogation either were cut out of key decisions (e.g., Secretary of State Colin Powell and his staff) or did not assert themselves until later against the Cheney–Rumsfeld team (e.g., National Security Advisor and later Secretary of State Condoleezza Rice and her primary legal advisor John Bellinger III).

Without going into the details of all the bureaucratic and legal maneuvering in late 2001 and early 2002, one can easily note several key outcomes which indicated the nature of administration thinking. The CIA was authorized to run secret prisons itself and thus engage in the policy of enforced disappearance. The intent was to isolate detainees so that they could be pressured into providing actionable intelligence. Early detention occurred in places like Thailand and Afghanistan, but also in places like Lithuania, Poland, and Romania, among other countries, in order to avoid legal obligations in U.S. jurisdiction. The basic rule of international law is that individuals are always to be considered legal persons with rights and never to be detained outside of legal arrest and charge. U.S. policy, however, was similar to Chinese and North Korean policies during the Korean War which featured isolation and pressure. From the start, Bush officials who devised the interrogation program knew they were on thin legal ice. Thus they sought authorizing memos from the Office of Legal Counsel in the Department of Justice which in effect gave those engaged in the abuse of prisoners a "get out of jail card."

Likewise, the Pentagon chose the military facility at Guantanamo Bay, Cuba, "leased" by the United States since 1898, to hold "the worst of the worst." Since Gitmo was not geographically in the United States, it was intended to be a legal black hole. No U.S. law presumably applied and it would be far from the media and other prying eyes. So while the Bush administration claimed to be involved in a "global war on terrorism," the laws of war were not supposed to apply. In reality, the main "terror suspects" were held and tortured by the CIA. Most of those initially held at Gitmo were either wrongly detained or had little actionable intelligence to give up, being at best "foot soldiers" for Al-Qaeda or the Afghan Taliban. Over time, perhaps 15–20 percent of those held at Gitmo were viewed as "high-value detainees" and subjected to abusive interrogation. Most of those detained at Gitmo were eventually released to their home country or to some friendly country, being of little political importance.

It fit with this scheme of things that a list of interrogation techniques was approved in writing for the CIA that included waterboarding (near drowning), slamming prisoners head first into walls, sleep deprivation, manipulation of hot and cold temperatures, confining in painful positions, removal of clothing, forced grooming (shaving of beards which is important to Muslim males), solitary confinement, and other abusive techniques. When used in combination, such techniques could add up to torture (infliction of severe pain, whether physical or mental). The intent was to dehumanize and disorient and essentially break the prisoner so that he became compliant and truthfully answered whatever question his captor might ask. The official quest was for actionable intelligence. There was also interrogation that exceeded approved guidelines—e.g., waterboarding hundreds of times, threatening a detainee with a power drill, threating to rape a detainee's female relatives, confining a claustrophobic prisoner in a small box with insects, and so on.

The approved techniques were similar for the military, but not completely so. Various lists of interrogation techniques were approved, rescinded, altered, and revised over time. For some military personnel in some places, it was not clear what the approved rules were. Once it was decided that the 1949 Geneva Conventions did not apply, not the P.O.W. convention for international war and not Common Article 3 covering internal war, over time it was not clear what specific rules did apply. Some principled military lawyers objected effectively to drafts of interrogation techniques that were circulating for approval, but the retraction of the draft rules or their revision contributed to the confusion.

It remained clear that Rumsfeld's office intended to implement harsh interrogation. This can be seen by the appointment of Geoffrey D. Miller to command Gitmo, with instructions to deal with prisoners harshly. With a background in artillery, he had no expertise in prisoner affairs but was appointed because of his willingness to run a harsh detention system. Indeed, the torture of the presumed 19th hijacker, Al-Qahtani, was supervised in Washington by Rumsfeld's office. Later Rumsfeld's office transferred Miller to Iraq in order to bring the chaotic Abu Ghraib prison under control. The intent was to "Gitomize" Abu Ghraib and make the mistreatment systematic and orderly rather than out of control.[10]

Likewise in U.S. military prisons in Afghanistan, early abuse of detainees that led to fatalities was more closely supervised and controlled, trying to ensure that mistreatment did not prove fatal. This was similar to certain other democratic detention polices—for example, by Israel.[11] (Indeed, the Bush administration consulted with certain allies known for past harsh detention and interrogation—e.g., Britain, Israel, Saudi Arabia. It also outsourced some of its detention and interrogation tasks to other allies known for harsh treatment—e.g., Egypt, Jordan, Morocco, and even Syria.) In addition, there were the military "take down" procedures in which a military team would burst into a detainee's cell and roughly subdue him on the pretext of some rule infraction. Prisoners were sometimes injured in this exercise. This was apart from planned sexual abuse in which a female member of the interrogation team would fondle the genitals of the Muslim prisoner or otherwise sexually torment him—e.g., by smearing fake menstrual blood on him. Still further, there are credible claims that U.S. special operations forces (JSOC) ran their own prisons in places like Iraq and engaged in such serious abuse of detainees that various U.S. officials objected.[12]

Confounding a neat separation of CIA activities from those of the military was the fact that the CIA operated in sectors of some military prisons, making lines of authority unclear—as in Afghanistan, Iraq, and Guantanamo. It was, however, clear in retrospect that some military personnel picked up some abusive techniques from observing these CIA operations, whatever the original bifurcation decided in Washington. At Abu Ghraib in Iraq, for example, some of the horrendous abuse meted out by American military personnel mimicked authorized techniques practiced elsewhere. Eventually there was agreement, as the Schlesinger report stated, that harsh interrogation techniques "migrated" across U.S. governmental agencies and personnel.[13]

At Gitmo, the ICRC was present from December 2001 because of lower level decisions in the military chain of command and not because Rumsfeld's office wanted Red Cross representatives on site. The ICRC was invited in because some uniformed military personnel assumed that when the United States was involved in armed conflict, prisoners were supposed to be treated humanely under ICRC supervision. This was what law and military tradition demanded. However, because U.S. policy as made in Washington was to detain assumed enemy prisoners harshly and interrogate them in abusive fashion, U.S. personnel at Gitmo tried to hide some "high-value detainees" from the ICRC. Most probably, U.S. policy was also to listen in on supposedly confidential interviews with detainees and sanction those prisoners who told the ICRC about abuse.[14] These tactics had been practiced by numerous other governments around the world, but usually by dictatorships. The ICRC was never allowed into CIA "black sites" but did interview some detainees formerly held by the CIA after they were transferred to Gitmo.

In concluding this section, one should note that much U.S. interrogation policy was driven by amateurish and controversial recommendations. Much of the planning and some of the implementation of U.S. abusive interrogation were given to two consultants involved in the Survival, Evasion, Resistance, and Escape (S.E.R.E) program. After the Korean War, the S.E.R.E. military program was designed to prepare U.S. security personnel to survive, evade, resist, and escape enemy detention and interrogation. It was then "reverse engineered" after 9/11 into a program to elicit actionable intelligence from enemy prisoners. Those running the program were not experts in the latter type of operation, nor were they experts on Arab and/or Muslim psychology. But they were still paid tens of millions of dollars for their role, even though their involvement was opposed by certain persons experienced in hostile interrogations who maintained that reliable information could be gained from non-abusive interrogations. In any event, particularly during the first five years after 9/11, U.S. abusive interrogation proceeded. It was to turn out to be the case that it was difficult to produce a consensus as to what exactly was obtained from this abusive process.

Relevant Evaluations

The ICRC has provided important information on the policies and behavior of the United States toward detainees after 9/11. The organization visits more detainees around the world than any other organization and has been engaged in prison visits since World War I. Starting as an amateurish agency, the ICRC is now an experienced prison inspector, familiar with the tactics of detaining authorities who pretend to cooperate but often do not fully do so. When President Bush decided to shut down the CIA secret prisons in 2006, 14 prisoners were transferred to Gitmo. (Other CIA prisoners, known to have been in that system, have never been publically accounted for.) With regard to the former CIA detainees, the ICRC concluded that some had been treated cruelly and some were tortured. For those detained by the military at Gitmo, the organization concluded that a certain percentage had been treated in ways that were "tantamount to torture." At the Abu Ghraib prison in Iraq in the fall of 2003, the ICRC suspended its visits as part of its quiet protest of major abuse there. The ICRC was also active in prisons in Afghanistan across time and space, with numerous and mixed evaluations of U.S. and Afghan policies.

ICRC judgments, initially delivered to U.S. authorities in a discreet process, fit with other evaluations. As for the treatment meted out to the supposed 19th hijacker, al-Qahtani, a U.S. official in charge of prosecutions in the U.S. military commissions, ruled that he had been tortured at Gitmo and the proceedings could not go forward. The F.B.I. and certain military agencies withdrew from the U.S. interrogation process at Gitmo once they observed its nature, disagreeing with the approach and knowing that it jeopardized successful prosecution of detainees later. It is a clear norm of American jurisprudence, both civilian and military, that coerced evidence is not admissible in court. The Schmidt Report by the U.S. Army about detention and interrogation at Gitmo did not differ substantively with what the ICRC had to say, and it recommended sanctions for the key commander there, Geoffrey Miller. Instead, the Bush administration gave Miller a medal for meritorious service.

The CIA, defying a court order, destroyed videos of waterboarding sessions and perhaps of other abuse. Just as the release in 2004 of unauthorized pictures of abuse at Abu Ghraib led to some efforts at reform in Congress by 2005, so the anticipated eventual release of videos of waterboarding sessions was feared by some in Washington and therefore destroyed. There was no punishment for this destruction.

As noted above, Vice President Cheney had been careful to obtain Justice Department approval for procedures that he knew would be controversial, if not obviously illegal and difficult to justify in a liberal democracy that talked frequently and loudly about human rights abuses by others. CIA Director George Tenet had insisted on written authorization for abusive interrogation, not wanting to be left out on a limb with sole responsibility for controversial CIA abuse.

In sum, most detaining authorities engaging in cruel treatment and/or torture call it something else. In the U.S. case after 9/11 it was called "Enhanced Interrogation Techniques." The Israelis approved "moderate physical pressure." The Nazis and cooperating French police in occupied France during World War II talked about "energetic interrogation." But it was clear that when prisoners were left traumatized on a cell floor in a fetal position, severe pain had been inflicted. When prisoners underwent simulated drowning hundreds of times, severe mental anguish had been inflicted. The fact that fingernails were not pulled out and electric shocks not applied to genitals only indicates that there are various ways of inflicting severe pain that do not disfigure and do not follow the traditional rule book of classic torture. The very process of painful forced feeding through nasal passages into the stomach while in a restraint chair, to end a prisoner hunger strike, raises serious question about the role of U.S. (and Israeli) medical officials in supervising such a process.[15] Then there was the matter of "rectal feeding."

To be sure, Al-Qaeda and the Afghanistan Taliban believed in few restraints. They attacked civilians on 9/11 in the United States and at other times and places. Like the self-proclaimed Islamic State at a later time, they consciously chose atrocities to instill fear as well as to provoke their targets into over-reaction and hence further troubles. These atrocities included torturing and killing prisoners. All of this leads to the point that absent reciprocity among fighting parties in trying to limit the violence, there tends to be a downward spiral of increased brutal behavior all around.[16] And despite lofty rhetoric about the American character and legal promises, the United States did not resist this trend. Facing an enemy who believed in total war, it went to the dark side itself—as particularly Cheney intended. Some U.S. officials argued the EHTs fell short of torture, but sometimes the facts indicated otherwise.

After Cruelty and Torture

Absent further major successful attacks on the homeland, the George Bush administration moved somewhat in a moderate direction from 2006. In some ways it had little choice. In the aftermath of the Abu Ghraib photos of atrocious American behavior in Iraq, Congress passed the Detainee Treatment Act in 2005, requiring the U.S. military to carry out detention and interrogation in keeping with prior military manuals based on the standards of the Geneva Conventions. The CIA was exempted, despite efforts by Senator John McCain and some others to include it.

McCain and others unsuccessfully used the argument of American exceptionalism—namely, that Americans shouldn't do torture, whether it be by the CIA or any other agency. In the words of Senator McCain on the Senate floor in 2014, reviewing past debates:

> I rise in support of the release—the long-delayed release—of the Senate Intelligence Committee's summarized, unclassified review of the so-called "enhanced interrogation techniques" that were employed by the previous administration to extract information from captured terrorists. It is a thorough and thoughtful study of practices that I believe not only failed their purpose—to secure actionable intelligence to prevent further attacks on the U.S. and our allies—but actually damaged our security interests, as well as our reputation as a force for good in the world. [...]
>
> I have long believed some of these practices amounted to torture, as a reasonable person would define it, especially, but not only the practice of waterboarding, which is a mock execution and an exquisite form of torture.

Its use was shameful and unnecessary; and, contrary to assertions made by some of its defenders and as the Committee's report makes clear, it produced little useful intelligence to help us track down the perpetrators of 9/11 or prevent new attacks and atrocities. [...]

But in the end, torture's failure to serve its intended purpose isn't the main reason to oppose its use. I have often said, and will always maintain, that this question isn't about our enemies; it's about us. It's about who we were, who we are and who we aspire to be. It's about how we represent ourselves to the world. [...]

We need not risk our national honor to prevail in this or any war. We need only remember in the worst of times, through the chaos and terror of war, when facing cruelty, suffering and loss, that we are always Americans, and different, stronger, and better than those who would destroy us.[17]

In June 2006, the U.S. Supreme Court ruled that the United States exercised functional sovereignty at the Cuban locale and that all detainees at Gitmo were protected by 1949 GC Common Article 3. In the view of the Court, this legal norm—which prohibited torture and cruelty—applied as a base line standard in all armed conflicts. And politically speaking, it seems that the president realized that certain harsh policy preferences by his Vice President and Secretary of Defense were not without their dangers and problems. He was encouraged in this new direction by Condoleezza Rice (who earlier, like Colin Powell, had attended White House meetings where Enhanced Interrogation Techniques were discussed).

Once in office President Obama's administration sought only a partial break with Bush's policies toward enemy prisoners. The president intended to close Guantanamo since especially in parts of the Muslim world it was seen as a negative symbol, but he had few options. Abuse of Muslim prisoners had indeed proved a rallying cry and recruiting issue for various Islamic militant groups. Various U.S. security officials testified that Gitmo was a drag on U.S. foreign policy. Congress, however, passed legislation forbidding the transfer of Gitmo detainees to the United States proper. This transpired despite the absence of evidence showing that anyone had ever escaped from a U.S. maximum security prison. Finding a new location for the detainees proved paralyzing. The Obama administration did close the CIA secret prisons and banned most of the EHTs. As for the eventual disposition of enemy prisoners, for those not released to home or friendly countries, the Obama team preferred to use the regular federal court system rather than controversial military commissions for trials of those attempting or carrying out attacks on U.S. targets. The military commissions were inherently controversial since they lacked the full procedural guarantees of regular courts and were widely seen as dispensing "rough justice."

Importantly, the Obama team did not seek the prosecution of those who had authorized cruelty and torture or had enabled that abuse through various legal interpretations. It was reasonably clear by this point that: 1) authorization for the EHTs had gone all the way to the level of president and vice president, and 2) these and other officials could present a reasonable defense—namely that the proper authorities in the Justice Department had said the interrogation techniques were legal. Even if the legal memos were flawed, they still constituted a viable defense for high officials—at least in U.S. courts. (Torture gave rise to universal jurisdiction, which meant that foreign courts could try Americans regardless of citizenship or place of the alleged crime. But what country wanted to take on the powerful United States and forfeit cooperation on various other issues?)

Obama seemed to be on politically sound ground in saying that he wanted to move forward rather than prosecute for past policies, given that parts of Washington and the country would criticize prosecution as partisan and dangerous to national security. Just as President Ford had pardoned Nixon for Watergate crimes in the 1970s, Obama sought political stability and agreement rather than a continuation of disputes. (Ironically, at approximately the same time, the Obama team pressed the victorious government of Sri Lanka to directly address past war crimes in the recently concluded armed conflict with the defeated Sri Lankan Tamil Tigers.) For Sri Lanka, the Obama administration argued the need to address the past for the sake of national reconciliation and future stability. For itself, it maintained just the opposite—namely that stability required bypassing past controversies.

Democrats in the Senate Armed Services Committee did review past military policies pertaining to detention and interrogation and issued a bi-partisan report that was critical in several respects.[18] In a companion move, Democrats in the Senate Intelligence Committee reviewed the role of the CIA on similar matters.[19] The highly critical executive summary of this report (the report itself has not yet been released) was rejected both by most Senate Republicans and by the CIA. (We noted Republican Senator John McCain's endorsement of the report above.) Senator Leahy, a Democrat on the Justice Committee, tried to stir up interest in a truth commission but this idea went nowhere.

Some 15 years after 9/11, partisan views clearly differed on many aspects of U.S. detention and interrogation policies. Moreover, disagreement persisted regarding what abusive interrogation had produced. Much factual information remained classified, which allowed the Cheney camp to argue that the EHTs had produced valuable information at least about Al-Qaeda's structure and manner of operations. Critics continued to claim that very little actionable intelligence had been obtained through abuse and no imminent attacks disrupted. This kind of debate centered on political effectiveness and not at all on legality and morality.

The underlying disagreements and conflicting policy preferences were also reflected in national public opinion surveys. Out of the vast number of public opinion surveys on the question of U.S. torture, it was repeatedly clear that Republicans were more supportive of harsh interrogation than Democrats and Independents. For example, Pew reported in 2009 that 45 percent of Republicans thought torture, which was named as such in the questions, was sometimes justified, as compared to 35 percent of Independents and 24 percent of Democrats. Against this background, it was not so surprising that Republican candidates in the 2016 presidential primaries endorsed Bush–Cheney–Rumsfeld policies on interrogation. Other polls show that Americans were not much concerned about past U.S. torture compared to other public policy concerns.

If one compares American views on torture to other nations, it is certainly hard to make the case for American exceptionalism as moral virtue. A global poll in 2008 asked if "limited torture" should be used on "terrorists" to protect "innocent lives." In the United States 31 percent agreed, which was high compared to most West European nations (e.g., 6 percent agreed in Spain, 12 percent in France). The U.S. figure of 31 percent was comparable to Russia (29 percent) and Turkey (34 percent). However, the U.S. response was more supportive of human rights in the case of torture than in India (47 percent), democracy there notwithstanding. In fact, Indian treatment of Muslim militants operating out of Kashmir, with possible Pakistani support, is quite harsh and has been for some time.[20] In sum according to this poll, American tolerance of torture was greater than in much of Europe, less than in some democracies like India and South Korea, and somewhere towards the middle of all nations sampled at that time. In other words, American views did not stand out as either exceptionally opposed to torture or exceptionally supportive of it.

The great number of polls on questions of torture leads to great debate as to what they actually mean. While several polls show growing American toleration of torture techniques from 2002 to 2014, some experts dispute simple interpretation of the numbers. One group of experts argues that the apparent trend toward more American acceptance of torture, even when called torture, is a reflection of various intervening variables. According to their polls, when Americans are asked about specific techniques like waterboarding and sexual humiliation of prisoners, they express overwhelming opposition.[21] (Recall the CIA destruction of waterboarding videos.) What can be said with some certainty is that beyond the clear partisan divide on the matter, many Americans are conflicted about how to stand for human rights while protecting national security. Given their concern for national security, some American show some tolerance for techniques like sleep deprivation and other manipulations of the environment (noise, temperature, food, water) which can be part of a no-touch torture policy which aims at psychological rather than physical pain.

At the end of the debate about detainee interrogations, there is little empirical evidence that Americans stand out as exceptionally virtuous, especially those on the conservative side of the political spectrum. Of course there is the view, often called the neo-con view, that the United States is such a force for good in the world that it is moral to use any means to defend it and moral to torture those who are clearly nefarious. In a book by former U.S. security officials, one finds this statement by Porter Goss, formerly head of the CIA:

What "must never happen again" is that we fail to understand that weakness—real or perceived—is a magnet that attracts "evildoers." … What "must never happen again" is for the United States of America to relinquish its leadership as the greatest force for good in the world …[22]

In other words, because we are so good, we must appear strong including if necessary the willingness to torture.

Conclusion

The United States after 9/11 treated presumed enemy detainees similar to the way Britain treated suspected IRA militants active in "the troubles" that centered on Northern Ireland in the 1970s and similar to the way Israel treated suspected Palestinian "terrorists" linked to the West Bank and Gaza since 1967. The prisoners were isolated, kept from the ICRC for varying amounts of time, abused in various ways, sometimes tortured, but mostly not killed. If prisoners died in the process, policy had been exceeded. Detainees may have been damaged psychologically, but mostly the system relied on pressures that did not leave permanent physical scars. It can be recalled that Bush officials consulted with Britain and Israel, as well as others before adopting the EHTs for both CIA and military detention. All of the detaining authorities were in search of information that would lead to fewer attacks on them, but in none of the cases did abusive interrogation prove decisive in controlling or ending the conflict. Whatever actionable intelligence was gained, it did not prove major, and the reputation of the democracy was damaged at home and abroad.

International law aside and national statues derived therefrom (which admittedly is a major consideration), evaluating the ethics of torture is somewhat like evaluating the death penalty. Regarding the latter, one can cherry pick the cases to focus on egregious behavior by defendants. One can thus say that the surviving Boston bomber behaved so badly in killing children and other innocents at the Boston marathon in 2013 that he deserved to die. On the other hand, if one takes a broader view of the system itself, one encounters certain facts: that in the United States there is discrimination in that the death penalty is more likely to be applied to racial minorities than to whites, and that mistakes have been made and innocent lives taken by the state. Some stress the horror of a crime; others stress the serious defects of the system.

Likewise with regard to U.S. torture after 9/11, one can say that Khalid Sheik Mohammed, the presumed mastermind of the attacks, was so evil that he deserved to be waterboarded 283 times. On the other hand, if one looks at the system at a whole, one has to acknowledge that U.S. detention and interrogation policies contributed to producing more criticism of the country, and more militants against it, especially in the Muslim world. The gains to national security remain unclear and debated. Moreover, there were mistakes, with innocent persons tortured. Particularly on the last point there are undisputed facts.

The case of Maher Arar is relevant. Seized in New York by U.S. officials on the basis of false information from Canada, he was "rendered" to Syria and tortured before being released. Canada apologized and paid reparations, the United States did neither. Likewise, relevant is the case of Khalid el-Masri. A German-Lebanese, he was seized in Macedonia, taken to a U.S. secret prison in Afghanistan, tortured, and then abruptly released when it was discovered he was not the right el-Masri. He currently suffers from various psychological problems. When interviewed, he told a reporter:

> People in the West are the last ones in the world that should talk about human rights. Look what they have done to me and others. There have been no consequences for those responsible. On one hand, they are great in pointing at others and criticizing them, but then they don't want to look inside and have accountability for human rights crimes.[23]

Notes

1 All statements of fact not otherwise referenced are drawn from David P. Forsythe, *The Politics of Prisoner Abuse: The United States and Enemy Prisoners after 9/11* (Cambridge: Cambridge University Press, 2011).

2 See further Stephen C. Neff, *War and the Law of Nations: A General History* (Cambridge: Cambridge University Press, 2005).

3 See further Brian D. Lepard, *Customary International Law: A New Theory with Practical Applications* (Cambridge: Cambridge University Press, 2010). Even if it turns out to be the case that some provisions of the 1977 Additional Protocols became part of customary international law and hence binding on the United States, the fact remains that Washington violated some of these norms in its policies toward enemy prisoners after 9/11.

4 See further William A. Schabas, "Spare the RUD or Spoil the Treaty: The United States Challenges the Human Rights Committee on Reservations," edited by David P. Forsythe, *The United States and Human Rights: Looking Inward and Outward* (Lincoln: University of Nebraska Press, 2000), pp. 110–130.

5 For one readable account see Gregg Jones, *Honor in the Dust: Theodore Roosevelt, War in the Philippines, and the Rise and Fall of America's Imperial Dream* (London: Penguin, New American Library), 2012.

6 Almost everything about the long American involvement in Vietnam is complicated, as is the U.S. record on torture there. For the argument that some U.S. military lawyers and diplomats tried to limit prisoner abuse, see Forsythe, *The Politics of Prisoner Abuse*. For one reliable account of the practice of torture by U.S. personnel, see Barbara Myers, "The Man Who First Blew the Whistle on CIA Torture," Moyers & Company, June 3, 2015. Available at: http://billmoyers.com/2015/06/03/conspirator-vietnam-anthony-russo-torture/. For an account of the CIA Phoenix program of torture and murder, see Douglas Valentine, *The Phoenix Program* (New York: William Morrow, 1990).

7 See further especially Alfred W. McCoy, *A Question of Torture: CIA Interrogation, from the Cold War to the War on Terror* (New York: Henry Holt, 2006). And Greg Grandin,

Empire's Workshop: Latin America, the United States, and the Rise of the New Imperialism (New York: Henry Holt, 2006).

8 James P. Pfiffner, *Torture as Public Policy: Restoring U.S. Credibility on the World Stage* (Boulder, CO: Paradigm Press, 2010).

9 On Cheney's view that 9/11 changed him, see Dick Cheney and Liz Cheney, *Exceptional: Why the World Needs a Powerful America* (New York: Simon and Schuster, 2015). On Cheney's own words about having to go to the dark side, see Jane Mayer, *The Dark Side: The Inside Story of How the War on Terror Turned Into a War on American Ideals* (New York: Random House, Anchor Books, 2008).

10 See further Philippe Sands, *Torture Team: Rumsfeld's Memo and the Betrayal of American Values* (London and New York: Palgrave Macmillan, 2008).

11 It is no secret that Israel uses various forms of coercion, such as shackling in painful positions, against presumed "high value detainees." See the numerous reports on this subject by both Human Rights Watch and Amnesty International, not to mention by various Israeli human rights groups such as B'Tselem.

12 See for example Jeremy Scahill, *Dirty Wars: The World is a Battlefield* (New York: Nation Books, 2013).

13 The 2005 Schlesinger report, named after a former Secretary of Defense who headed an investigative panel, was to some degree a cover-up. The panel did confirm atrocious abuse by U.S. military personnel in Iraq. But it never addressed the larger picture of how authorized abuse for both the military and CIA morphed into rampant uncontrolled abuse particularly at the Abu Ghraib prison. As usual in national investigations of national wrongdoing, the report focused on the rank and file and not at broad command responsibility including by civilian leaders. Likewise in a subsequent handful of military trials for events at Abu Ghraib, the focus remained on lower ranking military personal and not on those who authorized some abuse but created confusion over what was allowed and what was off limits. For the general trend, see Neil James Mitchell, *Democracy's Blameless Leaders: From Dresden to Abu Ghraib, How Leaders Evade Accountability for Abuse, Atrocity, and Killing* (New York: NYU Press, 2012). And Stephen Holmes, "The Spider's Web: How Government Lawbreakers Routinely Elude the Law," in *When Governments Break The Law: The Rule of Law and the Prosecution of the Bush Administration, edited by* Austin Sarat and Nasser Hussain (New York: NYU Press, 2010), pp. 121–152.

14 See Mohamedou Ould Slahi, *Guantanamo Diary* (New York, Boston, London: Little Brown, 2015).

15 For the tip of the iceberg about this controversy, see Patricia Klime, "Navy Will Not Discharge Guantanamo Nurse," *Military Times*, May 13, 2015. Available at: www. militarytimes.com/story/military/pentagon/2015/05/13/guantanamo-involuntary-feedings-nurse/27251657.

16 See further Mark Osiel, *The End of Reciprocity: Terror, Torture, and the Law of War* (Cambridge: Cambridge University Press, 2009).

17 "Floor Statement by Senator John McCain on Senate Intelligence Committee Report on CIA Interrogation Methods," December 9, 2014. Available at: www.mccain. senate.gov/public/index.cfm/2014/12/floor-statement-by-sen-mccain-on-senate-intelligence-committee-report-on-cia-interrogation-methods.

18 "Inquiry into the Treatment of Detainees in U.S. Custody," Report of the Committee on Armed Services, United States Senate, November 20, 2008. Available at: www. armed-services.senate.gov/imo/media/doc/Detainee-Report-Final_April-22–2009. pdf.

19 "Report of the Senate Select Committee on Intelligence of the Central Intelligence's Agency's Detention and Interrogation Program," December 9, 2014. Available at: www. gpo.gov/fdsys/pkg/CRPT-113srpt288/pdf/CRPT-113srpt288.pdf.

20 The ICRC has been visiting detainees held by India for a considerable time. The organization discussed Indian abuse of detainees with U.S. diplomats, hoping to generate pressure for change on Indian authorities. U.S. diplomatic cables on the subject were leaked to the public by Wikileaks, which generated difficulties for ICRC–India relations. All of this was covered by various media sources. For one example, see a detailed story by a leading Indian newspaper at www.thehindu.com/news/international/india-accused-of-systematic-use-of-torture-in-kashmir/article957003.ece.

21 On a huge subject one might start with Darius Rejali and his colleagues mostly at Reed College as per www.reed.edu/poli_sci/faculty/rejali/articles/US_Public_Opinion_Torture_Gronke_Rejali.pdf. For a useful point of comparison see www.gallup.com/opinion/polling-matters/180008/retrospective-look-americans-view-torture.aspx.

22 In the book *Rebuttal: The CIA Responds to the Senate Intelligence Committee's Report on its Detention and Interrogation Program* (Washington, D.C.: Naval Institute Press, 2015), former high CIA officials offer their defense of torture. See especially the discussion of this report at www.theamericanconservative.com/articles/the-cias-torture-defenders.

23 Souad Mekhennet, "A German Man Held Captive in the CIA's Secret Prisons Gives First Interview in 8 Years," *Washington Post*, September 16, 2015. Available at: www.washingtonpost.com/news/worldviews/wp/2015/09/16/a-german-man-held-captive-in-the-cias-secret-prisons-gives-first-interview-in-8-years.

Further Selected Readings

Cheney, D. and Cheney, L. *Exceptional: Why the World Needs a Powerful America.* New York: Simon and Schuster, 2015.

Forsythe, D. P. *The Politics of Prisoner Abuse: The United States and Enemy Prisoners after 9/11.* Cambridge: Cambridge University Press, 2011.

Grandin, G. *Empire's Workshop: Latin America, the United States, and the Rise of the New Imperialism.* New York: Henry Holt, 2006.

Holmes, S. "The Spider's Web: How Government Lawbreakers Routinely Elude the Law," in *When Governments Break the Law: The Rule of Law and the Prosecution of the Bush Administration*, edited by Austin Sarat and Nasser Hussain. New York: NYU Press, 2010, pp. 121–152.

Jones, G. *Honor in the Dust: Theodore Roosevelt, War in the Philippines, and the Rise and Fall of America's Imperial Dream.* London: Penguin, New American Library, 2012.

Klime, P. "Navy Will Not Discharge Guantanamo Nurse," *Military Times*, May 13, 2015. Available at: www.militarytimes.com/story/military/pentagon/2015/05/13/guantanamo-involuntary-feedings-nurse/27251657.

Lepard, B. *Customary International Law: A New Theory with Practical Applications*, Cambridge: Cambridge University Press, 2010.

McCoy, A. W. *A Question of Torture: CIA Interrogation, from the Cold War to the War on Terror.* New York: Henry Holt, 2006.

Mayer, J. *The Dark Side: The Inside Story of How the War on Terror Turned Into a War on American Ideals.* New York: Random House, Anchor Books, 2008.

Mitchell, N. *Democracy's Blameless Leaders: From Dresden to Abu Ghraib, How Leaders Evade Accountability for Abuse, Atrocity, and Killing.* New York: NYU Press, 2012.

Neff, S. C. *War and the Law of Nations: A General History.* Cambridge: Cambridge University Press, 2005.

Osiel, M. *The End of Reciprocity: Terror, Torture, and the Law of War.* Cambridge: Cambridge University Press, 2009.

Ould Slahi, M. *Guantanamo Diary*. New York, Boston, London: Little Brown, 2015.

Pfiffner, J. *Torture as Public Policy: Restoring U.S. Credibility on the World Stage*. Boulder, CO: Paradigm Press, 2010.

Rebuttal: The CIA Responds to the Senate Intelligence Committee's Report on its Detention and Interrogation Program. Washington, D.C.: Naval Institute Press, 2015.

Sands, P. *Torture Team: Rumsfeld's Memo and the Betrayal of American Values*. London and New York: Palgrave Macmillan, 2008.

Scahill, J. *Dirty Wars: The World is a Battlefield*. New York: Nation Books, 2013.

Schabas, W. A. "Spare the RUD or Spoil the Treaty: The United States Challenges the Human Rights Committee on Reservations," in *The United States and Human Rights: Looking Inward and Outward*, edited by David P. Forsythe. Lincoln, NE: University of Nebraska Press, 2000, pp. 110–130.

Valentine, D. *The Phoenix Program*. New York: William Morrow, 1990.

5

AMERICAN EXCEPTIONALISM REINED IN

The U.S. Supreme Court, Corporations, and the Kiobel Case

We usually think of U.S. foreign policy being made and conducted by the "political" branches, with only a minor and occasional role for the judiciary. But in the 2013 Kiobel case, the U.S. Supreme Court engaged in judicial activism to overturn some 35 years of settled law that favored a special U.S. role in protecting human rights abroad. Until then, the United States had demonstrated a rare situation of true American exceptionalism. The United States was the only country in the world to open its national (viz., federal) courts to civil law suits by foreigners (viz., aliens) who claimed to be the victims of major international human rights violations like torture.[1] In other words, the United States had established universal jurisdiction for violations of international law involving wrongs in civil law.

This chapter looks at the role of the U.S. Supreme Court and its treatment of private economic actors and their human rights policies. In particular, it looks at the Roberts Court, because it elevated concerns about international stability and corporate profit making over the protection of fundamental personal rights for all. For the Roberts Court, what was important was corporate profit making and the United States avoiding international complications that might upset stable inter-state relations. Unlike other U.S. courts, it was not interested in providing a remedy for victims of human rights violations. Legalities temporarily aside, the Kiobel judgment meant that when faced with the question of whether the United States should be a leader in allowing foreign victims to challenge human rights violations wherever they might have occurred, including by corporations and other private economic actors, the court was unanimous in saying no. How and why this happened merits our attention, as does the entire subject of corporate responsibility and human rights in U.S. foreign policy. What the Kiobel case demonstrates is that the U.S. record is no longer morally superior or even clearly positive when it comes to human rights violations by economic actors abroad.

Some History of International Criminal Justice

The United States has a rather long history of holding private economic actors responsible for aiding and abetting in human rights violations. After World War II, the principal victorious powers decided to hold trials for top political and military leaders in Germany and Japan who had engaged in aggression, war crimes, or crimes against humanity. The Nuremberg and Tokyo trials, which have much written about and which were international in composition, followed—with a leading role for the United States. (The Soviet Union and even Churchill's Britain at first wanted simply summary execution of the Nazi leaders then detained.) Less well known were the follow-on trials held by each of the victorious powers under the same legal principle of international criminal law—namely that individuals, not just states, could be held accountable for certain violations of international law.

In the strictly U.S. criminal trials of Germans, the decision was taken to prosecute corporate leaders as natural persons for complicity in violations of international law during the Nazi regime. Corporations themselves, legal persons in U.S. law, were not prosecuted. This was a tactical decision, because the judgment of prosecuting attorneys in the 1940s was that corporations themselves could have been prosecuted had time allowed and had not so much evidence already been collected about individual business leaders. Prosecution of Japanese business leaders was not pursued by U.S. authorities in the Far East.

In the U.S. trials of German business leaders,

> The defendants were four dozen leaders of six German firms, Flick, I.G. Farben, Krupp, Roechling, Hermann Goering Works, and Dresdner Bank, and the acts—slave labor, plunder, prewar takeover of Jewish- and Czech-owned plants, unconsented human experimentation, manufacture of poison gas, participation in the illegal rearmament for aggressive war—were charged as crimes against humanity, war crimes, conspiracy, and crimes against peace.[2]

Of most relevance for contemporary human rights were the charges regarding slave labor, manufacture of poison gas for use in genocide, pseudo-medical experiments on political prisoners, and various forms of persecution and discrimination.

In a final accounting of these trials, convictions were few and sentences were light. One reason was the "necessity defense" by defendants, namely that they had no choice but to do what they did in a totalitarian state featuring tight control of everything by Nazi top officials. Another reason was waning U.S. governmental interest in trials for war-time behavior, given the desire to integrate West Germany into the NATO alliance and to get the pro-West Konrad Adenauer elected as its Chancellor. The trials were also unpopular in West Germany and so U.S. strategic calculations shifted. Nevertheless, in law the principle was established that private economic actors could be held legally responsible for complicity, or aiding and abetting, in gross violations of internationally recognized human rights.

In general, international criminal law (featuring individual responsibility) was put into a state-induced coma from the late 1940s until the mid-1990s. Law professors debated the subject, and in the abstract states accepted the theory of universal jurisdiction. As a matter of legal principle, states agreed that at least genocide and major war crimes were so heinous that any state could try an individual so charged, regardless of nationality of defendant or place of alleged crimes. But few specific trials followed. It was not until 1993 and 1994 that certain states in the UN Security Council, troubled by the absence of decisive intervention to stop atrocities in the first Balkan War (1992–1995) and Rwanda (1994), moved to start a contemporary renaissance in the prosecution of individuals.

In the post-Cold War era, the focus in international criminal law was on "atrocity crimes" like genocide, war crimes, and crimes against humanity. One major result was the creation of the International Criminal Court (ICC) in 1998, a permanent international court. It began to function in 2002 when and if states were "unwilling or unable" to exercise their primary responsibility to act properly to investigate and perhaps prosecute natural persons concerning atrocity crimes. Its first case resulted in the conviction of a private individual—the leader of an African militia that engaged in the use of child soldiers. All of this pertained to criminal law and not civil law, but legal accountability of persons was at the core of developments.

In the meantime, there was a parallel development in the United States involving a here-to-fore obscure congressional act from 1789 called the Alien Tort Statute (ATS). This legislation, whose original intent has been mostly lost to history, reads: "district courts shall have original jurisdiction of any civil action by an alien for a tort only, committed in violation of the law of nations or a treaty of the United States." Most likely this law was designed to open U.S. federal courts to complaints by non-U.S. citizens involving piracy, breach of safe conduct passes, and violations of diplomatic immunity.

In 1980, American human rights lawyers were successful in utilizing the ATS in a case involving torture in Paraguay. Without replaying all the legal details, one can say that in the Filartiga case the U.S. appellate court agreed with plaintiffs that the torturer was similar to the pirate: both were "an enemy of all mankind."[3] Thus the Paraguayan relatives of Joelito Filartiga, who had been tortured to death in autocratic Paraguay, were entitled to seek damages from his torturer who at that time had been found within the United States. Damages were awarded to plaintiffs, although the losing defendant had been allowed to return to Paraguay. The victory was symbolic as the monetary judgment of about $10m was never collected. The case seemed to establish, however, that cosmopolitan values were the law of the land, as the court showed clear interest in remedies for human rights violations abroad, even if U.S. policy and American actors were not directly involved.

Filartiga was seminal (a movie was made about it and a book written) in that it led to many subsequent claims in U.S. courts by non-citizens alleging human rights violations abroad. Many of these petitions in civil law were screened out on various technical grounds. But about 75–80 cases were allowed to proceed. Some resulted in monetary damages being awarded to plaintiffs. Most of these financial judgments went uncollected because the defendant did not have assets within the United States that could be seized. Nevertheless, plaintiffs achieved some personal satisfaction or "closure" when they won their case. Human rights lawyers increasingly saw the ATS as a major instrument in trying to protect universal human rights. Interestingly, in no case did a major controversy erupt in international relations over the role of U.S. courts in passing judgment about human rights violations occurring abroad. Within the United States, academics as well as human rights activists followed developments, but the ATS was not controversial in Washington early on.[4] Within the D.C. beltway, few wanted to go on record as blocking a crackdown on torture and other atrocity crimes.

In the 1980s and 1990s, there was a growing movement to link corporate behavior and international human rights. Reference to the ATS was part of this social movement. It was perfectly obvious that corporate actors possessed much power and affected many lives in important ways. Prominent human rights NGOs like Amnesty International and Human Rights Watch devoted considerable attention to the subject. Specialized groups formed like the Business and Human Rights Resource Center. But it was equally clear that most states were not terribly eager to impose human rights standards on transnational corporations (TNCs) based within their jurisdictions concerning foreign actions. Human rights regulations might disadvantage home state TNCs in competition with others, perhaps driving them to locate their headquarters elsewhere (one form of relocation is called inversion), and deprive the home state of jobs and tax revenue. Business leaders often had much clout with governmental leaders whether the latter were left or right of center in national politics, since business leaders made sizable campaign contributions to politicians of leading political parties and were active in lobbying. States certainly had the legal authority to impose stringent human rights standards on TNC policies abroad, but it was perfectly clear they did not want to do so—regardless of how many human rights treaties a state might have ratified.

Hence, there was a proliferation of voluntary codes of conduct written for TNCs, and at the United Nations there was the development of the Global Compact under which corporations were asked to pledge to accept the central idea of social responsibility.[5] Part of the Global Compact embodied human rights standards as well as goals drawn from the idea of environmental protection (aka sustainable development). There were also specific social movements featuring consumer boycotts because of poor conditions for workers in the global supply chain of major TNCs like Nike, or Adidas, or The Gap clothiers. The Swiss firm Nestle was targeted early by protestors who questioned its marketing of infant formula in ways, times, and places that led to malnutrition in babies. Had states wanted to negotiate tightly worded treaties governing TNC operations, these "soft accountability measures" would not have been so prevalent. Independent experts in the UN Sub-Commission on Human Rights proposed specific standards for TNCs in 2003, but it went nowhere once that ball was passed to state representatives at the UN. In 2004 the parent UN Human Rights Commission (now the UN Human Rights Council), made up of states, declared that the draft norms for TNCs had no legal status.

In the 1990s, human rights lawyers had begun to go after corporations for complicity in human rights violations abroad, invoking the ATS. In a reversal of developments from the U.S. trials of Germans in the 1940s, the defendants were regarded as "legal persons" rather than individual business leaders as "natural persons." There was a proliferation of cases, about 150, charging TNCs with complicity in such violations as genocide, crimes against humanity, war crimes, torture, arbitrary detention, murder, persecution, and discrimination. The place of the alleged crimes varied but included Myanmar, the Philippines, Sudan, South Africa, Argentina, Ethiopia, and Nigeria. Companies targeted were often wealthy and included Royal Dutch Shell, Unocal, Exxon, the Ford Motor Company, Barclays Bank, Del Monte, Chrysler-Daimler but also many others that were small and unknown. The central logic was not complicated: if the ATS was intended for pirates, and if the torturer was essentially the same as the pirate, was not the abusive corporation in the same category?

As the cases proliferated, the business community and its friends in the George W. Bush administration (2001–2009) took notice and began to push back against such trends. They combined forces in the important 2004 Sosa case in the U.S. Supreme Court.[6] The U.S. Drug Enforcement Agency (DEA) suspected a Mexican doctor, Alvarez-Machain, of being implicated in the torture and death of a DEA agent in Mexico. It therefore hired Sosa and others to kidnap the doctor and render him to the United States for trial. (This exercise of bounty hunting violated an extradition treaty between the United States and Mexico, as well as the UN Charter and Charter of the Organization of American States.) Alvarez-Machain, upon his acquittal, sued Sosa under the ATS for unlawful detention. The doctor also sued the United States under other laws that need not concern us here, except to note that the U.S. Executive branch had ample reason to argue (which it did) that the Supreme Court should not view Alvarez-Machain with favor, since his private detention had been at the request of Washington.

The U.S. Chamber of Commerce could easily see the business implications of *Sosa*, namely that non-governmental actors might be held responsible under the ATS for violations—or complicity in violations—of human rights abroad. It therefore submitted an amicus brief (a friend of the court brief advising the court how it should rule) in support of Sosa and against Alvarez-Machain. A couple of foreign governments did likewise, acting on behalf of their corporations as headquartered abroad. The Supreme Court, deferring to these pressures in favor of judicial caution and deference to the political braches, reversed lower court opinions in favor of the doctor. The Supreme Court ruled in *Sosa* that the ATS applied only to a narrow range of wrongs supported by universal agreement on their nature, and not including arbitrary detention unless it was prolonged. In the opinion of the court, to rule otherwise would be to project the judiciary into sensitive subject matter best left to the political branches. The court did not specify what torts were covered by the ATS. The court ignored the fact that the primary dispute between the United States and Mexico centered on the U.S. bypassing their extradition treaty, not on the ATS.

One further set of facts brings us to Kiobel in 2013. Whatever the merits of prosecuting natural individuals under ATS, it is a fact that many TNCs have adopted policies that are at least complicit in, if not directly responsible for, human rights violations around the world. U.S. companies, for example, buy fish products that are produced via slavery: males looking for work out of places like Thailand and Myanmar are kidnapped and sold into slavery on fishing boats that spend long stretches at sea; the catch is part of the supply chain that often goes into the sale of food in American grocery stores.[7] Various minority groups have been forced into working on a pipeline in Myanmar (Burma) controlled by the previous military government there but organized and financed by Total in France and Unocal in the United States; repeated agitation by private groups and media coverage no doubt had something to do with Unocal deciding to settle the case out of court after being sued under the ATS.[8]

Caterpillar Inc. has repeatedly sold machinery to Israel that is used by others in collective punishments of Palestinians, as the homes of suspected "terrorists" are bulldozed in the occupied territories, sometimes with loss of innocent life.[9] Chrysler-Daimler was confronted with claims that during the time of a military junta in Argentina it was complicit in the kidnapping, torture, and murder of union activists at one or more of its plants in that country. The case was dismissed in the United States on jurisdictional grounds; the substantive claims were never adjudicated but are widely believed to be true.[10] Repeated exposure about the existence of "sweat shops" and other abusive labor conditions in the international clothing industry led to the negotiation of the Fair Labor Association, with periodic inspection of production facilities by independent monitors, such were the awful working conditions in places like Bangladesh and Honduras, among other places, in supply chains organized by major apparel brands in the West.[11] Various hi-tech or information technology companies in the West have sold expertise and software to repressive regimes which use the technology for spying on dissidents or blocking free speech and association via the internet.[12] For that matter it can be recalled that IBM and AT&T, among others including Fred Koch the billionaire member of the John Birch Society,[13] had contracts with the Nazi regime. There is no doubt that at various times and places, certain TNCs have at best been complicit in various violations of internationally recognized human rights.[14]

In brief summary to this point, it is clear that: 1) corporations are sometimes deeply involved in major human rights violations around the world; 2) the accountability that the United States demanded of German business leaders in the Nazi era has not been followed up consistently in succeeding years; and 3) recently, the U.S. judiciary has been the target of conflicting views—the desire by some to see that the United States does not become a safe haven for gross violators of human rights acting abroad versus the desire by others not to interfere unwisely with the authority of the political branches concerning foreign policy or with the activities of corporations producing benefits for the United States.

The Kiobel Case of 2013

Literally thousands of articles have been written about the 2013 judgment of the U.S. Supreme Court in *Kiobel*.[15] The triggering facts are well known. Several Nigerian refugees residing in the United States brought suit under the ATS, charging three business entities with complicity in violations of human rights such as murder, torture, denial of due process, etc. through actions in the delta region (aka Ogoni region) of Nigeria. The case eventually centered on Royal Dutch Shell, officially the Royal Dutch Petroleum Company, a partly public, partly private oil company reflecting combined ownership in both the United Kingdom and the Netherlands. The factual issue was whether Royal Dutch Shell had been a party to various abusive actions by the Nigerian government and its security forces as the latter sought to suppress protest actions by civilians concerned about oil extraction and transport by Royal Dutch Shell in the oil-rich Nigerian delta. The initial, primary legal issue was whether the ATS could be applied to a corporation rather than to a natural person such as a torturer.

Lower court judgments had addressed the question of whether corporations could be sued directly under international law and did not dispose of the case on those grounds. In the United States, corporations were considered legal persons with some rights and duties. But it was only territorial states that had full legal personality (also called subjectivity, as in subjects of the law) under international law. Perhaps because it was fairly clear that corporations had at least partial personality or subjectivity in international law,[16] key justices in the U.S. Supreme Court raised a new and different question on their own: regardless of the legal personality of corporations and their status in international law, should the ATS be applied to any action abroad by any type of actor? Was not the ATS intended to cover certain violations of international law when plaintiffs and defendants were both found within U.S. jurisdiction, or maybe where the United States had some connection to events? This shifting of the central question by the court itself represented judicial activism because this question had not been raised prominently by plaintiffs or defendants in lower court proceedings. Amicus briefs had not addressed it in depth.

It seems likely that the justices driving this shift intended from the outset to undermine the spreading use of the ATS for human rights reasons because: 1) amicus briefs in this and previous cases made clear that both the international business community and champions of judicial restraint in international cases favored limiting use of the ATS; and 2) *Kiobel* was a good case in which to limit the ATS, because all of the actions in question occurred within Nigeria with almost no U.S. interest in, or American connection to, events. According to the unanimous opinion written by Chief Justice Roberts, it was unwise for the court to project itself into matters wholly transpiring in another sovereign state, especially when the U.S. government as well as various business circles had advised caution. Similar wording in the *Sosa* controlling opinion, about how courts should proceed cautiously in these kinds of cases, gave the justices some prior reasoning to cite in *Kiobel* in this regard. In overturning over three decades of settled law regarding application of the ATS to human rights violations abroad, the justices could argue they were following some precedent as per the reasoning in Sosa. And, in exercising judicial activism to emphasize a different central question in the case, they did so in the name of judicial restraint. Various legal nuances aside, Justices Kennedy, Scalia, Alito, and Thomas joined the Roberts' opinion. None of them, excepting sometimes Kennedy, were known for great interest in the international law of human rights.[17]

The central logic of Chief Justice Roberts' controlling opinion was that if the ATS was intended primarily to allow the legal regulation of pirates, the latter operated in international waters. Thus, invoking the ATS in that kind of case did not intrude on events within sovereign nations. There was also an international consensus in favor of individual states taking unilateral action to deal with piracy. Otherwise, in cases dealing with events within sovereign states and where an international consensus in favor of decentralized action was not so clear, national courts should proceed with great caution. Technically, Roberts referred to a previous court judgment (Morrison vs. National Australia Bank), holding that if national legislation did not mention extra-territoriality, there would be a presumption against applying the act abroad.[18]

Since the ATS did not mention anything about application abroad, Roberts held that such a presumption should be applied. This line of argument had been used by government lawyers in the George W. Bush administration in different cases. Roberts and those who concurred in his opinion never mentioned, much less emphasized, any need to control for violations of human rights abroad, nor did his opinion address national legal prosecution as a major way to hold TNCs accountable. These issues were hidden behind discussions of foreign jurisdiction and judicial restraint. In fact, all three situations presumably associated with the ATS in 1789 involved international subject matter—pirates, protection of ambassadors, and safe conduct passes in war. Here was yet another case where internationally recognized human rights norms were intentionally undermined by arguments based on jurisdictional and other legal technicalities.[19] This is yet another case in which the Roberts Court showed great deference to corporate freedom of action.[20]

The first part of Roberts' reasoning was effectively contested by the concurring opinion of Justice Breyer, who agreed with the conclusion but not the reasoning. Breyer pointed out that when pirates operate, they do not do so just by moving around in international waters. They board ships, and ships are part of the jurisdiction of the nation whose flag they fly. When pirates board a ship flying the flag of Honduras or Liberia (our examples), they are acting within the jurisdiction of those nations. For Breyer, the better reasoning is that rather than discuss any presumption against extra-territoriality, one should allow cases to go forward under ATS where there is direct American connection to events such as: the alleged tort occurred on American soil or by an American defendant, or the United States has an important interest in developments, including ensuring that the United States does not harbor gross violators of human rights. In his view, *Kiobel* did not meet this test, and so he agreed to dismiss. Justices Ginsberg, Sotomayor, and Kagan concurred. In this concurring opinion there was reference to enforcing internationally recognized human rights as a U.S. national interest. Also, under Breyer's logic, presumably TNC behavior could be addressed, at least in certain cases.

Numerous amicus briefs were filed in this case, given the importance of the anticipated ruling. Most were predictable. Britain and the Netherlands argued for dismissal, not wanting the United States to review operations of one of their major corporations. They had also argued for judicial restraint in *Sosa* for the same reason. Other business interests also argued for dismissal, which was completely expected. Various human rights organizations argued for continuation of an expansive use of ATS for human rights reasons, also to be expected. Several former government lawyers in Republican administrations argued for judicial deference to the executive in important foreign policy matters, which was to be expected and which dovetailed with maintaining freedom of operations for TNCs—Republicans normally being friendly to big business (and forgetting Teddy Roosevelt's skepticism about big business and hence his "trust busting" efforts).

The first amicus brief by the Obama administration merits mention. (There is no clear rule in federal common law as to when a court should defer to executive preferences and when not. In previous ATS cases, Republican administration briefs had advised caution and Democratic amicus briefs had not, which fits the expected pattern. Conservatives tend to emphasize the quest for stability in world affairs whereas Progressives tend to emphasize attempts at improvement.)

Filed at the first stage of *Kiobel*, the Obama brief focused on the question of corporate liability for wrongful action under international law and whether such action fell under the ATS. It only mentioned extra-territoriality in passing. Signed by a variety of administration lawyers including the Legal Advisor for the Department of State, Legal Counsel for the Department of Commerce, and the Solicitor General, it argued that: 1) U.S. courts had broad discretion regarding how to apply international law, and 2) addressing corporate liability for torts fell within that discretion. Along the way it argued that the ATS imposed no distinction between natural and legal persons; that other legal instruments, including treaties did assign legal obligations to private corporations; and that while international criminal courts addressed only natural persons, not corporate persons, that was because of the nature of punishments available—namely incarceration. (One cannot sue a corporation in the International Criminal Court, but then one cannot put a corporation in prison.) In general the Obama administration through this amicus brief was fully supportive of using the ATS to impose accountability on TNCs. It argued that while under *Sosa* the substantive rule of international law at issue—viz., genocide, crimes against humanity, torture, etc.—had to be defined with sufficient specificity and broadly accepted by "civilized nations," the enforcement action had to meet no such criteria. Thus, the United States had freedom of action to choose its means of enforcing substantive standards in international law. In U.S. federal law, it was fully accepted that there was tort liability for private corporations.

With regard to *Kiobel*'s second phase, focused on extra-territoriality rather than corporate liability under international law, the substance of the Obama administration's second brief was much more cautious and represented a much noticed shift. It essentially advised more or less what the Roberts' judgment finally opined—namely, that plaintiffs' claim should be dismissed. With a slightly different cast of administration lawyers and the State Department Legal Advisor (Harold Koh) refusing to sign, the brief supported *Filartiga* and certain other unspecified ATS cases in which the United States was said to have an interest. Supporting the enforcement of certain internationally recognized human rights was said to be a U.S. interest. But where, as in *Kiobel*, what was at issue was action within a sovereign state's jurisdiction, implicating the government there, and involving action by a corporation based in a third state, U.S. courts should not recognize a cause of action in federal common law (or case law).

According to the brief, the ATS was jurisdictional only. This means that U.S. courts could hear a category of cases but also could stipulate further facts or conditions for an ATS case to go further (these are called causes of action). One of these causes of action had been stipulated in a general way in *Sosa*, namely that the violation of international law should be specifically defined and broadly accepted. In the view of the Obama administration's brief, other causes of action could be stipulated, but the brief advised the court not to try to do so in comprehensive fashion. The judiciary should proceed case by case, or category by category, taking into account the views of the political branches. Thus, in effect, the judiciary should continue to allow cases about torture by natural persons, but not about complicity in torture in Nigeria by non-American corporations. The brief left open the future regarding that kind of complicity by American corporations, neither recommending for or against. Thus the Obama amicus brief in *Kiobel* phase two was sensitive to questions of sovereignty and reciprocity (sometimes called comity), but also supportive of some type of continuation of use of ATS for some kinds of (unclear and not fully defined) cases. It was a surprising and tortured brief.

Perhaps by the time of the Obama administration's brief in *Kiobel* phase two, government lawyers had remembered what happened when Belgium passed a new statute on universal jurisdiction in 1993. The new law opened Belgian courts to claims for prosecution for war crimes, crimes against humanity, and genocide. The statute was praised by various human rights groups. But the courts were then flooded with petitions from various individuals of various nationalities regarding a wide variety of defendants, including Yasser Arafat, Ariel Sharon, George W. Bush, and others. A very good argument based on facts could be made that both Arafat and Sharon had committed war crimes. Likewise, a solid factual argument could be made that Bush had authorized torture in his so-called war on terrorism. But the fundamental political fact was that Belgium found itself embroiled in more controversy than it wanted. Even the International Court of Justice at the Hague, an arm of the United Nations, criticized Belgium for trying to indict a sitting Foreign Minister of the Democratic Republic of the Congo. The United States threatened to move NATO headquarters out of Brussels. In 2003 Belgium revised the controversial law, requiring some connection to Belgium for universal jurisdiction cases to be filed and moved forward. This quieted the controversy, even as it disappointed those who wanted to prioritize rigorous human rights enforcement.[21] There is the matter of the art of the possible in political context.

Kiobel is an important case but not the last word on the subject. Already there is more litigation in U.S. courts regarding the accountability of corporations. First, under both *Sosa* and *Kiobel*, as international law and state practice develop further, it is not always clear which international human rights norms are defined with sufficient specificity and are also widely accepted so as to allow a cause of action under the ATS. Second, under the Roberts and Breyer opinions and the Obama amicus brief, it is not at all clear what kinds of situations might touch upon the concerns of the United States with sufficient force to override any presumption against extra-territoriality. The general and vague wording as found both in Sosa and the Kiobel majority and concurring opinions invites further law suits to test the boundaries of any judicial deference to the political branches as they contemplate foreign affairs.

Suppose in Nigeria it had been an American corporation accused of complicity in torture? Suppose instead of Nigeria it had been a close ally like Israel and an American corporation? Suppose it had been Iran? Saudi Arabia? Would those alterations of fact make any difference in enforcement via federal common law? That is, what are the causes of action from U.S. case law that would allow an ATS case to move forward? What kind of U.S. "touch or concern" affects the disposition of cases? Surely, given other U.S. domestic cases about the rights and duties of corporations—do they have the right of freedom of speech and campaign contributions (Citizens United case), right of freedom of religion and avoidance of health care regulations (Hobby Lobby case) —we have not heard the last about corporate liability in relation to international law as processed according to the myriad and cross-cutting rules of U.S. federal courts.

Does Public Opinion Matter?

On the one hand, there is the old adage that at the end of the day, courts follow public opinion. On the other hand, federal judges are selected for lifetime appointments so they can presumably resist public opinion and concentrate strictly on legal interpretation. In other chapters we considered American public opinion in relation to elite policy making. Is there any reason to do so regarding the ATS and TNCs? As per our other chapters, does public opinion set the limits on what elites decide about human rights and business abroad?

Our conclusion is: probably not on this subject. First of all, it is expecting too much of the public to follow and understand the legal twists and turns of argument in matters pertaining to TNCs and the ATS. It is difficult enough for those with a J.D. or Ph.D. to follow the complicated facts and legal arguments in cases like *Sosa* and *Kiobel*. Second, we do not know what public opinion is on these matters. There is no precise and targeted survey research on TNCs and international human rights, or on attitudes toward corporate social responsibility (parts of which speak to ecology rather than most human rights norms).

The UN Global Compact is based on the underlying notion that corporations should develop socially responsible policies lest they face consumer criticism, boycotts, and loss of reputation and sales. Sometimes this does indeed happen. It can be shown via survey research that so-called millennials (or younger persons) *say* their purchases are affected by business reputation.[22] Sometimes this happens but sometimes it does not. Consumers will punish Volkswagen for cheating on environmental standards by not buying its cars, but Facebook and Apple have not been commercially punished for cooperating with Chinese repression and the curtailment of free speech in China.

Certain elements of European public opinion have pushed for, and achieved, some types of economic sanctions on Israel for its policies in the West Bank and Gaza. But no broad element of American public opinion has achieved sanctions on the company's cooperation with Israel in collective punishments in the West Bank. Certainly in the United States and probably elsewhere, public attention to TNCs and human rights violations is a murky and inconsistent and uneven thing. There are lots of international norms on human rights, lots of different kinds of products and services, lots of different kinds of corporations doing business in lots of different kinds of nations. Even the best-intentioned of consumers finds it difficult to be well informed and to prioritize cosmopolitan values in favor of global human rights.

Perhaps the best that can be said is that history shows that sometimes public opinion on human rights and business affairs matters. The Quakers in Britain led the charge against the slave trade and then slavery itself in the early 1800s. Over time this group defeated powerful economic interests embedded in the status quo. Starting in the 1960s, but implemented more widely in the 1980s, the disinvestment campaign in the United States (led by universities) put pressure on TNCs operating in South Africa because of the country's policy of apartheid. More recently, there has been a sea change in American public opinion in favor of gay rights and gay marriage, pushing hesitant politicians (like Barack Obama) to ride the wave or be submerged. Businesses in the United States, for example, that refuse to serve gay couples or gay weddings have been punished in the court of public opinion, sometime to the point of going out of business. TNCs have indeed come under pressure to improve workers' conditions in the global apparel industry. And even powerful companies like Apple have felt the heat of public opinion for how it treats workers in China. However, there is no indication that Apple's dealings in China or its dearth of workers' rights there has impacted sales. In general, TNCs have not been effectively pressured in other industries on other human rights issues—like freedom of speech and association via the internet.

There is much we do not know about public opinion and its impact on TNCs regarding human rights. In the meantime on subjects like TNCs and the ATS, political and judicial elites have much freedom to maneuver.

Conclusion

Without doubt TNCs are under more pressure to respect human rights in their international operations than a few decades ago, even as it is clear that most states do not want to legally regulate their actions—and the documented abuses pile up. A prevalent view is that states ratify human rights treaties for reasons of image but then violate those norms when they prove inconvenient. No doubt to some, it is inconvenient when a focus on human rights gets in the way of profits, jobs, and tax revenue. Some want to avoid the subject by talking about macro-economics and benefits over time. After China turned to more capitalism in the 1970s, vast numbers of Chinese were lifted out of poverty. Yet it is perfectly clear that when capitalism is insufficiently regulated, there is great exploitation and abuse in the process. Recognizing this fact has nothing to do with Marxist theory, and one can document the process of coercive and exploitative capitalism in impressive ways without the slightest reference to that convoluted theory.

Human rights lawyers were clever in utilizing the ATS circa 1980 in the *Filartiga* case. But in retrospect they over-reached when using that statute to go after corporations in the 1990s. That move led to a determined push back by TNCs and their many allies in many governments. The result in *Kiobel* was, at least for Chief Justice Roberts and his conservative allies, emphasizing a long-ignored rule mandating a presumption against extra-territorial application of statutes which provide no explicit guidance on the subject. The immediate result of *Kiobel* is to apply the brakes to attempts to prosecute various actors in various situations for direct or indirect violations of human rights abroad under the

ATS. The question of when will U.S. courts allow a case filed under the ATS to proceed has been greatly muddled. It is not clear what is a cause of action that allows litigation and adjudication of the merits of a claim. Wrangling over legal technicalities has obscured a focus on the realities of what happens to real people through murder, torture, unfair trials, arbitrary detention, and more, with private persons—including corporations—often involved.

The ATS itself, on the books since 1789, has not been completely foreclosed. There seems little opposition to its use in order to go after individual torturers as well as contemporary pirates. Congress could clarify causes of action under the ATS if it could rouse itself to do something beyond partisan bickering. It did so indirectly with the Torture Victim Protection Act back in 1991. Most likely future litigation in federal courts will clarify what are other actionable ATS claims beyond individual torture and piracy. Federal courts may well accept that sexual and other trafficking in persons, often controlled by business organizations, is a category of cases that should go forward. Recruitment and use of child soldiers might be another category. Then there is the matter of which situations "touch and concern" the United States in important ways—clearly a subjective and vague standard.

In the last analysis, mainstream TNCs will not be easily regulated under the ATS. They have too much power to mobilize governmental support, and too much favorable standing with conservative judges looking for technical rules to avoid human rights controversies. In Europe there are other avenues for controlling corporations, but that subject lies beyond this chapter.[23] For the United States, *Kiobel* mostly tosses the very real problem of corporate violation of human rights back into the realm of soft law: that is, to voluntary codes of conduct, media criticism, and citizen boycotts. Whatever the ultimate legacy of the Roberts Court, clearly it does not lie in support of cosmopolitan values like providing a remedy for corporate complicity in violations of internationally recognized human rights.

Notes

1 Civil law suits are between private persons and usually seek monetary restitution for harm (torts). Criminal law suits are about violation of public order and the values therein, often involving various forms of punishment. They are initiated by public prosecutors.

2 Jonathan A. Bush, "An Emerging History of CSR: The Economic Trials at Nuremberg (1945–1949)," in *Corporate Social Responsibility?: Human Rights in the New Global Economy*, edited by Charlotte Walker-Said and John D. Kelly (Chicago, IL: University of Chicago Press, 2015), p. 129.

3 *Filartiga v. Peña-Irala*, 630 F.2d 876 (2d Cir. 1980).

4 In 1991 the United States approved the Torture Victim Protection Act, allowing civil suits and monetary damages for that one type of action in foreign nations. Physical and mental torture was covered. This act overlapped with one category of cases under the ATS but permitted United States citizens as well as aliens to sue for torture and extra-judicial killings committed outside the United States.

5 For an overview of the subject see John Ruggie, *Just Business: Multinational Corporations and Human Rights* (New York: Norton, 2013). Ruggie was the UN point man on the topic as a Special Representative of the UN Secretary-General.

6 *Sosa* v. *Alvarez-Machain* (03-339) 542 U.S. 692 (2004).

7 Ian Urbina, "Sea Slaves: The Human Misery that Feeds Pets and Livestock," *The New York Times*, July 27, 2015. Available at: www.nytimes.com/2015/07/27/world/outlaw-ocean-thailand-fishing-sea-slaves-pets.html.

8 Reese Erlich, "Reports of Slave Labor on Pipeline Rouse Critics of Military in Burma," *The Christian Science Monitor*, October 12, 1995. Available at: www.csmonitor.com/1995/1012/12071.html.

9 Edith Garwood, "Caterpillar Inc.'s Role in Human Rights Violations in the Occupied Palestinian Territories," Amnesty International Blog, December 23, 2010. Available at: http://blog.amnestyusa.org/middle-east/caterpillar-incs-role-in-human-rights-violations-in-the-occupied-palestinian-territories.

10 "*Daimler AG v. Bauman*," 128 *Harvard Law Review* 311, November 20, 2014. Available at: http://harvardlawreview.org/2014/11/daimler-ag-v-bauman.

11 "Improving Workers' Lives Worldwide," Fair Labor Association website. www.fairlabor.org.

12 Craig Timberg, "U.S., Israeli Companies Supply Spy Gear to Repressive Regimes, Report Says," *The Washington Post*, November 9, 2014. Available at: www.washingtonpost.com/business/technology/us-israeli-companies-supply-spy-gear-to-repressive-regimes-report-says/2014/11/19/49da9b48-700b-11e4-893f-86bd390a3340_story.html.

13 Nicholas Confessore, "Father of Koch Brothers Helped Build Nazi Refinery, Book Says," *The New York Times*, January 11, 2016. Available at: www.nytimes.com/2016/01/12/us/politics/father-of-koch-brothers-helped-build-nazi-oil-refinery-book-says.html.

14 "Corporations and Human Rights: A Survey of the Scope and Patterns of Alleged Corporate-Related Human Rights Abuse," Working Paper for the Corporate Responsibility Initiative, No. 44, Harvard University, April 2008. Available at: www.hks.harvard.edu/m-rcbg/CSRI/publications/workingpaper_44_Wright.pdf.

15 *Kiobel* v. *Royal Dutch Petroleum Co.* 133 S.Ct. 1659 (2013).

16 See David Scheffer, "The Impact of the War Crimes Tribunals on Corporate Liability for Atrocity Crimes under US Law," in Walker-Said and Kelly, *Corporate Social Responsibility?*, pp. 152–174.

17 It was well known to scholars that justices on the Roberts Court differed about the wisdom of linking international law to interpretations of U.S. law. Justice Scalia was probably the most opposed to a broad use of international law in various ways in U.S. courts. Justice Breyer was probably the most supportive. Among many sources see the recent book by Breyer, *The Court and the World: American Law and the New Global Realities* (New York: Knopf, 2015). One chapter deals with the ATS.

18 561 U.S. 247 (2010).

19 See further Mark Gibney, *International Human Rights Law: Returning to Universal Principles* (Lanham, MD: Rowman & Littlefield, 2nd ed., 2015).

20 William Greider, "Thanks to the Roberts Court, Corporations Have More Constitutional Rights Than Actual People," *The Nation* blog, May 20, 2014. Available at: www.thenation.com/article/thanks-roberts-court-corporations-have-more-constitutional-rights-actual-people.

21 "Belgium: Universal Jurisdiction Law Repealed," Human Rights website, August 1, 2003. Available at: www.hrw.org/news/2003/08/01/belgium-universal-jurisdiction-law-repealed.

22 Andrew Swinard, "Corporate Social Responsibility Is Millennials' New Religion," *Crain's Chicago Business*, March 25, 2014. Available at: www.chicagobusiness. com/article/20140325/OPINION/140329895/corporate-social-responsibility-is-millennials-new-religion.

23 For example see Caroline Kaeb and David Scheffer, "The Paradox of Kiobel in Europe," *American Journal of International Law*, 107:4, October 2013, 852–857.

Further Selected Readings

Alston, P., ed. *Non-State Actors and Human Rights*. New York: Oxford University Press, 2005.

Bank, R. "The Role of German Industry," in *The Nuremberg Trials: International Criminal Law since 1945*, edited by Herbert R. Reginbogin et al. Munich: K. G. Saur, 2006.

Beckert, S. *Empire of Cotton: A Global History*. New York: Vintage, 2014.

Clapham, A. *Human Rights Obligations of Non-State Actors*. New York: Oxford University Press, 2006.

Cragg, W., ed. *Business and Human Rights*. Cheltenham, UK: Edward Elgar Publishing, 2012.

Frynas, J. G. and Pegg, S., eds. *Transnational Corporations and Human Rights*. New York: Palgrave MacMillan, 2003.

Hochschild, A. *Bury the Chains: Prophets and Rebels in the Fight to Free an Empire's Slaves*. Boston, MA: Mariner Books, 2006.

Howard Hassmann, R. *Can Globalization Promote Human Rights?* University Park, PA: Penn State Press, 2010.

Walker-Said, C. and Kelly, J., eds. *Corporate Social Responsibility?: Human Rights in the New Global Economy*. Chicago: University of Chicago Press, 2015.

Wettstein, F. *Multinational Corporations and Global Justice: Human Rights Obligations of a Quasi-State Institution*. Redwood City, CA: Stanford University Press, 2009.

White, R. A. *Breaking Silence: The Case that Changed the Face of Human Rights*. Washington, D.C.: Georgetown University Press, 2005.

6

HARD TIMES FOR HUMAN RIGHTS

The Role of Aspiring Powers

We are now in a transition to a more multilateral world, one in which there will be less talk of an American empire or American hegemony. There is thus much discussion about the rise of so-called "aspiring powers," also called BRICs (referring to Brazil, Russia, India, and China) and how their influence might shape international relations.[1] Although we believe that the importance of the BRICs has been exaggerated and the supposed demise of U.S. power has been overstated, it is still important to consider if a more multilateral world, presumably influenced more by BRICs, would also mean a more liberal world in which cosmopolitan values are better implemented. In other words, if American exceptionalism—understood as exceptional virtue—has proven mostly a myth, will the future look better when less dominated by Washington? Sadly, our conclusion is "no."

We submit that when and if power in international politics shifts, the influence of BRIC countries will make it even harder for cosmopolitan ideals—and in particular universal human rights—to prevail. BRICs are likely to become more active in international institutions, but their rise will spell even more bad news for the future of human rights. In this chapter, we show that although some BRICs hold certain cosmopolitan values, they still cling to parochial forms of nationalism rooted in national self-interest, state power, and non-interference. Their lack of real support for cosmopolitanism is thus not surprising, because many of these countries, China and Russia in particular, do not share many of "the liberal individualist foundations of the human rights regime."[2] And we submit that if these values are not found in domestic politics, they are unlikely to be consistently pursued in their foreign policies. The parochial nationalism of BRICs is demonstrated in many arenas, but given space constraints we focus largely on their views of humanitarian intervention and R2P. To the extent possible, we also address the role of public opinion. There are not many polls that ask citizens of

BRIC countries about policies of interest here, but what we do conclude is that because of domestic issues and local attitudes there is little impetus for leaders of these countries to prioritize human rights in their foreign policies.

Aspiring Powers and Parochial Nationalism

In the preceding pages we noted that the core of American nationalistic rhetoric was a certain kind of Providential Nationalism that inspired the United States to, on occasion, act on behalf of citizens in other countries. The core of American exceptionalism, as should be clear by now, is the widely repeated mantra that associates the actions of the United States with the advancement of personal freedom—both at home and abroad. It was possible to combine this supposedly divinely ordained self-image with isolationism, and the United States could be a beacon to the rest of the world. But as World War II began and American power and interests changed, the country became deeply engaged with the world and the rhetoric of an activist American exceptionalism became an integral part of its foreign policy.

During the Cold War, U.S. foreign policy was supposed to leave the world a freer and more democratic place. This national identity role, mythical to be sure in large part, did allow the country to sometimes promote universal human rights through the negotiation of treaties and diplomatic agreements. Hence, rhetoric about American exceptionalism overlapped significantly with the post-1945 international human rights regime. Both sought to advance personal freedom around the world, but they differed on the exact goals and the means to get there.

It is hard to speculate on the future behavior of BRICs without some background on their histories and identities. The following section addresses the degree to which any of the BRICs display a version of nationalism that supports cosmopolitanism. BRICs have different experiences, regime types, and national priorities, but none of them has either a history or national identity that can be linked to the consistent promotion of individual rights of those living outside its borders. In other words, there is no pretense in these countries that their identities are linked to cosmopolitanism, let alone a quest for a liberalized foreign policy that would act in defense of those outside its borders. Their leaders' speeches may pay lip service to a more just world order, but individual human rights do not loom large in their actions.

With the partial exception of Russia, the other BRICs are characterized by a core narrative that is based largely on victimization and exploitation—rather than doing good for others. Even Russia has often manifested the view of being encircled and victimized by a hostile West. Aspiring powers also emphasize strengthening (rather than weakening) the state and protecting their own ethnonational group (rather than all others). On the positive side, China, India, and Brazil do talk about downplaying the use of military force; they claim to be interested in strengthening international organizations; and they often endorse multilateral action in international politics. We are skeptical, however, that when the BRICs perceive the distribution of power to be in their favor, they will stick to these values or adopt cosmopolitan ideals. Despite important differences, these are countries that share a deep-seated reluctance to get involved in the domestic affairs of other countries. Yet, all but Brazil have not hesitated to use unilateral force in neighboring countries when national interests were at stake.

Russia is partially different from the others, because its leaders have sometimes claimed to be a liberating force in other countries. These concerns were not motivated by liberal ideals or cosmopolitanism, but by Russia's own version of Providential Nationalism. Russia is also different because it has a history as a great power that proclaims it to be a special country. One strain of presumed Russian greatness is linked to providential nationalism. Under the Tzars and again under Putin, Russia has claimed to be doing God's will with a foreign policy that is endorsed by the Russian Orthodox Church.

According to a Russian analyst,

> for centuries, Russia was torn by two cultural traditions. One of them, the Westernizing one, considers the rights of the individual to be its corner-stone. The other, the Slavophile, accepts authoritarian government and severe restrictions on human rights while seeing the source of the country's further development in its own particular traditions. The Westernizing tradition embraces universal rights, while Slavophiles emphasize cultural relativism and national particularism.[3]

The Westernizing tradition has always been weaker than the Slavophile one, but from time to time Russian leaders have shown a passing interest in human rights and liberal values. Usually its response to rights violations abroad was affected by notions of self-interest. Hence, Imperial Russia intervened to help stop nineteenth century atrocities in Bulgaria and Greece, which just happened to undermine control of those areas by the competing Ottoman Empire.

Russia's national identity is sometimes discussed in terms of its destiny as a great power, and there is a long history of those in the Slavophile tradition seeing Russia as threated by the West. Russia then claims to use its power abroad in defense of righteous causes: defending against Western aggression; spreading Christianity under the Tzars; liberating the exploited under the communist party of the Soviet Union; and countering the decadence of the West under Putin.

Russian leaders have provided both material and moral support for peoples who were oppressed or victimized. Again, though, their support was limited to certain people and specific places.

As mentioned, in the 1820s Russia (along with Britain and France) intervened on behalf of Greeks who were oppressed by the Ottoman Empire. Although not Slavic peoples, "the Greek cause aroused an enthusiastic reaction from nearly all sectors of Russian society, which for a long time held the notion that imperial

Russia had a vital role to play in protecting and liberating the Sultan's Orthodox subjects."[4] Later, Russia joined Britain and France in intervening on behalf of Bulgarians, which ultimately led to the creation of an independent Bulgarian state. Russia defended these people because of their Orthodox heritage, while elsewhere, for example, when Christian Armenians were massacred in even larger numbers by the Ottomans, Russia did not offer the same support.

There is no doubt that Vladimir Putin's ascent follows the Slavophile tradition. He described Mother Russia as a Eurasian third force between East and West, and he rejected most Western conceptions of human rights as excessively secular, individualistic, and licentious. Under Putin's influence, Russian national identity has been constructed in a way that undermines human rights at home, representing an autocratic quest for a regained great power status and blessed by the Russian Orthodox Church. The NGO *Freedom House* rated Russia as "not free" by 2016, its lowest category. Such a domestic situation makes it almost impossible to proclaim a genuine commitment to protect internationally recognized human rights abroad.

Chinese national identity is sometimes described as exceptional, but unlike the United States or Russia, Chinese exceptionalism is considered an "inward type of national exceptionalism" that supposedly emphasizes peace and cooperation.[5] As all countries do, Chinese scholars draw selectively from its history, highlighting China's peaceful culture and its dedication to pursuing harmonious relationships at home and with its neighbors. It is thus easy to find literature that traces Confucian values to the country's appreciation for agreement and leading by virtuous example to its current foreign policy behavior. Underscoring these values and highlighting only certain aspects of China's history, this self-serving discourse glosses over many inconvenient truths about the country's record, including: brutal campaigns against Tibetan monks; economic development strategies that privilege Han Chinese living in minority-dominated areas; or the government's repression of political dissidents, especially human rights lawyers.

Chinese historical factors pointing to persistent repression and parochial nationalism provide a weak foundation for Beijing in the twenty-first century to focus on the internal affairs of other countries or to engage in action on behalf of cosmopolitan values. Like Russia, seeing itself as Big Brother to ethnic Russians in neighboring states and smaller Slavic nations, on more than one occasion the Chinese government has taken issue with the discrimination of Han Chinese living in neighboring countries such as Vietnam and Indonesia. Again, by limiting its foreign humanitarian concerns to the treatment of its own ethnic group, Beijing demonstrates a traditional form of nationalism that values its own people over the rights and fate of others.

China experts maintain that while Beijing's leaders—past and present—do not hold Western notions of individual civil and political rights, this does not mean that the country's leadership has ignored human rights completely. Almost two thousand years before the concept of state sovereignty emerged in Europe,

Chinese philosophers were discussing the responsibilities of national rulers. But from a Confucian perspective, the most important government obligation is the duty to secure the conditions for peoples' basic means of subsistence. Thus, when China thinks about human rights—at home or in other countries—it thinks primarily about the government and the obligation of rulers to alleviate poverty and provide assistance for all—but especially children and the elderly. Human rights rhetoric is thus collapsed into a push for economic development. This partially explains why China has ratified the UN Covenant on Social, Economic, and Cultural Rights; although Chinese citizens are not free to exercise personal rights in demanding its implementation—and China does not manifest independent courts that might compel authorities to take that ratification seriously. China has not ratified the companion UN Covenant on Civil and Political Rights.

Despite the fact that China has consented to about two dozen international instruments on human rights, China under Xi Jinping views universal human rights as dangerous and rejects them in favor of national priorities. Particularly after Gorbachev's effort to inject more civil rights into Soviet communism led to the implosion of that regime, the Chinese ruling elite has reaffirmed its view that extensive personal rights undermine stability. Beijing has never forgotten the chaos in the years before 1949, and the Western imperial penetration that fragmented and held back the country's development. The periodic upheavals during Mao's Cultural Revolution and great leap forward reaffirmed the current elite's quest for stability and development. In place of the dangerous idea of human rights, President Xi has stressed Confucian principles, including top-down leadership, and the people's duty to defer to that leadership in the name of national harmony. Thus, Chinese nationalism as articulated by national leaders has precious little in common with universal human rights properly understood.

As for India, political discourse on the country's national identity sometimes emphasizes the country's exceptional qualities, such as a presumed moral preeminence and ability to synthesize different values and traditions. But even more so than China, Indian nationalism reflects the country's enduring concern with power politics, specifically its own exploitation at the hands of Western colonial powers. Its foreign policy behavior is regularly rationalized, because of its position "somewhere between the powerful and the powerless" and a presumed national identity that reflects its uncertainty about where it belongs in the international system.[6] Such themes can be linked to historical facts like Mahatma Gandhi's successful nonviolent movement for national independence, and the need for political compromise in a large, multi-cultural, and multi-sectarian nation with pronounced regional differences.

Indian leaders' notions about their presumed moral superiority was probably reinforced by the country's leading role in the non-Aligned Movement after 1955, a movement which officially rejected both the East and West in the Cold War in favor of efforts to develop mainly post-colonial states into a supposedly benevolent political force. Diplomatic articulation of these themes was so vigorous early on that they led to widespread "[p]erceptions of Indian diplomats as 'self-righteous, moralistic, and preachy', and as displaying 'cultural arrogance' and a 'peculiarly chauvinistic world-view'."[7] Although several factors combined to lessen India's moralistic tendencies in its foreign policy, the result was that India's approach to internationally recognized human rights became more defensive over time. Rather than being confident in the export of the Indian political experience through a moralistic foreign policy, New Delhi sought to fend off criticism about its own torture, ethnic violence, and chauvinistic political parties.

Over time, India became more inward-looking while it continued to stand up for sovereignty and non-interference. As its economic power grew in the 1990s, Indian leaders gave more attention to domestic problems and strengthening its own democratic institutions, while it embraced a unique form of nationalism that was both rooted in the Global South but separate from it. Experts on Indian foreign policy thus maintain that while India's foreign policies will no doubt change as its power grows, certain aspects of Indian nationalism are unlikely to shift, particularly its concern that states be treated equally and that sovereignty be upheld. Like China, India does not have a history of Providential Nationalism that will allow its leaders to exploit messianic ideals to rationale geostrategic goals. Indian nationalism, instead, has been mostly inward-looking, focused on strengthening the country's ethnonational identity while ensuring that national interests are served.[8] India's domestic policies are usually more liberal than both Russia and China, but there is still little reason to believe that it will prioritize, much less take costly action for, human rights in other countries. That smacks of neo-colonialism to Indian eyes.

Among the BRICs, Brazil has been the most supportive of human rights in both domestic and foreign policies, but its interest and commitment have been quite recent. Brazilian nationalism is also not linked to any global project focused on universal human rights. Discussions of Brazilian foreign policy instead emphasize: the country's longstanding suspicion of great powers; its commitment to the peaceful resolution of disputes, but mostly its desire for independence. In the early 1900s, for example, the United States supported the creation of an International Court and a Court of Justice, while Brazil opposed it. Explaining its position, the Brazilian government warned of the disproportionate influence of great powers, "questioning the exclusive management of the world order by the major powers."[9] Despite Brazil's historical friendship with the United States, it has always sought independence from its northern neighbor—seeking distance without wanting to antagonize it.

Brazil joined the Allies in World War II, but a more lasting legacy on its foreign policy was the authoritarian and military dictators that ruled the country for decades, often brutally. Because of the country's authoritarian past (1930–1945) and then military leadership (1964–1985), human rights do not figure prominently in the country's identity. Its history of military rule has however made Brazilians wary of the use of military force. Even as the country alternated between authoritarian and democratic regimes and Brazil remained allied with the United States, national discourse underscored the importance, if not urgency, of a foreign policy that was independent and supposedly promoted a more peaceful and just world order.

Brazilian diplomats like to suggest that because of the country's cultural diversity and historical experiences as a middle power, its foreign policy is guided by four main principles: national self-determination; non-intervention and the peaceful solutions of disputes; multilateralism; and a preference for avoiding military confrontation with other countries. Although Brazil has not shown outright aggressiveness toward its neighbors, it is important to remember that its commitment to these principles has come only after years of authoritarianism and repression at home. Since Brazil's democratic transition in 1985, however, different administrations have emphasized some importance in promoting liberal values domestically and in foreign affairs.

Brazil's recent foreign policies, specifically its support for international criminal justice and occasional endorsement of humanitarian intervention, are justified by the government as being in line with the country's diverse culture and national values—which are supposedly rooted in conciliation and peacefulness. In adopting such rhetoric, elites have had to overlook their country's own dark spots—particularly its treatment of indigenous groups and its staggering economic inequality. In sum then, Brazil joins India as the only BRIC countries likely to support some types of diplomacy in favor of international human rights in the future. Yet, given its historical suspicion of great powers and its deep commitment to sovereignty and non-interference, it is likely to demonstrate only soft support for such policies.

Brazil, India, and even China hold some cosmopolitan ideals, and they may, in their own ways, try to create a more just and inclusive international system. Yet, their pragmatic, realist world views mean that they are unlikely to prioritize universal human rights over states' rights and national interests. Up until this point in time, their foreign policies suggest that they are more concerned with outdoing or replacing the West than they are with liberal principles aimed at restructuring world order. After Haiti's earthquake in 2010, for example, Brazil and China both engaged in "disaster diplomacy," claiming they were committed to helping both the people and the state recover. They also claimed that they could respond more quickly and efficiently than Western powers that dithered over the conditions they would place on the host government. In the case of aid to Haiti, China's involvement could be seen as part of its effort to demonstrate a global reach, as well as perhaps a point of leverage in weaning Haiti away from its recognition of Taiwan. For Brazil, it was partially about demonstrating that it was a regional, if not global power with the resources to help others.[10]

As aspiring countries, BRICs may indeed want to create alternatives to international institutions dominated by the West, but there is little reason to believe, based on their histories or national identities, that the future world order will be any better for human rights. At first cut then, the fate of human rights after U.S. hegemony is not that bright.

Aspiring Powers and International Priorities

Our goal here is not to provide a thorough analysis of the foreign policies of aspiring countries, but instead to give a brief sketch of their policies, mainly on humanitarian intervention and Responsibility to Protect (R2P) which has been covered a good deal. BRIC summit declarations indicate that these countries hold some cosmopolitan ideals, but a close examination of their policies shows that such ideas are rarely backed up. Instead, they remain suspicious of Western efforts to promote international standards and universal human rights, because they limit sovereignty and interfere with domestic priorities. Such international efforts are generally seen as a mask for expanding Western influence.

Since the Soviet Union's collapse, different Russian governments have tried to focus international attention on human rights violations in the former Soviet space, and a few times it has used military force to make its point clear. In 2014, it violated Ukraine's sovereignty by detaching Crimea, ostensibly to protect ethnic Russians living there. But despite rhetoric that Putin's Russia is greatly disturbed by human suffering outside its borders, Russia's human rights agenda, to the extent that it even exists, is limited to policies that enhance Russian influence in its "near abroad." One would be hard pressed to find clear examples of when Russia has shown an obvious concern with the rights of others or tried to save distant strangers.

In his first presidential address to the Russian Federation's Federal Assembly in 2000, for example, Putin criticized Western humanitarian intervention, calling it a pretext for Western powers to infringe on the rights of weaker countries. Russia has endorsed some interventions with a humanitarian remit, but when Western democracies accepted Kosovo's declaration of independence in 2008, without demanding security guarantees for Serbs (Russia's Slavic cousins), Moscow became even more suspicious of the West. The U.S.-led intervention of Iraq only strengthened Putin's position and his distrust of so-called humanitarian interventions.

According to one observer, Russia's opposition to Western-led intervention and its real indifference to the R2P are less about obstructing efforts to save strangers than they are about "Putin's commitment to a global order which prizes the sovereignty of incumbent rulers."[11] This is probably why Putin used military force in Syria in the fall of 2015 to support Assad's government and supposedly help it defeat ISIS. Although Putin was opposed to the West's trying to pick winners and losers, in Syria, Russia intentionally tried to ensure who ended up on top, and wound up on the side of a brutal autocratic regime that had authorized numerous atrocities.

Russian parochial nationalism is not caused by Putin alone, but is rooted in the country's dominant political structure and the ideas shared by many elites. But regardless of the cause, Russia's authoritarian tendencies and its desire to challenge the West have pushed it to provide financial and moral support to anti-democratic forces throughout the former Soviet Union and beyond, in part to counter the democracy promotion agenda of the European Union and the United States. Domestically, it has tried to prevent Western governments and NGOs from interfering with Russian affairs, and its recent foreign policy behavior, including bombing groups that oppose Syria's President Assad, are based on Russia's desire to challenge the United States and the liberal policies it has promoted, explicitly those that favor humanitarian intervention, democracy promotion and international criminal justice.

For Putin, liberal policies are not only intended to reaffirm the position of the West, but they do more harm than good. The use of unilateral force outside the auspices of the United Nations Security Council, particularly in support of one party to a conflict that leads to regime change, does not alleviate the suffering of the population but risks pushing the country into a full-scale civil war. But this view is hard to square with Russia's support for violent movements in eastern Ukraine or similar policies that tried to carve out independent areas from Georgia (e.g., Abkhazia and South Ossetia).

The best that can be said for contemporary Russian policy on human rights is that sometimes it was not obstructionist. For example, it abstained and did not veto certain UN Security Council resolutions (creating a no-fly zone in Libya to prevent attacks on civilians or referring atrocities in Sudan's Darfur region to the ICC). It also worked with the United States in Syria both to reduce the government's stockpile of chemical weapons and to institute a partial truce in the deadly fighting from 2016. However, it is hard to see how Russia, particularly under Putin, could ever make genuine attention to universal human rights a priority in its foreign policy.

China's record on cosmopolitan causes is not much better, though there is some internal elite debate over how the country should best manage its rising status. Some of the rhetoric suggests that it is trying to be a more responsible international stakeholder, acting cautiously in foreign affairs to discourage any perceived threat but also to attend to its domestic priorities. In 2015, China sided with the United States, Britain, and France in support of a proposal to improve compliance with the rules of war. Unfortunately, Russia, along with India and others, led successful efforts to defeat the measure.

Some in China want the country's leadership to adopt a more assertive position in international affairs. As one Chinese scholar put it, "China has become a leading actor on the international stage"; thus, it must "have the courage to speak out and contribute its ideas to the world."[12] Although China is developing a global agenda when it comes to alleviating poverty and strengthening international organizations, it clearly does not share most Western ideas about humanitarian intervention, democracy promotion, or the strong enforcement of the international law of human rights.

All BRIC countries are generally opposed to humanitarian intervention, but China was once among the most outspoken critics. In the early 1990s, China (along with India) adamantly opposed the use of military force in other countries, regardless of the reason. When the United States wanted to intervene in Kosovo in 1999, China maintained that even if a massive humanitarian crisis took place, the country in question should consent and international organizations should lead the intervention. Until the early 2000s China steered clear of this cause. Yet, by late 2015, Chinese elites had come to accept the legitimacy of multilateral involvement to resolve certain kinds of crises but in particular ways.

In 2006, China's behavior in this area started to change. While on a visit to Darfur, President Hu Jintao tried to encourage Sudan's President al-Bashir to cooperate with the United Nations. A year later when visiting Sudan, President Hu reaffirmed his country's respect for sovereignty and the integrity of Sudan but also acknowledged the importance of resolving issues peacefully, the need for the Africa Union (AU) and the UN's involvement, and the urgency of improving conditions for local people. Some even credit China's involvement with forcing the hand of the Sudanese government to allow peacekeeping troops into the country. Since the Sudanese were opposed to the presence of White, European troops on their territory, China's idea of a hybrid UN–AU force with troops largely from Africa provided Sudan's President al-Bashir with an opening to agree to an international presence, ultimately helping to moderate the crisis. China still agreed to host al-Bashir on two occasions, even though the ICC had issued a warrant for his arrest. And the UN–AU security force has been less than a great success.

China still opposes international interference in the domestic affairs of other countries, but it now recognizes the importance of taking a position when such an international crisis develops. Some suggest that because of its desire to be a responsible international stakeholder, China is actively trying to shape the rules under which international intervention takes place. It would be "wrong to conclude that China has recognized a right of humanitarian intervention," but "it would be equally mistaken to suggest that China's position on humanitarian intervention has demonstrated little change or no flexibility since the end of the cold war."[13] The challenge for China will be maintaining an independent position on humanitarian intervention that allows it to avoid looking like it is indifferent to human suffering.

To maintain this balance, China has articulated its own guidelines on when and how the international community should respond. International interventions should be a policy of last resort, multilateral, led by international organizations, and they should prevent or react to crises created by natural disasters. In line with others who support R2P, China is intent on securing host states' consent to international involvement. China is clear that decisions on future humanitarian interventions should rest with the United Nations, "as the core of the collective security mechanism, plays an irreplaceable role in international cooperation to ensure global security."[14] For China, as for others, hard and fast rules tend to fall victim to circumstance. Thus, when Syria was discussed in the UN Security Council, China sometimes vetoed resolutions seen as burdensome to the Assad government, yet later voted for the right of trans-border humanitarian assistance to civilians regardless of what the Assad government might wish.

China imports more oil from the Middle East than the United States, and it is understandably concerned with the region's stability. China also does not want enemies that might someday restrict its access to this natural resource. Thus, in 2011 China initially defended Libya's sovereignty and opposed humanitarian intervention. Later, as Western countries found consensus and Arab and African countries made their views known, Chinese leaders called for a peaceful resolution of the crisis, abstaining from but not vetoing a UN Resolution to intervene. In accordance with its own principles, Chinese leaders indicated that it deferred its decision on Libya to the UN, Arab countries, and regional organizations like the Arab League and the AU.

China's abstention helped clear the road for international intervention, but instead of being rewarded for its "passive followership," the Chinese were criticized both at home and internationally for siding with the West and compromising their principles. According to a prominent Chinese strategist, the West and Arab states did not show any appreciation for China's efforts, labeling it an "irresponsible power" for not taking part in the military campaign. Realizing its difficulties but still wanting to maintain its commitment to sovereignty, when it was time to take a position on the Syrian crisis China sided with Russia to block Western sponsored resolutions in the UN Security Council. More recently, the Chinese government developed a "wait and see" policy, choosing not to side with either Assad or the opposition, stepping up its mediation efforts, lobbying for a political alternative, and reaching out to allies in the region. China's views on R2P have softened, but its position on Syria has been rather consistent, opposing the imposition of solutions from the outside, putting faith in the UN and regional players, and looking for a political solution.

Given domestic politics in authoritarian China, it is not surprising that China has given little attention to democracy or civil-political human rights in other countries. And when Chinese leaders have addressed these issues, it is to criticize the West for interfering in the domestic affairs of other countries. Like Russia, China's Communist Party recently passed legislation to counter the influence of foreign NGOs. Although officials claim that the new law will provide a much needed legal status for NGOs, which would allow them to work more effectively, many are worried because the legislation specifically stipulates that NGOs in China cannot receive foreign funding. In the future, all NGOs must partner with an official sponsoring organization, and the government will be intimately involved in monitoring their activities.

But it is not just NGOs with foreign funding that are finding it difficult to operate in China. President Xi Jinping has also cracked down on other promoters of what the Chinese government sees as Western liberalism, detaining a former head of a reformist think-tank in Beijing and putting researchers, lawyers, as well as activists on warning. According to a former Western diplomat in Beijing, the Chinese are saying, "We don't want any of your values, we'll do things our way."[15] And since China itself is criticized for its non-democratic practices, even using an array of torture methods against government opponents and activists, it has little to say about the use of torture by other countries. Thus, as with Russia, there is no reason to believe that China anytime soon will embrace cosmopolitanism or defend human rights in other countries. It seems the best that one can hope for is that China will not block efforts led by others to stop atrocities, as when China did not veto the UN Security Council vote authorizing action to protect civilians in Libya in 2011.

Although India is the world's largest democracy, its record defending human rights abroad is, in fact, quite similar to other BRIC countries. Like Russia and China, India opposes most proposals to use forceful humanitarian intervention— although its position on a diplomatic R2P is less about opposing the West and the liberal order than it is a reflection of the country's own cultural values and reluctance to press change on others. As suggested earlier, non-violence is one of India's most important values, shaping its foreign policy and specifically the use of military force. Thus, Western-led intervention can look like neo-colonialism to India, especially given its Buddhist and Hindu traditions and its own history of exploitation.

Like others, India has not always followed its high-minded principles or kept its promises. For example, India initially argued that its intervention in East Pakistan in 1971 was humanitarian, because of the indiscriminate killing of unarmed civilians and other atrocities—not to mention as a response to a massive refugee flow into India. Most countries rejected India's claims, despite the fact that more than a million died; and the raping and pillaging by the East Pakistani army were well established. Yet, it was also true that India's use of force helped create Bangladesh and its efforts were calculated to weaken Pakistan.

Perhaps India learned its lesson, because before it used military force in Sri Lanka in 1987, it concluded an agreement with the Sri Lankan government that consented to Indian peacekeeping troops to help end the country's civil war. The Indo-Sri Lankan Accord was a demonstration of India's willingness to use force to save others without undermining the inviolability of state sovereignty. As with Russia and China, India's behavior was motivated by traditional ethnonational ties, specifically pressure coming from ethnic Tamils living in southern India to help their ethnic kin living in Sri Lanka. Thus India's military engagement in Sri Lanka, while partially driven by a concern to lessen violence, was not part of a crusade to institute an international order respectful of human rights. Absent domestic Tamil pressures, India would not have expended the costs of involvement.

In 2005 India, along with 149 other countries, including all the BRICs, endorsed the UN General Assembly's resolution that included two paragraphs on R2P. Yet, India, along with much of the developing world, insisted on language indicating that international action against atrocities had to be in compliance with international law. Without a doubt this general language implied that such action, since it would not qualify as self-defense, would have to be authorized by the UN. Unilateral action is thus presumably ruled out.

Later, when it came to deciding its position on Libya in 2011, it sided with the other BRICs (and Germany) by abstaining from the UN Security Council's vote authorizing action to protect civilians. India's abstention generated considerable internal debate, but leaders were, prophetically, concerned about the lack of clarity surrounding international actions and what would happen after intervention.[16] Importantly, its decision on Libya was directly shaped by China's position; had India voted in favor of the resolution while China abstained, this would have allowed Beijing alone to stand as the champion of the weak in Africa, Asia, and Latin America.

India's position on Libya disappointed many of its Western friends, but this aspiring power did not fundamentally change course when the international community turned to the civil war in Syria. Like China, India's challenge was squaring its historical commitment to non-interference and state sovereignty with what might appear to be indifference to human suffering. India tried to hedge its bets, sending a delegation to meet with members of the Syrian government as well as leaders of the opposition group without breaking any ties to Assad.

After non-violence, pluralism and tolerance have had the strongest influence on India's position on humanitarian intervention but also democracy promotion and international criminal justice—which India also opposes. While proud of its own diversity, democratic institutions, and legal practices, India generally does not have a strong desire to impose democracy elsewhere or to create international criminal courts. India, like China and Russia (and the United States and Israel), has never ratified the Rome Statute creating the International Criminal Court. It does not want such a court to review its military actions in places like Kashmir, where it is now public knowledge that Kashmiri Muslim insurgents have been tortured in detention.

India, like the United States after 9/11, has also been the target of Islamic terrorism. Like the United States during the George W. Bush administration, it has resorted to very tough anti-terrorism policies. Moreover, Prime Minister Modi's government has increasingly sought to promote a Hindu-based nationalism that has led to violent clashes with Muslim and Christian communities. He is accused of shrinking the space for freedom of expression and association in India.

In 2010, India started to work with the United States and the United Nations on global democracy initiatives, becoming the second largest donor to the UN's Democracy Fund. However, the government maintains that its attitude and implementation in this matter are different from Western countries, because civil society organizations in India are reluctant to impose or criticize those in other countries. For India, democracy promotion is about educating others and partnering with states, not admonishing them. India maintains that it wants be a model of democracy and rule of law without however forcing others to model it.

Brazil has adopted the most positive foreign policy of any of the BRICs in the area of human rights and humanitarian affairs. Although its policies are rather recent, it has gone from opposing international efforts to defending human rights to becoming a strong advocate of liberal values. Brazil has ratified all the core international human rights treaties, put in place a domestic infrastructure for better human rights policies, and it has developed broader goals to demonstrate that it is a responsible international citizen. It signed and then ratified the Rome Statute of the International Criminal Court, and it has since opened its borders to human rights inspectors, sent various reports required by the various human rights treaties, and created a national human rights plan.

Although Brazil (along with India) has the closest relationship with the United States of the BRICs, its commitment to the peaceful resolution of disputes influences has sometimes puts it at odds with its northern ally. During the Libyan crisis, for example, Brazil held the rotating presidency of the Security Council. But it (along with Russia, India, China, and Germany) chose to abstain from voting on UN Resolution 1973, which put into place an international response to the unfolding events. Brazil also did not support other international efforts in Libya, because Brazilian leaders were not convinced that the use of force in such an open-ended manner would achieve desired goals. After the bombing campaign carried out by certain NATO and Arab states, Brazil's opposition hardened even more because of the loss of civilian lives. As a Brazilian policy analyst put it, when it came to Libya many people in Brazil believed that the "rules of the game are too easily bent to serve the interests of the most powerful nations."[17]

Despite its general opposition to humanitarian intervention and the use of force internationally, Brazil has maintained a close relationship with Western countries, supporting engagement in countries when there is consent of the authorities in the targeted country. While generally supportive of many international liberal norms, like India, it has been reluctant to compel their implementation. Like China, it has tried to strike a balance between respecting state sovereignty on the one hand, but on the other preventing atrocities and human suffering. Agreeing with the main principles of R2P, Brazil has called for a widening of the concept of humanitarian intervention to include non-military, diplomatic mechanisms that would monitor actions and try to prevent the deterioration of the situation. In Haiti, for example, Brazil took a leading role in providing peacekeeping troops in 2004. Ambassador Antio de Aguiar Patriota explained the country's position thusly: while "Brazil remains committed to the established principles of international relations, such as noninterference in internal affairs, President Lula has been formulating another, equally important concept: the notion of non-indifference to other people's plights."[18]

Late in 2011, Brazil coined the concept of "responsibility while protecting" (RwP) to push debates and actions in a new direction. Vexed by the notion that members of the international community, which largely means the West, can take any means necessary in another country, Brazil maintained that the use of force often does not bring about the promised end or the protection of civilians. As Brazilian leaders explained to the UN Security Council members, it generally supports R2P, but it is still concerned about *how* it is implemented. This is because there is a growing perception that R2P might be misused for purposes other than protecting civilians, such as regime change. This perception may make it even more difficult to attain the protection objectives pursued by the international community. Brazil's RwP is, thus, an attempt by Brazilian elites to positon themselves as mediators between pro-interventionist voices in the West and more reluctant rising powers like China and Russia.

Brazil's ability to strike the right balance between state sovereignty and individual human suffering is not easy, as its position on Ukraine demonstrates. When the UN General Assembly criticized the referendum held in Crimea after Russia's intervention, Brazil refrained from taking a position, trying to maintain some independence from both the United States and other Western countries and its BRIC partners. Brazil will no doubt face similar situations in the future where it will be forced to take a position. However, it has not always chosen to withdraw and avoid the fray. Its racial policies at home and involvement in the LGBT rights, for example, have made Brazil a leader in these areas of human rights. Its leadership style is also acknowledged, because Brazil reluctantly votes for resolutions that single out specific countries in the highly visible General Assembly and instead criticizes governments within the more obscure UN Human Rights Council. Nevertheless, in the latter body, Brazil has an active diplomacy supportive of most pro-human rights measures that are introduced there.

It is easy to see why some refer to Brazil as a "pivotal player" in global governance, given its role as an advocate for global governance reforms, its efforts to foster South–South relations, and its regional leadership role. Even before Brazil started to democratize, it cultivated a strong relationship with the United Nations, participating in peacekeeping missions that began in the 1950s. Recently, Brazil has made significant contributions to peacekeeping in Angola, East Timor, Haiti, and Lebanon and is now one of the top contributors of personnel to UN peacekeeping. These UN peacekeeping missions usually have a human rights dimension.

Brazil may want to lead in some areas, but there is still little evidence of its willingness (or ability) to expend much diplomatic capital on the promotion of human rights abroad. Regionally, it has only expressed hopes and offered mild diplomatic support for democratic, liberal changes, seeking a more prominent international role in the area of conflict prevention and resolution. Given Brazil's economic problems and various scandals among the elite, there is a weak base at home for an activist human rights policy abroad.

To promote their foreign policy priorities, BRIC countries often stand together in international fora. In the UN General Assembly for example China votes with Brazil, India, and Iran over 80 percent of the time, and with the United States about 12 percent of the time. UN statistics further confirm that among the BRICs, Brazil tops even India in actively using international mechanisms to advance human rights and other liberal values. In 2006, the UN Human Rights Council was created as follow-on to the Human Rights Commission to promote human rights globally. Although BRICs have become members of this body, with China and Russia always there, and Brazil and India sometimes elected, it is difficult to generalize on their voting records because of the variety of recommendations made and the need to understand each particular context. However, *Human Rights Watch*, which monitors Council members' behavior closely, regards Russia, India, and China as generally hostile and obstructive to the goals of the Human Rights Council. On the other hand, this respected NGO regards Brazil's record favorably. This was not only because of Brazil's voting record but also because it frequently acted as a "recommending State"—hence taking a diplomatic initiative to address human rights issues in other countries.

China and Russia, moreover, have weak records at home and were often on the receiving end of many Universal Periodic Review (UPR) recommendations. This is a process in which each member state in the UN Human Rights Council has to submit to a review of its public policies. But both used the Human Rights Council and UPR mechanisms to shine the light on selected issues of poverty and development (for China) and minority rights (for Russia, in its near abroad with Russian speaking minorities).[19] Alone and as a group, each BRIC country may claim to advocate certain cosmopolitan ideals, but their behavior, particularly as it relates to humanitarian intervention and R2P is lacking. And Russia, China, and India are downright hostile to most human rights developments in the UN's Human Rights Council.

Domestic Politics and Public Opinion

As we noted in our initial discussion of American exceptionalism and in other chapters, it is hard to assess a country's foreign policy without some consideration of what is happening domestically. It has long been true that domestic public opinion sets the limits on what political elites can do over time, especially in genuine democracies but also in autocracies. What then can be said of domestic politics within BRIC countries? How might domestic public opinion influence future foreign policies on human rights? Again, we have little good news to deliver.

In addition to national discourses that are inward-focused, emphasizing sovereignty and narrow self-interest above all, aspiring countries face political, economic, and social challenges at home that are unlike to fit easily with cosmopolitanism. As we know from the United States, domestic challenges and even opposition from the population do not necessarily prevent its leaders from occasionally acting on liberal concerns internationally. Our contention here is that if BRICs became concerned with human rights abroad, it might undermine domestic priorities; thus, domestic realities only reinforce parochial nationalism and the tendency to focus on narrowly defined national goals.

The first and most important domestic consideration is the nature of human rights policies within BRIC countries. There are various ways to measure a country's human rights record, but by any of the existing measures our four aspiring countries do not score well. Using annual reports published by *Amnesty International*, the U.S. State Department, and *Human Rights Watch* reports, the Political Terror Scale (PTS) measures the repression carried out within a country's border, as an indication of a country's respect for personal integrity and civil and political rights. Attention to socio-economic rights is not covered. From 2000 to 2014, all of the BRICs consistently demonstrated evidence of extensive political imprisonment, political murders, and brutality, earning scores of a four (out of five) on the PTS (one is the highest and five is the lowest score.) This means that civil and political rights violations in these countries have expanded to large numbers of the population, and murders, disappearances, and torture are a common part of life. On the other hand, *Freedom House*, a center-right American NGO, uses different measures, and it gives Brazil and India higher scores, declaring them "free states." Russia and China are listed as "not free," missing even the category of "partially free."[20]

Although BRICs have different experiences, regime types, and national priorities, they do have much in common when it comes to their lack of interest in a world order based on human rights. Given the free and fair elections in India and Brazil, as well as their records on judicial independence and most measures of political and civil rights at home, these countries may, at some point, adopt more activist foreign policies to defend human rights abroad. Russia and China have different human rights record, as is their competition with, if not hostility toward, the West and its liberal values. Their human rights policies have been particularly criticized. Since 2006, members of the UN Human Rights Council made 422 recommendations to China (by 127 states) and 365 recommendations to Russia (by 99 states), making them among the countries to receive the most human rights recommendations for improving their countries.

The fact is that BRIC countries face a whole host of domestic problems that restrict their ability to think about citizens outside their borders, including but not limited to: political instability; ethnic or regional tensions that may even include violent attempts by minority groups to separate from the country (such as Chechens in Russia and Uighurs in China); high rates of poverty; economic inequality; and severe environmental problems. Russia and China may have the worst human rights records of all the aspiring powers, but Brazil and India also suffer from paralyzing economic inequality and unfair legal practices, regularly pushing people to the streets to protest their government's perceived illegitimacy, incompetence, or corruption.

Despite economic improvements in India, almost 30 percent of the population still lives in poverty. And while Indians are generally satisfied with their country's direction, recent surveys indicate that Indians are increasingly concerned with a range of domestic issues, including crime, unemployment, economic inequality, and basic sanitation. Since Indian national identity traditionally lacks a sense of Providential Nationalism (although Modi is trying to emphasize a Hindu-based identity), it is hard to imagine a scenario in which Indian leaders are compelled to move toward a more cosmopolitan foreign policy because of domestic urgings.

Even Brazil, whose human rights record is more positive than the others, is criticized for being a regional laggard. It has not been all that supportive of the Organization of American States (OAS); it was one of the last OAS members to recognize the jurisdiction of the Inter-American Court of Human Rights (ICHR); and it has only reluctantly been involved with the Inter-American Commission on Human rights (IACHR). Recently, it did create a Truth Commission to conduct a massive investigation of the murders and disappearances during Brazil's military rule (from 1946 to 1988), but this came only in 2012, many years after other countries in the region created such bodies. In other words, while it may continue to strengthen human rights mechanisms in domestic and foreign policy, its capacity for shaping outcomes will remain limited because it lacks a strong history or reputation in this area.

Brazil is a multi-ethnic country that has struggled to overcome legacies of slavery, discrimination, and domestic brutality. The increasing pluralization of Brazilian society has expanded the opportunities for human rights activism, but the professionalization of Brazil's human rights organizations puts the Brazilian government in a difficult spot, having to defend its policies and account for its behavior. It has worked hard to build an inclusive society, but it is still increasing participation of previously marginalized sectors of society and its need to develop economically has contributed to gross human rights violations against indigenous people and communities in the Amazon region. Brazilian companies and the government are criticized for their lack of regard, if not open disinterest, in sustainable development. In the summer of 2015, Brazilians took to the streets to protest government corruption and economic downturn, and by the beginning of 2016, Brazil's economic situation had deteriorated so much that many questioned the country's status as a rising power.

BRIC countries may have risen economically during certain eras, but they are still fragile, middle-range countries with many issues to address. Not only Brazil and India, but also Russia faces acute economic problems, and even China's remarkable economic growth has slowed. Thus, while these countries' leaders may want to become more engaged internationally, they will face a range of domestic issues, as well as some skepticism from a growing middle class that is better educated on its international activities. In the last two decades, China, Brazil, and India have also become international donors, promising to behave differently than Western countries. If their rhetoric rings true, these aspiring powers may provide some unique and important opportunities for poverty reduction, economic development, social well-being, and environmental sustainability globally. But they must still deal with these same issues at home, and none of these issues, as seen from the capitals of aspiring powers, emphasize fundamental, individual rights.

Research on BRIC countries and their development policies leads to mixed conclusions. Some claim that BRIC development policies and aid are more focused on national self-interest at the expense of poor people while seeking to undermine liberal global governance. Others are more complementary, explaining that these new aspiring powers offer recipients greater choices in their sources of financing and assistance, providing alternative models and approaches to economic growth that may prove more effective. It remains true that unlike Western countries, the BRICs never put human rights conditions on their bilateral aid and grant programs. In 2016 the United States suspended aid to Tanzania because of concerns about fair and free elections. It is inconceivable that any of the BRICs would emulate such a policy.

Depending on the country and issue, there is significant potential backlash against spending money overseas when domestic needs are so high. In Russia, for example, the people are interested in a government that promotes the economic well-being of those living within its borders, though they still obviously care about national security and restoring the country's pride and position. Just four years ago, chants of "Russia without Putin!" were heard throughout the country as thousands demonstrated in response to Putin's return to the presidency, with his approval ratings at 63 percent, his lowest in over a decade. However, after the annexation of Crimea in 2014, Putin's ratings soared to nearly 90 percent.[21] And they have not dropped significantly ever since. Thus, while Russians are concerned about economic growth, the environment, and other things at home, narrowly defined national interests, such as being recognized as a great power, still matter greatly.

Not many surveys exist on how citizens of BRIC countries feel about hypothetical foreign policies aimed at protecting universal human rights. A World Values Survey that looked at Brazil, Russia, India, China, and South Africa however asked a series of questions related to domestic policies and foreign priorities. These surveys from 2010 to 2014 indicate that most citizens of BRIC countries do not in fact believe that individual human rights are strongly respected in their countries.

While more than 20 percent of Indians and almost 18 percent in China indicated that individual rights were strongly supported elsewhere, views were more negative regarding rights at home. This is somewhat encouraging news, because it may signal a desire for more attention to individual and human rights at home. But in terms of the aims of the country, there was a significant consensus on the top three priorities: focusing on economic growth, strengthening defenses, and providing people with more of a say in jobs and their community.

TABLE 6.1 Country Priorities according to the World Values Surveys, 2010–2014

Respect for human rights in different countries

	TOTAL	BRAZIL	CHINA	INDIA	RUSSIA	SA
A great deal of respect for individuals	11.4%	4.6%	17.9%	20.4%	2.5%	12.4%
Fairly much respect	41.6%	33.1%	51.4%	41.6%	39.1%	40.6%
Not much respect	30.4%	36.2%	12.5%	26.9%	45.9%	30.2%

Aims of country: first choice

	TOTAL	BRAZIL	CHINA	INDIA	RUSSIA	SA
A high level of economic growth	51.3%	50%	47.2%	43.5%	60.4%	45.8%
Making sure this country has strong defenses	19%	11.4%	22.8%	27.1%	9.8%	22.7%
Making sure people have more of a say; jobs and their communities	17.9%	27.8%	7.9%	13.4%	30.2%	23.6%

Most serious problem in the world

	TOTAL	BRAZIL	CHINA	INDIA	RUSSIA	SA
People living in poverty and need	51.4%	59.2%	42.5%	36.7%	55.7%	57.4%
Discrimination vs. girls & women	12%	10.1%	5.1%	25.4%	3.7%	17.3%
Poor sanitation & infectious diseases	10.8%	10.5%	8.5%	11.6%	9.9%	12.7%
Inadequate education	9.7%	14%	12.1%	11.1%	5.3%	8.8%
Environmental pollution	13.2%	5.8%	21.6%	14.2%	22.7%	3.8%

Confidence in the United Nations

	TOTAL	BRAZIL	CHINA	INDIA	RUSSIA	SA
A great deal	11.9%	7.9%	8.2%	27.4%	4.7%	14.3%
Quite a lot	28.1%	29.3%	23.4%	31.3%	29.1%	28.6%
Not very much	23.3%	20.1%	12.6%	27.2%	24.6%	28.8%
None at all	14.9%	23.1%	3%	13.3%	17.1%	18.4%

Source: Data from World Values Survey wave 6 (2010–2014). Available at: www.worldvaluessurvey.org/WVSDocumentationWV6.jsp.

TABLE 6.2 Views of China Generally Favorable

	Favorable	Unfavorable
United States	35%	55%
United Kingdom	47%	38%
France	47%	53%
Germany	28%	64%
Russia	64%	28%
Israel	49%	50%
Egypt	46%	53%
Pakistan	78%	3%
Bangladesh	77%	22%
Indonesia	66%	25%
Venezuela	67%	26%
Tanzania	77%	10%
Kenya	74%	16%
Median	49%	32%

Source: Data from "Global Opposition to U.S. Surveillance and Drones, but Limited Harm to America's Image," Pew Global Attitudes Survey, Spring 2014 Q15b. Available at: www.pewglobal.org/2014/07/14/chapter-2-chinas-image.

There is also a consensus among the BRICs about the most significant problem facing the world: people living in poverty. In fact, in all of these countries except India, almost half of the population responded that poverty was the most significant problem facing the world. At the same time, despite rhetoric within China, India, and Brazil about the centrality of international organizations and multilateralism, when people in these countries were asked about their confidence in the United Nations, only about one-third of people had "quite a lot" of confidence in this body and only India had "a great deal" in the United Nations with almost 30 percent.

In considering the ability of BRIC countries to shape the future of world order, it is useful to consider global public opinion and how these countries are regarded. In this regard, only China is viewed as a potential alternative to the United States. Few doubt China's growing power in the world and recent public polls are favorable about this country's economic rise. This is true even in countries that are strong allies of the United States.

Surprisingly, large percentages of people in Africa and parts of Asia indicated that they believed that the government of China respected personal freedoms. Although this is hard to interpret, this may mean that people in these countries viewed personal freedoms differently from those in democratic countries in Europe, Latin America, and Asia.

When it comes to debates about the future, China's foreign policies, especially in Africa, have attracted the most attention. The United States and other Western

TABLE 6.3 Views on China's Respect for Personal Freedom, 2014

Does the government of China protect the personal freedom of its people?

	YES	NO
United States	14%	78%
United Kingdom	15%	75%
France	12%	88%
Germany	6%	91%
Russia	46%	32%
Israel	26%	68%
Egypt	42%	48%
Pakistan	52%	5%
Bangladesh	66%	27%
Indonesia	51%	30%
Venezuela	47%	32%
Tanzania	59%	23%
Kenya	74%	10%
Medium	36%	39%

Source: Data from "Global Opposition to U.S. Surveillance and Drones, but Limited Harm to America's Image," Pew Global Attitudes Survey, Spring 2014 Q15b. Available at: www.pewglobal.org/2014/07/14/global-opposition-to-u-s-surveillance-and-drones-but-limited-harm-to-americas-image/pg-2014-07-14-balance-of-power-2-04.

countries have accused China of adopting colonialist-like policies, claiming that it is only interested in extracting natural resources. Yet, cross-sections of Africans hold favorable opinions on the Chinese government, and African leaders often describe the relationship with China "as neutral and business-oriented."[22] This is also true of China's involvement in Latin America, particularly in countries that are politically at odds with the United States like Ecuador and Venezuela—where Chinese money is going to build roads and bridges. Since China does not attach human rights strings to its foreign assistance and development loans, developing countries and particularly non-democratic ones are quite happy to have an alternative to the West.

Such responses might be in reaction to Western countries' bad behavior or because of China's ability to lift African countries out of poverty. Yet, its involvement has not been uniformly positive and its activities have fueled complaints and even anti-Chinese riots. While the debate over China's foreign policy intentions continue, it is clear that in some places and in certain sectors, China is providing an alternative to the West, its aid practices, and to relationships that condition aid and investments based on countries' record on human rights and democracy. China, indeed, presents a powerful alternative and likely an attractive one to countries that do not respect liberal values or civil and political rights.

Conclusion

One has to be wary about sweeping generalizations, but it is clear that BRIC countries not only have different histories and nationalisms, but their foreign policy orientations are not always cohesive. It is the case, however, that all of the BRICs are determined to strengthen states and the principles of sovereignty and non-interference, minimizing the ability of international actors to undermine domestic priorities. However, as these countries have risen they have started to acknowledge their unique role and responsibility in addressing and responding to certain but not all global problems. For BRICs, democracy and human rights are far less important than economic development and the maintenance of political and social stability. Thus, while they might be willing to play a leadership role in areas like economics and trade, their growing influence will likely not have a dramatic effect on cosmopolitan ideals.

In many ways, China is in a league of its own in this grouping, given its population, steady economic growth, and its long-term vision of where it wants to go as a country. Its GDP (and capacity to pollute via greenhouse gases) now rivals the United States, and some international surveys even put China's economic power ahead of the United States. Yet, the U.S. economy is not only strong in terms of its overall GDP, but it possesses the high-tech innovation, financial reserves, and sophistication that China lacks. China will continue challenging Western norms and the U.S. position on many issues, but it is likely to do so in a more indirect way (certainly than Russia), ignoring or discounting political and civil rights while claiming to be committed to advancing economic and social rights internationally and deferring to the United Nations.

For its part, Russia has been able to disrupt the status quo in Europe (with military force in Georgia and Ukraine) and it has used force unilaterally in Syria (with the assent of the Assad government). Despite its obvious military might, its ability to challenge the West in the future is far less certain; its struggling economy, unfavorable demography, and tenuous political environment will make it difficult for Russia, even under a tenacious Putin, to remain a major international player without first attending to domestic issues.

Together, China and Russia have successfully blocked various Western initiatives in favor of human rights in various international fora, but often these rising powers are not on the same page internationally, competing rather than cooperating with each other. Brazil and India, while more supportive of human rights and Western liberal policies, are much weaker than either China or Russia, and their foreign policies often side with Western countries. However, since they are both experiencing significant problems at home, they are far more likely to focus on domestic priorities than risk a foreign policy that might affect them negatively or undermine their country's stability. Brazil in particular is increasingly preoccupied with domestic concerns, specifically a sagging economy and government corruption. Indeed, in March 2016 with the country's economy in dire straits, Brazil witnessed the largest protests ever.

On balance, the national identities and domestic priorities of China, India, and Brazil might have some impact on the evolving international human rights regime, but it is likely to be marginal at best. Under the right conditions, these rising powers might indeed work to strengthen some aspects of the United Nations, encourage more equal treatment of states, or focus on socio-economic development. And as positive as this might be, theoretically, for the future of world order, there is little evidence to suggest that cosmopolitan ideals will be high on the list of priorities. In fact, there is little reason to believe that any of the BRICs has the history, the interest, or the capacity to someday soon adopt a more cosmopolitan world view and seek to advance or protect the rights of others outside their borders.

Notes

1 For more on these countries, see H. R. Nau and Deepa M. Ollapally, eds., *World Views of Aspiring Powers: Domestic Foreign Policy Debates in China, India, Iran, Japan and Russia* (Oxford: Oxford University Press, 2012).

2 Tim Dunne and Sarah Teitt, "Contest Intervention: China, India, and the Responsibility to Protect," *Global Governance*, 21:3, July–September 2015, 371.

3 Sergie Chugrov, "Russian Foreign Policy and Human Rights: Conflicted Culture and Uncertain Policy," in *Human Rights and Comparative Foreign Policy, edited by* David P. Forsythe (Tokyo: United Nations University Press, 2000), p.149.

4 Theophilus C. Prousis, "Russian Philorthodox Relief During the Greek War of Independence," *History Faculty Publications*, 1985. Paper 17, 32. Available at: http://digitalcommons.unf.edu/ahis_facpub/17.

5 F. Zhang, "The Rise of Chinese Exceptionalism in International Relations," *European Journal of International Relations*, 2011, 1–24.

6 Aseema Sinha and Jon P. Dorschner, "India: Rising Power or a Mere Revolution of Rising Expectations?" *Polity*, 42:1, 2010, 75.

7 Kate Sullivan, "Exceptionalism in Indian Diplomacy: The Origins of India's Moral Leadership Aspiration," *Journal of South Asian Studies*, 37:4, September 2014, 149.

8 Sinha and Dorschner, "India: Rising Power or a Mere Revolution of Rising Expectations?" 88.

9 Gelson Fonseca, "Notes on the Evolution of Multilateral Brazilian Diplomacy," *Global Governance*, 17:3, July–September 2011, 377.

10 W. Alejandro Sanches Nieto, "Brazil's Grand Design for Combining Global South Solidarity and National Interests: A Discussion of Peacekeeping Operations in Haiti and East Timor," in *Global South to the Rescue*, edited by Paul Amar (New York: Routledge 2014), p. 174.

11 Derrick Averre and Lance Davies, "Russia, Humanitarian Intervention and the Responsibility to Protect: The Case of Syria," *International Affairs*, 91, 2015, 813.

12 Rosemary Foot, " 'Doing Some Things' in the Xi Jinping Era: The United Nations as China's Venue of Choice," *International Affairs*, 90:5, 2014, 1086–1087.

13 Jonathan Davis, "From Ideology to Pragmatism: China's Position on Humanitarian Intervention in the Post-Cold War Era," *Vanderbilt Journal of Transnational Law*, 44:2, March 2011, 272.

14 Lui Tiewa, "China and the Responsibility to Protect: Maintenance and Change of Its Policy for Intervention," *The Pacific Review*, 25:1, March 2012, 162–163.

15 "Uncivil Society," *The Economist*, August 22, 2015. Available at: www.economist.com/news/china/21661819-new-draft-law-spooks-foreign-not-profit-groups-working-china-uncivil-society.

16 Dunne and Teitt, "Contest Intervention: China, India, and the Responsibility to Protect," 381.

17 Melinda Negron-Gonzales and Michael Contarino, "Local Norms Matter: Understanding National Responses to the Responsibility to Protect," *Global Governance*, 20:2, 2014, 268.

18 Esther D. Brimmer, "Is Brazil a 'Responsible Stakeholder' or a Naysayer?" *The Washington Quarterly*, 37:3, 2014, 142.

19 The Universal Periodic Review (UPR) is a State-driven process created in 2006 which involves a review of the human rights records of all UN Member States. Operating under the auspices of the UN Human Rights Council, it provides the opportunity for each State to declare what actions they have taken to improve the human rights situations in their countries.

20 Freedom House receives some funding from the U.S. government, but also from other democratic governments as well as from private foundations such as Ford. It is widely regarded as independent from the United States.

21 "Vladimir Putin's Unshakeable Popularity," *The Economist*, February 4, 2016. Available at: www.economist.com/blogs/graphicdetail/2016/02/daily-chart-4.

22 S. Zhao, "A Neo-Colonialist Predator or Development Partner? China's Engagement and Rebalance in Africa," *Journal of Contemporary China*, 23:90, 2014, 1034.

Further Selected Readings

Alden, C. "China in Africa," *Survival (00396338)*, vol. 47, no. 3, 2005, 147–164.

Averre, D. and Davies, L. "Russia, Humanitarian Intervention and the Responsibility to Protect: The Case of Syria," *International Affairs*, 91, 2015, 813–834.

Bhagwati, J. "China Shows Trade Is Best Route Out of Poverty," *NPQ: New Perspectives Quarterly*, vol. 22, no. 2, 2005, 46–51.

Blaxland, M., Shang, X., and Fisher, K. R. "Introduction: People Oriented: A New Stage of Social Welfare Development in China," *Journal of Social Service Research*, vol. 40, no. 4, 2014, 508–519.

Breslin, S. "Debating Human Security in China: Towards Discursive Power?" *Journal of Contemporary Asia*, vol. 45, no. 2, 2015, 243–265.

Brimmer, E. D. "Is Brazil a 'Responsible Stakeholder' or a Naysayer?" *The Washington Quarterly*, vol. 37, no. 3, 2014, 135–151.

Chan, L-H., Lee, P. K., and Chan, G. "Rethinking Global Governance: A China Model in the Making?" *Contemporary Politics*, vol. 14, no. 1, 2008, 3–19.

Chen, D. "Opening the Black Box: Domestic Sources and China's Human Rights Foreign Policy," *Conference Papers—International Studies Association*, 2006.

Chen, D. "Explaining China's Human Rights Foreign Policy: An Identity-Based Approach," *Conference Papers—International Studies Association*, 2007.

Chugrov, S. V. "Russian Foreign Policy and Human Rights: Conflicted Culture and Uncertain Policy," in *Human Rights and Comparative Foreign Policy*, edited by David P. Forsythe. Tokyo: United Nations University Press, 2000.

Davis, J. E. "From Ideology to Pragmatism: China's Position on Humanitarian Intervention in the Post-Cold War Era," *Vanderbilt Journal of Transnational Law*, vol. 44, March 2011, 217–282.

Fabio Bertonha, J. "Brazil: An Emerging Military Power? The Problem of the Use of Force in Brazilian International Relations in the 21st Century?" *Rev. Braz. Politic. Int.*, vol. 53, no. 2, 2011, 107–124.

Fleay, C. "Transnational Activism, Amnesty International and Human Rights in China: The Implications of Consistent Civil and Political Rights Framing," *International Journal of Human Rights*, vol. 16, no. 7, 2012, 915–930.

Fonseca, G. "Notes on the Evolution of Multilateral Brazilian Diplomacy," *Global Governance*, vol. 17, no. 3, July–September 2011, 375–397.

Foot, R. "'Doing Some Things' in the Xi Jinping Era: The United Nations as China's Venue of Choice," *International Affairs*, vol. 90, no. 5, 2014, 1085–1100.

Gang, K. H. and Xiuli, C. W. "Analysis Finds U.S. Newspapers Use Six Frames for 'Made in China'," *Newspaper Research Journal*, vol. 35, no. 2, 2014, 6–23.

Glanville, L. "Retaining the Mandate of Heaven: Sovereign Accountability in Ancient China," *Millennium (03058298)*, vol. 39, no. 2, 2010, 323–343.

Hurrell, A. "Hegemony, Liberalism and Global Order: What Space for Would-be Great Powers," *International Affairs*, vol. 82, no. 1, 2006, 1–19.

Hwang, E. L. "China: The Growth of a New Superpower and the Extinction of Universal Jurisdiction," *Wisconsin International Law Journal*, vol. 32, no. 2, 2014, 334–354.

Jordaan, E. "South Africa and Abusive Regimes at the UN Human Rights Council," *Global Governance*, vol. 20, 2014, 233–254.

Joshi, D. "Does China's Recent 'Harmonious Society' Discourse Reflect a Shift Towards Human Development?" *Journal of Political Ideologies*, vol. 17, no. 2, 2012, 169–187.

Klein, R. "An Analysis of China's Human Rights Policies in Tibet: China's Compliance with the Mandates of International Law regarding Civil and Political Rights," *ILSA Journal of International & Comparative Law*, vol. 18, no. 1, 2011, 115–165.

Krickovic, A. "All Politics is Regional," *Global Governance*, vol. 21, no. 4, October–December 2015, 538–579.

Krumbein, F. "Media Coverage of Human Rights in China," *International Communication Gazette*, vol. 77, no. 2, 2015, 151–170.

Lee, P. K., Chan, G., and Chan, L-H. "China in Darfur: Humanitarian Rule-maker or Rule-taker?" *Review of International Studies*, vol. 38, iss. 02, April 2012, 423–444.

Li, S. and Ye, L. "How Do Americans Evaluate China's International Responsibility? An Empirical Assessment," *Journal of Contemporary China*, vol. 24, no. 92, 2015, 222–239.

Lui, A. "China Rising, Human Rights and 'Hard Times': The Foreign Policy Implications of an Asian Century," *Conference Papers—American Political Science Association*, 2010, 1–35.

Macdonald, B. "China's Policy of Non-Interference in Sudan," *Undercurrent*, vol. 7, no. 3, 2010, 6–14.

Mawdsley, E. "Human Rights and South-South Development Cooperation: Reflections on the 'Rising Powers' as International Development Actors," *Human Rights Quarterly*, vol. 36, 2014, 630–652.

Nathan, A. J. "Human Rights in Chinese Foreign Policy," *The China Quarterly*, 139, 1994, 622–642.

Nau, H. R. and Ollapally, Deepa M., eds. *World Views of Aspiring Powers: Domestic Foreign Policy Debates in China, India, Iran, Japan and Russia.* Oxford: Oxford University Press, 2012.

Negron-Gonzales, M. and Contarino, M. "Local Norms Matter: Understanding National Responses to the Responsibility to Protect," *Global Governance*, vol. 20, 2014, 255–276.

Noesselt, N. "China and Brazil in Global Norm Building: International Law and International Criminal Court," *Pap Polit Bogata (Columbia)*, vol. 18, no. 2, 2013, 701–718.

Ofodile, U. "Trade, Aid and Human Rights: China's Africa Policy in Perspective," *Journal of International Commercial Law & Technology*, vol. 4, no. 2, 2009, 86–99.

Peerenboom, R. "Assessing Human Rights in China: Why the Double Standard?" *Cornell International Law Journal*, vol. 38, no. 1, 2005, 71–172.

Qi, Z. "Conflicts over Human Rights between China and the US," *Human Rights Quarterly*, vol. 27, no. 1, 2005, 105–124.

Sudo, M. "Concepts of Women's Rights in Modern China," *Gender & History*, vol. 18, no. 3, 2006, 472–489.

Sullivan, K. "Exceptionalism in Indian Diplomacy: The Origins of India's Moral Leadership Aspiration," *Journal of South Asian Studies*, vol. 37, no. 4, September 2014, 640–655.

Tiewa, L. "China and the Responsibility to Protect: Maintenance and Change of Its Policy for Intervention," *The Pacific Review*, vol. 25, no. 1, March 2012, 153–173.

Wan, M. "Human Rights Lawmaking in China: Domestic Politics, International Law, and International Politics," *Human Rights Quarterly*, vol. 29, no. 3, 2007, 727–753.

Weiss, T. and Erthal Abdenur, A. "Introduction: Emerging Powers and the UN—What Kind of Development Partnership?" *Third World Quarterly*, vol. 35, no. 10, 2014, 1746–1758.

Wu, C. "Sovereignty, Human Rights, and Responsibility: Changes in China's Response to International Humanitarian Crises," *Journal of Chinese Political Science*, vol. 15, no. 1, 2010, 71–97.

Xue, H. "Chinese Observations on International Law," *Chinese Journal of International Law*, vol. 6, no. 1, 2007, 83–93.

Zhang, F. "The Rise of Chinese Exceptionalism in International Relations," *European Journal of International Relations*, 2011, 1–24.

Zhao, J. "China and the Uneasy Case for Universal Human Rights," *Human Rights Quarterly*, vol. 37, no. 1, 2015, 29–52.

Zhao, S. "A Neo-Colonialist Predator or Development Partner? China's Engagement and Rebalance in Africa," *Journal of Contemporary China*, vol. 23, no. 90, 2014, 1033–1052.

CONCLUSION

Liberalized Realism in Today's World

It should be clear by now, based on the facts we have presented and the public opinion polls we have cited, that American society is not much given to liberal crusades to perfect the world. This is certainly so for human rights in foreign policy. Should any president choose a policy based on a crusading version of American exceptionalism, launching an effort to correct the human rights violations of others, that policy would surely come to grief. This is especially the case when U.S. security personnel die because of the policy, or when other interests seen as vital are damaged. Recall that in Somalia during 1992–1993 a rare case of humanitarian intervention devoid of self-interest, authorized by George H. W. Bush and pursued by Bill Clinton, was abandoned when American soldiers were killed and wounded in a dubious exercise that had morphed into coercive state-building. Intervention in Somalia was supposed to benefit the Somali nation, but when costs escalated, popular and congressional pressure compelled a different direction. In the years since there is no shortage of evidence undermining the enduring myth of crusading American exceptionalism.

On top of all the evidence we have compiled, not just about American political culture and American forceful intervention, but also about democracy promotion, regulating transnational corporations, and torture, we can add the debacle of the American presidential primary campaigns of 2016—particularly pertaining to the Republican Party. Rather than debating genuine policy positions and serious options for the future of the country, many Republican presidential candidates much of the time hurled personal insults at each other and wound up discussing the presumed size of candidates' genitals. How anyone could believe that such an exceptionally bad spectacle derived from an exceptionally good people was difficult to fathom. Ironically, polls show that more Republicans than Democrats believe in American exceptionalism.[1]

The fact was that a surprising number of Americans supported the Republican nominee, Donald Trump, who had openly disparaged women and Hispanics and Muslim emigrants—as well as having repeatedly made false or otherwise outlandish statements on a variety of topics. Even by the usual standards, recognizing that politicians campaigned in poetry but had to later govern in prose, Trump's campaign statements regularly ran afoul of various fact checkers. His campaign was a sorry spectacle to any thinking observer and recognized as such by a variety of leading Republican personalities—from office holders to journalistic pundits. Trump echoed the worst of American political history, appealing as he did to racism and bigotry and know-nothing nativism. He played to the dark underside of American society with his appeals to the anger and frustration of social segments left behind by events, although plenty of well-off citizens and various elected officials supported his campaign as well.

How was it that such a miserable development as the rise of Donald Trump in the Republican Party, on top of the facts of American slavery, Jim Crow laws, persistent racism, statistics on poverty, demeaning views of women, bouts of anti-Semitism and anti-Catholic vitriol, police brutality, and a host of other real defects in American society had not killed off the myth of American exceptionalism? Why was it that various political leaders returned time and time again to that venerated concept—and would no doubt do so in the future? How could it be that Washington repeatedly presented itself as a leader for human rights in the world when its real history at home revealed so many violations of human rights? Did no one care about the facts of U.S. torture in different eras, not to mention U.S. support for various disreputable autocrats?

One part of this puzzle is explained by the presidential election of 1980. Most Americans like to hear they are a good people with a bright future and a beneficial can-do attitude. Ronald Reagan, with a certain intuitive political genius, recognized this with his theme of "Morning Again in America." On the other side, incumbent Jimmy Carter came across as an Old Testament Jeremiah, forecasting gloom and doom, the need to recognize a malaise in American society, with the concomitant need to tighten belts and do with less. Reagan won handily and repeated the feat four years later against Walter Mondale. It is clear that Americans like to be told they are an exceptionally good and capable people, whatever the facts.

To be sure, the Carter years were characterized by the facts of stagflation at home and disappointments abroad, such as the Soviet invasion of Afghanistan and the takeover of the American Embassy in Iran. Reagan endorsed some traditionally popular American positions, specifically his hawkish posture toward Russian-led communism and his enthusiasm for the private for-profit sector. Yet, our point remains true that Reagan's genial optimism played well in contrast to Carter's cautionary views about dangers to the natural environment and limits to growth. Reagan unabashedly resurrected the theme of America as a shining city on a hill, capable of all sorts of wonderful achievements. This played well in the electorate.

Never mind that worrying figures on economic inequality in American life date from about 1980, especially after Reagan and his Republican successors basically undid the inclusive New Deal of Franklin D. Roosevelt.[2] Such facts are ignored by politicians and people who thrive on bravado, taken in by promises to make America "great again" by adopting an "American First" foreign policy.[3]

As we repeatedly explained in the preceding pages, there is much good on the American record as well as the blemishes. Perhaps the two most important are maintaining some kind of democracy since the late eighteenth century (moving from more restricted to less so), and engaging in self-struggle to remove the warts stemming from racism, gender stereotyping, and lack of attention to the hard edges of crude capitalism. But it also true that other democratic societies like Britain and those in northern Europe also have a long history of constitutional democracy and also have developed a broader sense of inclusiveness and human dignity. While Trump was rising, London elected a Muslim mayor. So even on the matter of democratic self-improvement over time, the United States does not stand out as exceptional.

We tried to keep matters in proper perspective by speculating about the future and whether the so-called aspiring powers of Brazil, Russia, India, and China might provide hope for a more dynamic and balanced attention to human rights in world affairs. If the United States presented such a mixed record on human rights as part of a liberal world order, might these others do better? Perhaps because China and Russia were included in our comparative group, our answer was decidedly pessimistic about a future world order featuring an enhanced role for these two states. China and Russia have never featured strong liberalism with its focus on individual rights, and their contemporary foreign policies consistently reflect the illiberal values so evident in their domestic politics. If we reflect on Brazil and India, the prospects are slightly more encouraging, but only if we skip the subject of forceful intervention abroad in the name of human rights. India has paid into a democratic fund to promote democracy through the UN, and Brazil has a good voting record in the UN Human Rights Council and lively interest in the UN notion of R2P especially through early diplomacy to head off atrocities. These states (and some others) show considerable interest in advancing human rights by diplomatic means. That is somewhat encouraging for the future, but no aspiring power shows much of an interest in using its resources or political capital to actually sacrifice for liberal causes in the global arena.

We concluded that none of the aspiring powers have constructed a national identity and a form of nationalism that fits very well with internationally recognized human rights. American exceptionalism, despite its penchant for being used in hubristic causes, presents a mythical content that can actually be put to positive use on occasion. We noted that President Obama did so with regard to heading off atrocities in Libya in 2011. Since the United States supposedly stands for the advance of personal freedom at home and abroad, this self-defined role may at least make Washington uncomfortable when it supports dictators or otherwise fails to leave situations more free than previously. Just as the theory of revolutionary Marxism proved embarrassing to a conservative Soviet Union in its later years, so the theory of America as a shining city on a hill proves embarrassing when contradicted by the evident realities of U.S. foreign policy. The big problem for a clearly realist foreign policy by Nixon and Kissinger (circa 1969–1977) was that it failed to demonstrate the usual American concern for uplifting the persecuted. The Nixon–Kissinger over-riding quest for stability in world affairs lacked the usual veneer of American optimism about a better future built on personal freedom—which Kissinger admitted in an indirect way after the fact.[4] Jimmy Carter exploited this shortcoming, winning the 1976 election amid much discontent about the lack of ethics in U.S. foreign policy during the preceding eight years.

The notion of American exceptionalism can overlap at least partially with universal human rights, thus permitting leaders of both major American parties to agree on some international projects such as UN democracy promotion. And when the United States departs from its traditional values, which also at times find expression in international human rights, as when George W. Bush implemented policies of torture, not only many Democrats but also some Republicans react adversely. So despite the danger that American exceptionalism, defined to mean a special rather than ordinary people, can lead into a dangerous chauvinistic nationalism, the idea can also lead to support for universal human rights. Some other nations, lacking a comparable national identity linked to personal freedom, find a more difficult fit with internationally recognized human rights.

Toward the end of his tenure, President Obama gave a revealing interview which was published in *The Atlantic* magazine.[5] Much of what he said is relevant to our discussion here in that it addresses the extent to which U.S. foreign policy can implement universal human rights. The following quotes would seem to suggest that Obama sees himself as a liberalized realist—one who starts with both American exceptionalism and U.S. self-interest, but one who tries to advance global human rights where not too costly:

> "For all of our warts, the United States has clearly been a force for good in the world," he said. "If you compare us to previous superpowers, we act less on the basis of naked self-interest, and have been interested in establishing norms that benefit everyone. If it is possible to do good at a bearable cost, to save lives, we will do it." ...
>
> "I am very much the internationalist," Obama said in a later conversation. "And I am also an idealist insofar as I believe that we should be promoting values, like democracy and human rights and norms and values, because not only do they serve our interests the more people adopt values that we share ... but because it makes the world a better place."
>
> ...
>
> "Having said that," he continued, "I also believe that the world is a tough, complicated, messy, mean place, and full of hardship and tragedy. ... we've

got to be hardheaded at the same time as we're bighearted … There are going to be times where our security interests conflict with our concerns about human rights. There are going to be times where we can do something about innocent people being killed, but there are going to be times where we can't."

This kind of general orientation leaves to specific decision making exactly what is too costly and what is not, and hence when can one act for human rights abroad and when not. One of Obama's most controversial policies had to do with Syria—whether to use military force in response to Bashar al-Assad's use of chemical weapons, and more generally whether to act decisively to end the major and prolonged suffering in that long-running internationalized civil war. Refugees from Syria had roiled U.S. allies in Europe and elsewhere. Apparently, Obama was satisfied with his record there and believed that locals would have to sort out their problems over the course of several generations. Obama's Syrian policy gave rise to much criticism, however, with a number of foreign policy "experts" seeing the president as weak and unwilling to stand up to other powers like Putin's Russia. Questions about what is truly in the U.S. security interest are often answered only with hindsight—e.g., to avoid another Middle Eastern quagmire or to stand firm against Russian efforts to extend its influence.

Despite Obama's willingness to tolerate much injustice in Syria and elsewhere, in the words of the journalist Goldberg, "he consistently, and with apparent sincerity, professes optimism that the world is bending toward justice. He is, in a way, a Hobbesian optimist."[6] The phrase Hobbesian optimist is helpful in sorting out the contradictions found in Obama's views. While believing the United States on balance is a force for good in the world, he admits that U.S. history in dealing with countries like Iran, Indonesia, and Nicaragua has not been perfect and mistakes have been made.[7] Also, he is aware that American exceptionalism can slide into chauvinistic nationalism, so he has indicated a preference for multilateral action where U.S. vital interests are not seen to be threatened. He sees multilateralism as a check on crusading exceptionalism.

At the end of the day, it seems that labeling Obama a liberalized realist is correct. This is more or less the same as an optimistic Hobbesian. As Goldberg explains, "Obama generally does not believe a president should place American soldiers at great risk in order to prevent humanitarian disasters, unless those disasters pose a direct security threat to the United States." So U.S. security is the key factor, and action for human rights can occur when it does not jeopardize that security interest. We would also add that rarely does any U.S. administration act for human rights abroad when major economic self-interest is jeopardized. One sees this in U.S. high-level silence about serious human rights violations by China, Saudi Arabia, and other important trade partners.

The fundamental tension between national self-interest and, in our focus, implementing universal human rights as part of a liberal world order, is an old one. By centralizing the idea of American exceptionalism we have highlighted that tension. One could wait for world government to replace the nation-state system. That would greatly reduce if not eliminate the concept of national interest. But that would be a very long wait. Or one could recognize the difficulties of acting for rights in a nation-state system and abandon human rights in foreign policy, which Nixon and Kissinger mostly did. But for those who seek to combine in some fashion the security and wealth of a nation with the advancement of universal human rights, as the late Stanley Hoffmann wrote some decades ago, "anybody who believes that there is a simple road to progress [on human rights] has my sympathy."[8]

Notes

1 Jeffrey M. Jones, "Americans See U.S. As Exceptional," Gallup, December 22, 2010. Available at: www.gallup.com/poll/145358/americans-exceptional-doubt-obama.aspx.
2 "Inequality in America: The Rich, the Poor and the Growing Gap Between Them," *The Economist*, June 15, 2006. Available at: www.economist.com/node/7055911.
3 Michael Hirsh, "Why George Washington Would Have to Agree with Donald Trump," *Politico*, May 5, 2016. Available at: www.politico.com/magazine/story/2016/05/founding-fathers-2016-donald-trump-america-first-foreign-policy-isolationist-213873.
4 Henry Kissinger, *Diplomacy* (New York: Simon and Schuster, 1994), p. 50: "[Woodrow] Wilson's historic achievement lies in his recognition that Americans cannot sustain major international engagements that are not justified by their moral faith." See also p. 834: "In traveling along the road to world order ... American idealism remains as essential as ever, perhaps even more so."
5 Jeffrey Goldberg, "The Obama Doctrine," *The Atlantic*, April 2016. Available at: www.theatlantic.com/magazine/archive/2016/04/the-obama-doctrine/471525.
6 Thomas Hobbes emphasized the need for a strong state in a nasty world.
7 The United States along with Britain overthrew the elected Iranian Premier in 1953, it supported murderous repression in Indonesia in the mid-1960s, it repeatedly intervened in Central American to prop up repressive officials.
8 Stanley Hoffmann, *Duties Beyond Borders: On the Limits and Possibilities of Ethical International Politics* (Syracuse, NY: Syracuse University Press, 1981), p. 140.

INDEX

Italic numbers indicate tables.